You Can Make It Happen

How Breakthroughs in Neuroscience Can Transform Relationships

Eva Berlander
EVA DOZZI

Illustrations by Eva-Lena Martinsson

ISBN: 1470191490
ISBN 13: 9781470191498

Orginal Swedish/ 2011 - ISBN 978-91-7437-192-5

You Can Make it Happen

To Sven, Anders and Nicholas

Contents

Foreword

It's no coincidence that the first personal conversation I ever had with Eva Berlander was about differentiation. Like old friends, we jumped into a deep discussion about how you can maintain your individuality while at the same time be connected in relationship. Two things stood out to me then and still do now: (1) the woman knows what she's talking about; and {2) she practices what she teaches.

This made a great impression on me because when it comes to differentiation, it's important to understand it at a personal level because it is a cornerstone of healthy love as well as compassion and support. Knowing where I stop and you begin; understanding how my personal history and issues affect my relationship with you; being able to distinguish old brain habits from current behavior; and delineating physical problems from emotional problems is vital to creating mature relationships.

Eva Berlander is one of the few professionals I know that can speak to all of these issues with authority and experience. I am thrilled that this book is now available so that others can reap the benefits of her wisdom. We need this wisdom because most of us have a love /hate relationship with differentiation. There's good reason for this: the human brain is designed to be quite subjective; it's always looking out for Number One—you. For this reason, it's easy to see the faults of others, i.e. how they offend you, but difficult to see how you might be contributing to the very problems you dislike. This is why individuals and couples coming for help are frequently inclined to give great discourse on how and why their *partner* is causing so much conflict and consternation.

Differentiation, by contrast, challenges us to ask such questions as: "What is it like to live with *me*?" "What am *I* like as a partner?" "'What is *my* role in creating the nightmare I dread?" "How does *my* physiology make me prone to behavior unbecoming of a partner?" Through the pages of this book, Eva Berlander guides you gently through these questions to the shores of true love. Enjoy the journey, and welcome to the world of knowing yourself through conscious relationship.

Pat Love, Ed.D.

Pat Love is an international trainer on couple's therapy and past president of the International Association for Marriage and Family Counseling She is the author of *The Emotional Incest Syndrome*, *Hot Monogamy* and *The Truth About Love*, and co-author of *How to Improve Your Marriage Without Talking About It* and *Never be Lonely Again*.

For love in the time of conflict

When the gentleness between you hardens
And you fall out of your belonging with each other
May the depths you have reached hold you still.
When no true word can be said, or heard,
And you mirror each other in the script of hurt,
When even the silence has become raw and torn,
May you hear again an echo of your first music.
When the weave of affection starts to unravel
And anger begins to sear the ground between you,
Before this weather of grief invites the black seed of
bitterness to find root,
May your souls come to kiss
Now is the time for one of you to be gracious,
To allow a kindness beyond thought and hurt,
Reach out with sure hands
To take the chalice of your love,
And carry it carefully through this echoless waste
Until the winter pilgrimage leads you
Toward the gateway to spring.

Poem by John O'Donahue

Lisa and Michael

The End or the Beginning?

"What's wrong, Mike?"

"Nothing."

"But you don't say anything!"

"What am I supposed to say, Lisa?"

"We can just talk to each other. We *need* to talk, Mike! I've tried to arrange a nice evening and you just sit there sulking, staring into space."

"I'm not sulking… and I'm not staring."

"You are! You look at everything but me."

The couple sat in the kitchen with their empty plates and a glass of wine each between them on the oak table. The kids had eaten dinner earlier and from the TV in the rec room, loud music could be heard. *American Idol* had just begun.

Lisa's chest ached with disappointment. She'd made a real effort to arrange a cozy Friday supper, with Carpaccio for starters and lamb chops for main course – meat-lover Michael's favourite. She'd gone to all this trouble because she and Michael really needed to talk. He had been away from home even more than usual this fall, and the contact between them was almost nonexistent.

But she'd hoped that if they just had a serious talk about it, maybe they could get closer again. Maybe even have sex. She had dressed nicely in her new green dress with the matching earrings. She even wore high heels! Yes, she was looking good, she was. But he didn't see it, because he didn't see her anymore. And he never listened, either.

They ate their dinner in silence, since all of Lisa's attempts to make conversation just died out. She asked him about work and how he was, but got monosyllabic replies. Finally, Michael's eyes turned to her. But there was no warmth, just fatigue and irritation. Lisa froze. She knew she shouldn't have said anything; she should have kept silent, played the game, and given him a big, false smile in spite of the pain in her chest. But it was too late: she had punched a hole in the cozy evening that never was and now never would be.

"Please, Lisa. Don't start." Mike's voice was toneless, dead. "I've had a rough week, stressful as hell." He raised his voice. "I don't want to talk! All you want to talk about is problems, I can't take it."

"No, that's just it! You never can talk to ME. You can talk to everyone else, but not me! You can talk to everyone at work and you can work sixty hours a week but you can't talk to your wife."

"It's no use. You never listen."

"What is there to listen to when you never *say* anything?" Lisa pounced on his comment. "You don't listen to me, either!" There were tears in her eyes. She felt so incredibly sad, deserted and small; the loneliest person in the world.

Michael looked at his wife. He had been hoping for a nice quiet evening, a conflict-free dinner with good food and a couple of glasses of wine, and then some effortless talk about everyday things, the kids, the neighbours, some TV--to simply relax, which he needed very much. But he soon realized that the cozy dinner came with a secret agenda: She wanted to "talk about things." He knew what was coming, so he went silent. Better to keep quiet than to lure the bear out of the cave.

But his tactics had failed and now it was too late. Lisa's face would soon be smeared with mascara and she would sob and fire away all the bitter questions: *Is there something wrong with me? Do you think that I'm ugly and boring? Or are you perhaps thinking of someone else? Don't you love me anymore?"* And his stomach would hurt from anxiety and guilt and bad conscience blended with rage in a terrible mixture, and there would be no way out. He felt the panic rising.

"Lisa, stop it, that's not true. I do talk to you."

"Yes, you say, 'pass me the butter' or 'where are the sports pages.' But that's about it."

And Michael knew that she was more or less right. He avoided his wife, and even more so after what happened at that conference in June. It just wasn't possible to play happy family anymore. He couldn't take it. But for now, it was all about calming Lisa.

"Lisa," he said, trying to fill his voice with confidence and authority; his manager voice, the one he used on difficult colleagues. "I'm really whacked after a week at work. You have to respect that, Lisa."

She looked at him for an instant with an open gaze, and he saw something move in the big brown eyes, and a hopeful impulse told him she would accept this. But then her eyes went black again.

"So? You're whacked? *You* are whacked? What do you think I am after a day at work and everything else at home afterwards? Should I stop talking to my husband because I'm *tired*? There wouldn't be much said here then, would it!" Her eyes narrowed. "What are you thinking about all the time when you look into thin air? Work? Or is it *someone else*?"

Her voice rose and cracked with a little squeak with the final words.

"Now stop it, Lisa." He said with a sigh. "I just can't dwell on problems when I come home tired. Can't you just accept that?"

Now the sobs came. "Fuck you!" she yelled. "Poor you, who has to *strain* yourself to be with your wife. Poor Mike, it must be so HARD on you," she hissed between her teeth as she suddenly rose, cleared the table and dumped the plates in the sink with a rattle. "I made an effort tonight with food and cleaning, making things cosy and I dressed up, but you don't even notice that I *exist*. Fuck off, Mike."

"Okay," he said with clenched teeth. He rose violently, took long strides to the hallway, grabbed his coat and put his feet into a pair of shoes. The panic was getting bigger in his chest, he was falling into a black abyss, he must get away and he would not let Lisa's suggestion pass unnoticed. He would fuck off.

"No… please Mike, don't go, I didn't mean it like that!" Lisa's voice was now trembling, pleading. Her eyes, red with tears, met his in the dark hallway. Her fingers began to search his neck, and suddenly he felt as though he were being strangled. He tore loose from her hands, pushed passed her and threw open the front door. The last thing he heard before he slammed the heavy door shut was her yell:

"No, Mike, don't go!"

Preface

Now, you may be wondering, what is this? The latest chick-lit offering? A script for a soap opera?

No, it's just Michael and Lisa, a quite ordinary, middle-class couple in their early fifties who are approaching the pit of a deep, drawn-out crisis in their marriage. Divorce is knocking on the door. Later on, you'll find out how things work out for them. I have used this couple to introduce the method of dialogue and communication that is the focus of this book. It's an understatement to say that currently, Michael and Lisa are not communicating well! I suspect that quite a lot of readers will recognize parts of their story. And while they are similar to many couples that I work with in therapy, Michael and Lisa are the product of my imagination. And, as they say, any resemblance with actual persons is unintended.

In 1989, I ended a passionate but very stormy relationship. Love--so intense it should have lasted forever--had ended in black despair. I started to suspect that a happy and lasting relationship was not possible for me. I also saw more and more clients and friends having great difficulties in their close relationships. I wanted to understand why. I wanted to be a better partner, and a better therapist, and I couldn't understand why life with another person was so *damn hard* for me and so many others! So I started to look for better answers and a new understanding.

In recent years I have worked with many hundreds of couples in Sweden and in workshops abroad, in addition to the work in my therapy clinic. I get so many grateful e-mails from men and women who learnt to listen to each other and regained the closeness in their relationship as a result of this new understanding. In this book I will try to sum up what I have learnt during these past twenty years.

You can make it happen is not an ordinary fix-it kind of book. It doesn't teach you to "find yourself" or "save your marriage" or "do this and everything will be fine." I have written it to spread knowledge about the role of the human brain and our mind, in our relationships and about a new way of communication that leads to better mental health and more loving relationships.

In my work as a couple therapist and trainer in positive psychology, I meet couples every day that are in actual combat with each other, who find themselves in a disillusioning routine, or who have simply lost contact with each other. Many feel unheard, unseen and "dead" inside.

In despair they ask themselves: is it possible to have a loving relationship once the fire and the closeness is gone? Can you rediscover love when everything has deteriorated into arguing and emptiness? Is it possible to be heard and understood? Is it necessary to break up families and change partners, or can you learn to love the same person once again? Simply, can you create and keep long, loving relationships?

My answer: Yes you can.

For some couples, it's easy to find the way back. Of course, I feel great satisfaction when people get in touch with me a year after a workshop and tell me that their life together is better than ever – and it stays that way! Others have a more difficult time finding the way back to a loving relationship, and they have to work harder. There are some who decide to divorce all the same – but in a better way, a way that reduces the risk for continued conflict after the fact. All of them have acquired important new insights and skills.

Much of the time, however, I have seen that it is possible to change a wretched situation and find a way back to a loving connection. And since I'm a living proof of this myself, I'm so bold as to include scenes from my own marriage in the book (with clearance, of course, from my husband!) And while this book is meant primarily for couples in crisis, I'm convinced that *we all* have to find new, more effective ways to communicate with each other, with our children, our friends, and colleagues – in all of our relationships! So in this way, the book is for everyone who wants a more loving, compassionate relationship with someone in their lives.

You can accomplish this by making *new tracks in the brain* and altering old fruitless patterns and behaviour. I work with a dialogue process or way of communicating that I call "crossing the bridge. This beautiful name and metaphor of "crossing the bridge" to someone else, first came from my teacher, mentor and friend Hedy Schleifer. Using this process, we can safely and consciously get into each other's brains and minds for a visit, to take an empathetic walk in each other's "shoes." From a neurobiological viewpoint, safe and empathic communication can lead to new integration in the brain – and also between the brains of two individuals. This is a perfect way to calm the nervous system and create a feeling of safe attachment.

But do note: this book is not supposed to make all couples stick together no matter what. While continuing together is often the *result* of using this concept, it is not the goal. The goal is to inspire you to become more mature and aware in your relations with intimate others, and enjoy them. I want to point to the alternatives. I hope that you will feel encouraged to slowly, steadily develop a competence that will lead to a life of loving relationships. The goal is for you to become your own expert.

The dialogue process "crossing the bridge" is a fantastic opportunity to create contact, harmony, and integration. But it is vital to understand that isn't all about talking – discussing, arguing, interpreting, negotiating, bargaining, or otherwise verbalizing problems. We can do that until our tongues fall out, but it won't change anything in our brains or hearts. Instead, it is a question of listening and "be attuned to" another person, taking in that person's signals and integrating the message in ourselves. By doing this, we create a safe connection. We are truly present as we visit the interior of another individual, as well as our own.

The book is *not* about solving problems or bargaining about time, responsibilities, housecleaning, money, and so on. I don't think that the answers can be found outside. Instead I want to focus on the ability to look inward and make an exciting expedition into our personal history.

Contingent communication [1] does change the brain. But to be able to change the brain on purpose, you have to understand how it works. So I will attempt to clearly describe the fascinating discoveries in recent brain research, as well as new discoveries about how human attachment, development, and "emotional resonance" [2] work.

It is not at all easy to listen to someone whom you think of as an enemy. But having witnessed hundreds of couples make the journey from struggle to closeness (as well as trudging around in the marshes of argument with my husband) I have started to understand how the process works. Because of that I'm convinced about the importance of a book that can inspire the art of listening. The "crossing the bridge" dialogue is not the only approach to better communication. But in my experience, it is a uniquely powerful way to listen, connect, meet, change, heal oneself, and heal together.

My hope for this book is to inspire as many people as possible to develop, and experience, the joy of a loving relationship. That's the best gift we can give ourselves and our close ones--not least our children.

---

1 Explanation for contingent communication, Bonnie Badenoch, *Being a Brain-Wise Therapist; A Practical Guide to Interpersonal Neurobiology,* Page 57

2 Explanation for emotional resonance - Bonnie Badenoch, *Being a Brain-Wise Therapist; A Practical Guide to Interpersonal Neurobiology,* page 39, Daniel Goleman, *Social Intelligence; The New Science of Human Relationships,* page 40 - 45, Sue Johnson, *Hold me Tight; Seven conversations for a Lifetime of Love*, page 159-162

Out beyond ideas of wrong doing
and right doing, there is a field
I'll meet you there

R U M I ,

Persian poet, philosopher and mystic, 1200s

1

I Feel Pain

How Did We End Up Here?

Many of the couples that get in touch with us at the Swedish Relationship Institute are desperate, angry, sad, and hurt. They may be a husband and wife living in a constant power struggle, unable to free themselves from their knot of mutual anger and blame. Some carry with them betrayals that can't be forgotten. Others are quite recently married and can't understand how they could fall so quickly from the heights of love to a swamp of bickering, hopelessness and perhaps infidelity.

Some couples that come to us are still in love, but want to create a solid foundation for their marriage from the start. They might have been through a divorce and realized that it takes awareness, maturity, and determination to live well in a relationship. We also meet people who are involuntarily single, who've been turning themselves inside out in their attempts to find love, and are determined to understand who they are, in order to finally find a partner.

We also meet couples that have been married for many years, which have managed through difficulties but feel dejected and disappointed. The joy in their life together is gone: daily life may be peaceful, but also a little dead. They feel they have nothing in common any longer. They live under the same roof in a "parallel marriage," each of them having their own friends and interests. Will they ever be able to love their partner again? Or is it time to cut the ropes and find someone else who can offer the love, joy and security that they long for? Some have already fallen in love with someone else and are torn between the needs of lover and spouse.

Then we have couples that come here after they've separated, but realized that life didn't get much easier after the divorce. The conflict with the old partner remains, and there may already be friction in the new love relationship. I see both types of couples--ex-spouses still trying to work out their ancient conflicts and divorced individuals who arrive with new partners, wondering why they are facing the same old conflicts with a brand new person.

Hurray!

Most people who come to us are in pain. It is *painful* when the dream of the perfect relationship falls into pieces; it's painful to fail, and it's painful to never find lasting love. It's painful to not be heard. But here is the good news: conflict may be the very thing that can help us create a more profound and satisfying relationship. When it occurs, we should really say "Hurray!" Conflict puts a spotlight on the needs and desires that we usually hide deep inside. If we use this awareness and our means to communicate, we can calm our nervous system. When we can "cross the bridge" and actually listen, take in the world of another individual and understand it, we can differentiate ourselves from each other, while at the same time becoming curious and connected. And at that exact place – in the area between the brain halves of an individual as well as between our two brains, in the landscape of implicit and explicit memories – we

2

can change things. In this *gap* we can build understanding, attunement, resonance, empathy, harmony, and true intimacy.

So you see, there is reason to be hopeful.

A Very Young Therapist

I grew up in a loving family and my parents did their best. But in spite of all the love I received, I was a lonely, alienated, and frightened child. My father, who came from England, was an alcoholic and later died from his illness. My mother, who was Swedish, was co-dependent and often overwhelmed with feelings.

I grew up very rapidly. My parents divorced when I was four, only to marry again shortly afterward. When I was ten, they divorced once more.

As though it were yesterday, I remember when my dad left us to live far, far away in Australia. He was "gone" forever. But sometimes, when he was drunk and his longing (especially for my mother) got too great, he called and cried over the phone.

"Nobody loves me anymore," he would weep. "Poor me! Everyone deserts me. I'm so lonely!"

I can still feel the pain and emptiness that filled my little body as I heard him cry. I felt guilty for abandoning him.

I also remember the hatred I felt for my mom when she threw him out. I was astonished and enraged that she could hurt poor Dad so. Later, I came to realize that mother made a necessary choice in her life: either he goes under himself, or the entire family will be pulled down with him.

Alcohol invaded dad's life and slowly, steadily sucked all life from his skinny, withered body. When he passed away at age 54, he weighed 81 pounds. My wonderful, beloved dad died confused, haggard, with a bleeding ulcer, a twisted mind, and a mangled soul. Longing, fear, guilt, and a feeling of powerlessness froze in me as a child, and these feelings have reappeared a number of times to mess up relationships, between me and my husband and other people close to me.

Dad's drinking affected me deeply. His alcohol abuse made him irresponsible, despairing, helpless, overcome, martyred, and sometimes aggressive. All in all, he was more like a child than a grown man.

Mother had a genuinely positive attitude. But she had to struggle constantly and often became ill, exhausted, lonely, and in despair. She was very emotional and prone to weeping – there was a lot of *drama* about my mother. But her positive personality and her sense that everything is possible rubbed off on me. This has been a real gift. A negative factor was that I had to cling to her too tightly in order to survive in a hostile world. My mother influenced me more than anyone else, since she was the one who was present. She remains a great source of inspiration.

My Parents' Luggage

Since my father worked in Nigeria, which was then a British colony, West Africa was my home for almost ten years. As a child, I felt the hot red sand of Africa under my feet. As I played outside in our large yard, I smelled the rich aromas of bananas and tomatoes from our beautiful garden. At night, I listened to crickets and the sounds of family members singing.

We were the only white people in our area. Auta was the name of the man who was our steward. He and his family lived beside our house. I loved them! My father tried to help black people and asked Auta and his family to live in our house, but they didn't feel comfortable doing so. They called us Sir and Ma'm. We had a dog called Nadja and a rabbit named Kalle kanin. I felt especially close to my rabbit, because it was white like me.

My paternal grandparents lived and worked in various countries in Africa, so for my dad it was natural to leave England at seventeen and work on a farm in what was then Rhodesia – the country where my grandfather had worked as a prison manager. Grandfather brought a number of horrible stories into the family. During World War I, he fought on the Western Front and carried with him terrible experiences from that period. In the thirties and forties it was not safe for white children to grow up in Africa. At least that was the reason my grandmother gave for leaving her two sons in London during the war, while she continued to live in Rhodesia.

Since her parents died young, Grandmother herself grew up in a Catholic convent, and when she was a parent herself she did what she thought best for her children. She placed her eldest son, Dad, in a boarding school south of London at the age of six. His younger brother, five years younger, followed suit several years later. It was a fine and expensive school, and grandmother thought that her children would be safe there. But when I asked my dad about that period, he just laughed and said: "Yes, you can survive anything." That's all he ever said.

During their school years, Dad and his brother saw their parents very seldom; they lived in a tropical country far from their children. So, Dad learned to manage without his parents from an early age.

My maternal grandparents lived in the beautiful, 17th-century house Lång Lassesgård in Västerås, Sweden. It was an amazing house, one of the oldest in Sweden, a low-roofed, wooden structure with small windows and a small garden inside the house. Our wooden floors clicked and clacked when we walked over them. When we returned from Africa, the house by the church became our home. For a blessed period of about 7 years, my brother and I had the privilege of growing up with our mother, grandmother and grandfather, all in that house.

Mother was the eldest of three children. Grandmother and Grandfather were loving parents who adored their children. In their marriage, hugs and kisses was a natural part of everyday life. Grandmother was a soft, warm, and round woman who put her faith in the hands of God and Jesus. According to my mother, my grandfather became an atheist, in spite of the fact that his father was a Lutheran minister. To him there existed no God; instead, science was his truth.

When they were newly engaged, Grandmother wished that her fiancé would choose to become a priest. But Grandfather wanted to be a journalist or writer. But at that time and with their position in society, it wasn't considered "good" enough. So, he became an engineer. That way, he could walk the thin line between his own needs and other people's wishes.

In the loving family that Mother grew up in, she was especially close to her father. She quickly learnt to be his scientific and academic little girl, a capable lass who could bask in the appreciation of her father. Mother learnt to be a clever girl early on – with few needs of her own.

These are some of the things that my parents carried with them.

Here are some of mine.

My Luggage

As a small girl, I didn't understand that I lived in a world filled with danger. I didn't understand why mother often was so sad, or sick or worried. I didn't understand why my father turned into another person when he became intoxicated. I didn't understand, but I desperately tried to grasp and piece my world together.

These experiences triggered my interested in personal development in various ways. It was my background that drew me to psychotherapy and to take various courses that in time led me to my profession as a couple's therapist. As an adult, I also sought a rewarding and lasting relationship, but that turned out to be very complicated.

Imago Relationship Therapy

In 1991, I met Sven, my husband-to-be, and I felt I'd been struck by lightning – so much in love was I! Shortly after our meeting, my mother, who also was a therapist, suggested that I participate in a workshop for couples in New York City. Sven went with me, but he didn't feel quite up to participating. The method was called "Imagotherapy." The leader of the seminar was Harville Hendrix, who created the foundation for Imago Relationship Therapy. The seminar was very enlightening and an important milestone for me.

After a couple of years, conflict came knocking on the door for Sven and me. Suddenly we were "in the middle of it," mired in arguing and conflict. We decided to go to another Imago seminar, this time for our own sake and not for professional purposes. The leader of this course was Hedy Schleifer, the woman who later became my, friend, teacher and mentor, and her husband Yumi. The seminar allowed us to fall in love again. After that powerful experience, I decided to continue my professional Imago training and focus on working with couples. Hedy became my teacher. In 1995, I started one of the first European Imago institutes, in Stockholm.

Imago means, "image" in Latin. Imago therapy is a structured method where a couple learns to understand why they keep arguing about the same things over and over again – and why this never leads anywhere. We can find out which "images" in the brain play tricks on us. With knowledge, presence, resonance, awareness and a clear structure. we can build an intimate relationship once again and feel heard and understood.

My work rests on four corners: Imago Relationship Therapy, mental training (positive psychology), mindfulness and IPNB (interpersonal neurobiology), all of which rely on evolving research on the brain, the mind and relationships.

Our children are waiting for us to arrive

DANIEL J SIEGEL

2

The Brain: From the Cradle to the Wall

Bonding

In order to understand what happens when we "lose the love" in our relationship, we must take a closer look at how human bonding and development work.

We are animals with the program for our development coded in our genes. We begin our lives in a relaxed and happy state and we feel connected to everything and everyone. When we are born, our dominating impulse is to bond, *belong,* to attach. If our parents, other guardians or important people close to us (from here on I will simply use the word parents) understand and fulfil our needs, hear and understand our signals, and offer contact, warmth, safety and food, we will feel happy and alive. We experience balance and harmony. We go out into life with self-assurance, for we know who we are and our worth. We know where we end and where other individuals begin.

But of course, it's not that easy. Not even under the best of conditions can parents provide a perfect upbringing. There is no parent who can be available to fulfil the needs of their children every minute. There is no such thing as a perfect parent – and that is fortunate because it means that we, as parents, can let go of that guilt feeling! It's not a question of a good or a bad childhood, and it's not my intention to speak ill of parents. I don't want to hand out guilt and with great affection for my parents (and their parents, and all other parents, myself included) I know that it is tremendously hard work to lead, reflect and support children in their development.

Here we deal with something much greater, with everything that our forefathers and we have been affected by and thus registered in our brains, minds/ bodies and nervous systems. These stored "images" sooner or later appear in our close relationships. This is especially clear in loving relationships, but it is also evident in how we behave with our children, colleagues, parents, and friends. The images often appear in the shape of conflicts that consume a lot of energy, and usually we don't know where they come from.

Being a parent may be the most difficult, happiest and most important work in the world. No matter how hard we try to do our best for our children, we parents will provide them with experiences and images that affect their personalities, both negatively and positively. We do this partly through our actions as parents, but perhaps mainly by the emotional luggage that we unconsciously carry along--our own early experiences and the experiences of numerous generations before us. This is called *the implicit memory*, which encompasses memories that aren't understandable and logical to us, and thus have not been integrated into our consciousness. (Chapter Five will explain the various types of memory in more detail.)

Nonetheless, with knowledge, new insights and skills, we can learn to make conscious, loving choices each day.

So, our brain stores images that we carry along. When we fall in love, we are "drugged" with hormones and with this strong cocktail we produce and are blinded by the *positive* images that we see, those that make us feel warm, safe, and loved. Just like any other drug, it makes our life seem wonderful – temporarily. The grass is greener, the food tastes better, and we feel strong, wonderful, and beautiful. The levels of testosterone rises, which increases the sex drive in both genders.

When the drug subsides and the first stage of love ends, we return to a "normal" state. Now we more quickly see the *negative* images. We do this automatically, since – and this is important *– for our survival, it is better to conclude that a stick is a snake than to believe that the snake is a stick.*

With attuned communication, as for example, "crossing the bridge," we help each other and ourselves to fit the present, the past, and the future together, systematically using the conscious part of the brain in order to integrate the left and right halves of the brain – *but also in order to integrate both our brains.* We help each other to "heal," and neuro-biological facts can now explain what happens. We can heal by being attuned, visiting each other, telling our stories and seeing *the logic* in our behaviour. With empathy, curious presence, and adult awareness, we create new tracks in our amazing brains; we create bonding and new memories for the future; we create *in the present* the positive images that we choose ourselves and then can carry along to the next generation. *We can learn that a stick is not a snake and that our partner is not our enemy.*

We don't dwell overly on what we find, but we do see where our habitual autopilot responses lead us. We understand these responses in order to create new, more healing memories.

The Great Library

In order to more clearly describe these phenomena with memories that we "carry along," I use the word *images*. Every image can contain frozen, or congealed, emotions that have both a positive and negative effect on us, in relation to others as well as to ourselves.

You can think of these images as photographs that our brain has taken of everything around us. The camera of the mind is always taking photos--every hundredth of a second--of everything we see, dream, feel, smell, hear and say – *click-click-click-click!* This continues all our life.

Innumerable images are registered, sorted and stored in the filing cabinet of the brain and mind. It could be compared to a great number of photo albums that we carry along. Or, if you wish, you can picture the brain and mind as a library with walls stacked with bookcases filled with albums, where each album can represent one day or perhaps one year, in your life. Every picture is there, stored in the brain. Each one has made such a mark on you that it has become a part of your identity.

Now we know that we also carry along images that our parents have had in their library in *their* brains and minds. They are stored in our brain and thus we inherit them and pass them on to our children.

In addition, now we know that our brains mirror each other's neurons (nerve cells) in *all human contact*. What´s going on in your brain registers in my brain, and build our fantastic nervous system on these experiences and meetings; our brains seem to move into each other and "contaminate" each other – with both good and bad things. For example, when you smile, I am likely to smile. When you yawn, I will definitely yawn! When you get angry, I feel my own defensive anger rise up. And when I write about the brain, I don't see it as separated from the body. The brain is an integrated part of the body, and together they create the experience of a soul – which we call the mind.

In spite of the fact that I've just invited you to play with words like "images" and "albums" in order to make the memory process more vivid, our memories, of course, aren't actually stored as videotapes or still photos. They are stored as electrochemical tracks in great networks in the entire brain. These tracks are called *electrochemical patterns*.

A number of scientists have contributed to our understanding how our interactions with the surrounding world affect the brain. The psychiatrist and brain researcher Eric Kandel, professor of biochemistry and biophysics at the Columbia University in New York, spent fifty years studying memory. He was the first person to realise that the brain actually "rebuilds itself" when it stores memories. He proved this by studying, among other things, a modest sea slug, *Aplysisa californica*. He found that learning involves creating special circuits for communication in the brain, and that these circuits are formed on the basis of our experiences. Eric Kandel thus showed that learning and storing memories lead to *physical* changes in the brain, and his work was awarded a Nobel Prize for medicine in 2002 (together with Paul Greengar and Arvid Carlsson).

The Copycat Cell

What is it that leads to intimacy, contact, and love and sometimes makes us tread deeply into the quicksand of love?

With the aid of this recent research, such questions can much more easily be answered and understood. A number of scientists now agree that the human brain contains the answers to many of our questions about relationships.

One revolutionary discovery was made in the early 1990s by an Italian brain researcher, Giacomo Rizzolatti, at the University in Parma. His group studies the Motor neurons (nerve cells specialised in movement) in monkeys. The monkeys had small sensors surgically placed in their brains that could register all activity in specific nerve cells. When the monkey saw a nut on a table, the neurons started to work, the instrument responded and the monkey went up and took the nut.

But it was during these studies that, by coincidence, they discovered a fantastic thing: the neurons were activated and the instrument beeped – when one of the *researchers* took the nut! Rizzolatti was amazed. He expanded the experiment and let a second monkey go up and take the nut. The sensors in the first animal used in the experiment beeped just as though she'd picked up the nut herself!

Rizzolatti had discovered the mirror neuron.

The researchers in Parma conducted a number of further experiments: they tested monkeys gripping peanuts and raisins, monkeys watching people do the same thing, monkeys watching other monkeys doing it, people watching other people grasping things, people watching other people putting things in their mouths – and so on. Only after four years of persistent experiments did Rizzolatti dare publish the article that would revolutionize psychological and neurobiological research. In the article, they showed that both monkeys and people possess these kinds of reflecting brain cells, which have come to be called "mirror neurons."

It has been noted that we imitate other people, from birth, often unaware that we are doing so. Some cells in the brain are activated no matter whether we *perform* the action, *plan* it, or *see someone else* perform this action. The discovery of the mirror neuron has made it clearer how learning (among other things) works. It proves how deeply we humans interact, and how important we are to each other.

Rizzolatti's discovery has been vitally important. Researchers all over the world have further developed his experiments, and we now know that the human system for mirror neurons, called "the resonance circuit," is more advanced than in a monkey. Our brains mirror each other, we experience each other's feelings; *we are within each other.* In his book, *Mirroring People; The New Science of How We Connect with Others,* Dr. Marco Iacoboni describes research showing, for the first time in history, that mirror neurons provide a plausible neurophysiological explanation for complex forms of social cognition and interaction. By helping us recognize the actions of other people, mirror neurons also help us to recognize and understand the deepest motives behind these actions. [3] Iacoboni believes that this study of mirror neurons will force us to radically rethink the deepest aspects of our social relations and our very selves. [4]

---

3 Marco Iacoboni, *Mirroring people; The Science of Empathy and How We Connect with Others,* page 6
4 Marco Iacoboni, *Mirroring people, The Science of Empathy and How We Connect with Others,* page 8

A Sensitive Animal

The mirror neuron and our resonance circuits explain how we can scan the moods of other people. We can watch an action and imitate it. Thanks to the mirror neuron, we can *foresee* an action that someone else is going to perform. This neuron also explains why bodily expression and facial expressions are infectious: yawns, smiles, wrinkled foreheads, threatening postures, grumpy faces. The mirror neuron imitates. It also means that we can be sensitive to other people's emotions, and that our emotions infect people around us and vice versa. The mirror neuron makes it possible to experience something that someone else is experiencing. This is the basis for human empathy.

As we see someone else do something – whether it is scratching the nose, falling down laughing or behaving anxiously – our mirror neurons respond as if we did it ourselves. Researchers call this *resonance*. Just as with a musical instrument, where one string vibrating makes other strings vibrate without anyone touching them, we activate each other's brains.

To attune, listen and mirror each other is so important that it can cure and heal another person. Not doing it may be fatal. Contact is essential for life. A person who is disconnected from mirroring will despair and wither.

Ski Tracks in the Brain

Daniel N. Stern is an American physician and psychiatrist working at the University of Geneva in Switzerland. He has been performing systematic observations of mothers and infants--their interactions, emotions, and communication--for decades. He has found that we can learn early on to feel empathy for each other and create what is called *intrasubjective contact*. We continually register and mirror each other and each other's nerve cells, thus creating experiences that, put simply, make *tracks* in our own brains. These tracks, in turn, form our behaviour and what we perceive as our reality.

If the tracks are "used" many times, because of repeated experiences, they get deeper and become "furrows." They become tracks that live (and sometimes make a mess!) in "the space" between two individuals.

The first person to write about "the space" was the Jewish philosopher, theologian and editor (1878 -1965) Martin Buber. In his groundbreaking 1923 book, *Ich und Du* (*I and Thou*), he claimed that human encounters were not about you or me, or even about us. Everything is really about the space between us, the interval. [5] So, the relationship exists not only in You or in Me, or even in the two of us together, but in the living space between the two of us. In this space, *everything* we carry along exists and gets activated. – and becomes our relationships!!

Our connection to our own experiences and the images that we store in the brain greatly influences our ability to communicate with others. Whether we learned to accept or despise ourselves as children, this early template will have a great impact on our adult relationships – especially with our intimate partners and others who are emotionally close.

I think that everyone carries along both acceptance and rejection of themselves. Of course, the amount and depth of each varies from person to person, depending on the particular experiences and mirror images that we carry along. We will meet our partner with acceptance or rejection, depending on what we feel for ourselves – *consciously or unconsciously*. Our self-image, in turn, is created by the image our parents have of themselves, as well as the image that our parents (and other important persons) have of us.

You may be thinking: How will I ever be able to do anything about the fact that Grandma lost her mother at the age of three or that Grandpa got beat up as a kid? Well, it's not easy. But I persist: you can change your brain. Researchers such as Kandel, Rizzolatti, Siegel, Doidge, Iacoboni, Bauer and many more proved it possible. Their discoveries also explain to me why the dialogue, "crossing the bridge," works. Listening, presence, mirroring, and empathy all produce *emotional attunement.* That is the basis of healing and change.

---

5 Martin Buber by Walter Kaufmann, *I and Thou,* page 66

The Armani Suit

From the beginning, we have the instinct to survive and maintain contact at any cost. Because of this survival instinct, each of us developed defence strategies early on. Jokingly I call these strategies "Armani suits" – because they are of prime quality, but also because they remind me of "armours." The design of these armours varies a lot, depending on our experiences of those that care for us, partly from the culture and ideals we grow up with, and partly from the amount of neglect we experienced as children. Our ways to protect ourselves from pain – our Armani suits – are thus very distinctive.

Put simply, we either turn our energy outwards or inwards. Some readily cry to get attention or comfort. Others become aggressive as soon as they feel pain, and live by the principle "attack is the best defense." We may withdraw from touch and attention, closing down our emotions in an attempt to deny that we have any needs. Still others use jokes and humour in painful situations. There are many strategies; we utilize most of them unaware. We use them automatically in an attempt to calm down our nervous systems.

But, no matter how clever our defense and how handsome our Armani suits are , they serve as barriers to finding the love and response we so desperately seek.

Free to Go, Safe to Return

The urge to bond is only one of a number of impulses that we develop as we grow. When we are attached to someone and feel safe in the relationship (the so called *bonding phase*), the need to explore the world grows. We need freedom to move away from our parents. At the same time, we need to know that the safety of the parents is still there when we return. Even here (in the so called *explorer phase*), our ability to manage the task depends on how well our parents have realized this impulse themselves, as well as how successfully the foundation has been laid through our bonding with our parents. And our development goes on this way: the impulse to explore the world paves the way for the next impulse: to establish a sense of identity (*the identity phase*): who am I in relation to other people and my surroundings? May I say no when others say yes? May I be another person than you?

Next comes the *competence phase*, in which we acquire abilities and feel that "yes, I can!" Finally, we reach the phase that involves the ability to care and be close to others (*the caring phase*) – and then we've gone full circle. Every phase is based on the previous one, and every "need not fulfilled" along the road lessens our ability to deal with the next phase. We need to link, differentiate, link and differentiate, link and differentiate again.

Of course, our ability to develop in a healthy way depends on much more than what Mom and Dad do and don't do. Predicaments such as poverty, war, illness, loss, unemployment, and so on, can also be powerful influences. Once again, this is not about having had a "good" or "bad" childhood. It's about the fact that our unfulfilled childhood needs will return to haunt us later on in life – *as long as we fail to understand why we put on the Armani suit in the first place.*

Everything that we experience during our whole life, especially during childhood is incorporated into us, and we also incorporate the history of our parent indirectly – especially all that they are not aware of that they carry along. Everything is in *the space*.

How Shall I Be?

Parallel with family influences, we are shaped by our society – we become social partly as a result of the culture we grow up in. We constantly get messages about what to do, what to say, how to behave, dress, talk, and move, in order to be approved. We find models for our behaviour in friends, teachers, classmates, idols, celebrities, and so on. All the while, we continue to be influenced by our relationships with our parents, and by the relationship *between* our parents. Observing and mouldable as we are, we learn how to behave in order to be loved and accepted.

We survive and are enriched as far as our parents, and others close to us, have been able to support our development through all phases, and have allowed us to be who we are. How well they manage this, in turn, depends on the contents of their luggage and brains from generations back.

Most of us have had good *enough* parents – we manage. Others have been less lucky, and their lives have been limited by deep, unfulfilled needs. We all try to take care of our lives as well as we can, but pain from the past sooner or later appears in our important adult relationships. The protective Armani suit we put on once to survive doesn't fit anymore--it's too small, tight, wrong or limiting in some other way. This suit is now stopping us from getting what we want and need. By this time it's a part of our identity, and since we are not aware that we wear it, we can't get out of it and move on, free and naked, ready to meet love! Instead, we exist through our defences, in suits that are long out of fashion.

We survive, but we don't live. Until…

I'm in Love!

When we fall in love, we feel deliciously alive and we are convinced that we have found salvation. Finally, we have found our way home, met our second half, and discovered the person the makes the world go around! Suddenly we see our life in a new light. We nibble at each other's ears, sit constantly entangled and reveal all our secrets. We become sexy, smart, funny, happy, and generous. We want to give *everything* to this wonderful person that makes us feel so good! We decide that we cannot live without this person. Finally, we feel whole and can be ourselves! We sigh with relief and liberation and relax for a moment. Unconsciously, we shrug off the Armani suit and put it on a chair by the bed… we don't need it anymore. We are naked and still safe. We dare to be naked because someone looks at us with loving eyes!

For a while, everything seems to be fine. Bright skies fill the future, and if there are clouds, they are small and far away at the horizon, nowhere near. We aren't alone, and together with our beloved we can fly. Hormones are flowing and for a while we are numbed by a wonderful intoxication, as we discussed earlier. We see what we think we see--what we *want* to see. With our bodies pumped full with the drugs of love, we look at each other with our most loving eyes, and in this intoxicated state we make each other feel safe by constant confirmation, tokens of endearment, caressing, gifts of love, appreciation, and cute little notes, flowers, and on and on. We find ourselves extremely tolerant towards our loved one:

"What? You dropped my mobile phone in the toilet? Well, well, such things happen."

"Oh, no problem that you're late, I've just been waiting for forty minutes."

"Of course I forgive you for shrinking my favourite sweater in the washing machine!"

We know there was no ill intent.

But as the "love drugs" slowly and relentlessly leave the system, we wake up to reality and begin to see the beloved and flawless one in a new light. Once again, we respond to what we *think* we see – but now we've lost the loving eyes. Since the drugs have left the system, our feeling of security may decrease or diminish, and our eyes are now sometimes filled with criticism, dissatisfaction, and bitter disappointment because the loved one doesn't respond to our needs in the same way as before. Or, we are filled with a sense of emptiness and feel that love is simply gone.

Slowly and steadily, we put the Armani suit back on.

The End of Infatuation

It now turns out that our love god or sex goddess has qualities that we can't stand. Even personality traits that we used to admire now irritate us. Old wounds start to hurt when we *get the impression* (since we now see with fearful eyes) that our partner will not be able to give us the love that we need. Our dreams crash into the wall.

But that is as it should be. We shall not be in love forever. The hormones go back to normal levels. We must remember: *it is normal.* We are not intended to sustain this increase of hormones in our body, and couldn't manage physically if we did.

For some of us, this is a huge crisis: we believe that we are out of "love" and all hell breaks loose. We argue, hurt each other, threaten, and maybe even resort to physical violence. Maybe we flee head over heels from the relationship, crawl into a cave and lick out wounds. Or, maybe we throw ourselves into a new relationship for comfort and to once again be high on the drug of love.

But for many people, the crisis isn't such a drama. You have simply sobered up, taken the rosy red lens from the camera and placed the partner closer to earth. He or she wasn't quite the one we'd hoped for, but... well, nobody's perfect! A lot of us reason this way: well, my darling turned out to have some serious flaws, but if I can only make the little darling understand that I can make him/her change, things will be fine again!

Still others slide into the next phase without even noticing.

Power Struggle

Quite often, tensions start when we decide to make our relationship more serious, move in together, get married or have children.

Our feelings of powerlessness and misery may turn into anger, disconnection, tears, revenge, manipulation, threats, criticism, jealousy, resignation, indifference, ……… (you can fill out the missing ones!) Since we no longer believe that our partner will give us what we need, we change tactics and unconsciously do what we *think* will give us what we need. We want to be looked upon with warm eyes! We need to be heard and understood! We simply want to be respected and loved for who we are. But since we don't feel that we are, we find ourselves on a quagmire and often behave counter- productively. Now, it's hard negotiations! We argue, discuss, and make compromises about time, chores, presents, and sex. We measure our success in terms of plus and minus points, gains and losses. We try to control our partner by accusing, sulking, crying, controlling, and so on. It can also be full-scale war. Clad again in our protective Armani suits, we throw grenades of guilt, bombs of accusation, landmines of threat, and projectiles of tears into the space between us. The power struggle is in full swing.

Some couples pursue their power struggle in a more subtle way, by filling the space with cold indifference – the same space that had been once filled with so much love! Others sweep the problems under the carpet and fill their life with other things, such as sports, work, alcohol, pets, or the children. Others simply experience that there is an end to the love and, without much drama, slip into a dull and lonely existence.

But these are not the only choices. Some couples slowly move into the next phase and begin to share a calm, fine and *good* life. They solve their conflicts and rediscover love.

Ghosts from the Past

Sooner or later, scenes that remind us of our previous experiences will surface and when they do, there is a great risk that we will once again *see what we saw before*, and thus create a reality that corresponds with this. And the feeling that this "reality" triggers will be felt with the same force as when we were children. If we have once felt alienated or abandoned, then our brain will interpret the smallest sign of this as a truth. We see what happens in the present, but we make our own interpretation of it – we see what we think we see, namely the images that we carry along the library of our brain and mind.

We are especially vigilant about negative experiences. We automatically see things that we believe can threaten our survival faster than the positive and pleasurable ones (remember the stick and the snake). We defend ourselves in the way we *think* is best and that nature early on taught us to use--attack, flight, manipulation, aggression, deceit, tears, silence--in order to try to survive.

Conflicts are Normal

All of this seems a fine recipe for disaster. It may seem puzzling that everything works in such a sad way. We are caught in old perceptions and behaviours. How can we sort this out and stop hurting others and ourselves? Can we renew our love and avoid "serial monogamy" and repeated divorces that involve great pain, not least for our children?

Yes, we can. I have seen couples achieve this, over and over again. A bit humorously, you could say that I want to encourage sustainable, ecological relations! And then *awareness* is the first step. Awareness about the nature of conflicts offers a unique possibility to help our "difficult" partner through the obstacles. The partner will be our pathfinder simply by treading on our sorest toes.

First we must accept that *conflicts occur*. It's natural! The harsh reality is that the basis for a relationship is difference and incompatibility. It is with this insight that conflicts can be constructive. Conflicts can be seen as a gift.

In our culture, we are not aware of the role and meaning of conflicts. We don't understand that contrast is the road forward. Instead we honour the romantic ideal that there exists "the right one" who is "made for me." And if we can just find this wonderful person, we can live happily together all our days. It's a *static* ideal, just like in fairy tales. We are deluged by films, books, and songs that hammer home this familiar message If you hang on to this naïve view of love, differences and conflicts will of course be a reason for divorce.

When the initial love fades and love turn sour, many people just switch off and think: well, that's the end of love. Current societal values then give us permission to move on and keep up the illusion that we simply chose the wrong person. It will be better with a new partner! We are even encouraged to "trust the feeling" – if you're not in love any more, then end it. Internet dating can be a fine way to meet a partner, but these websites also feed the dream that the grass is always greener on the other side, and thus make it much easier to alter the object of your love – maybe easier than it should be.

The truth is that there are no ideal, conflict-free relations. The dream of the perfect love and the ideal partner is a twist of the natural process of human relationships. It is often based on a naïve and unrealistic longing for happiness--a longing that, ironically, usually leads to unhappiness.

Divorce May Not be the Answer

Too often, divorce doesn't solve the problems we face in creating a healthy relationship. We may get rid of our partner, but unfortunately, we usually hang on our problems and move them along to the next relationship. We just drag along the worn, out-of-fashion Armani suit to the next house.

Here, I want to add that we sometimes *must* leave a destructive relationship. It may be one that involves physical violence or threats to life and limb of our children. I *don't* mean that a couple should stick together at all costs. What I mean is that we shouldn't get a divorce because we're no longer in love. That is supposed to happen. It's natural that emotions will change and that we will move on to the next phase.

This may sound a bit dreary, but I persist with my good news: when we get stuck in a power struggle, we *can* end it and begin conscious communication. Then we can look forward to a much better life together.

Real love starts in the area between two persons. *In the space*. What we choose to put there – both *explicit* memories (that which we remember that we remember) and *implicit memories* (that which we don't remember that we remember) – becomes our relationship. Our attitude towards each other becomes our relationship. We can learn to shed our defences, let go of being powerless, create positive goals, and start to live the life together that we want to have. We can choose to live in a loving relationship.

When we change the way we look at things
The things we look at change

UNKNOWN

3

The Biology of the Brain

The Age of the Mind

During my lectures and workshops I sometimes get the question: why do we have to understand how the brain works? You just have to start to work and solve the problems! They see my enthusiasm about the new scientific findings, but don't quite realise why they are so important.

I have realized that it is fundamental. I have worked for many years with mental training and couples therapy, developing my method and seeing that it really works – but I haven't really, really understood why. Now, there is clear and logical proof, via the latest research in interpersonal neurobiology. The basis for my enthusiasm perhaps also lies in my own difficulties with reading and writing and my desire to understand my own experiences. I have always wanted to understand why and how I do the things that I do, so that I can more quickly let go of things that don't lead me where I want to.

First of all, we must stop looking at conflict as a problem. We need to approach it from a different angle. In order to create a *shift* in ourselves, we must turn our gaze and look at difficulties with newly compassionate and curious eyes.

The more I learn about how the brain works the more enthusiastic and optimistic I become, and I want to transmit this enthusiasm to you! Even the simplest understanding of the brain can have profound effects on your love and compassion for both you and your partner. Maybe you're worried that this information about brain research will be a bit difficult to get through. From experience, I know that many clients call and want help quickly, and they don't understand why they need to start by understanding the brain. Then, once they have this knowledge they realise how important it is to their change process. It *is* very important to understand this in order to be able to maintain lasting change. So please be patient!

A number of researchers have called the 1990s the Decade of the Brain, while the 2000s are often called the Age of the Mind. The psychiatrist and professor at UCLA, Daniel J. Siegel, defined *the human mind* an embodied and relational process that regulates the flow of energy and information within the brain and between brains.[6]

Our knowledge in this area is growing very rapidly, to a large extent because sensors now can be used to scan the active human brain. We are gaining increasing knowledge about how this complicated organ works, even though we have just begun to study its potential. We know so little, and yet much more than just ten years ago. Still, we are at the beginning of understanding basic neural processes and the function of various brain structures, both as individual groups of neurons and as part of the brain's complex process of interconnectivity.

Following is a short basic course for the layperson on the biology of the brain.

6 Daniel J Siegel, *Mindful brain; Reflection and Attunement in the Cultivation of Well-Being,* page 5

A Hundred Billion Neurons

There are two types of brain cells, neurons (nerve cells) that communicate with each other and the rest of the body, and *glial cells*, that are needed to keep everything moving. The brain consists of close to a hundred billion nerve cells. It is believed that they create and receive up to ten thousand transferences – called *synapses* – to other nerve cells, creating 2 million miles of neural highways in our brains. Electric and chemical contact can take place in one thousandth of a second. That is an indication of our capacity for learning.

The nerve cells don't communicate connecting physically, by touching each other. Instead, they discharge something called *neurotransmitters* that are collected and read by other nerve cells. Let's take a brief look at how we got our fantastic brain.

The Reptilian Brain

Our brain has been formed by evolution in three steps. Hundreds of millions of years ago, we evolved the *brainstem*. It is also called *the reptilian brain* or *the old brain*, and is (of course) the oldest part of the brain. Here, basic body functions are regulated, including sleep, wakefulness, heartbeats, breathing, and body temperature.

The reptilian brain also exercises continuous control if we are in danger, with the aid of *amygdala* in the "mammalian brain" (see below). The reptilian brain houses our basic survival tactics: fight, flight, and avoidance.

The Mammalian Brain

About 150-200 million years ago, conditions on the earth changed. During a period of about 50 million years, a group of animals adapted to laying eggs internally – as compared to reptiles and birds that lay their eggs externally. During that period, the mammalian brain, also known as the *limbic system, limbic area,* and *limbic brain,* evolved. From the point of view of survival, it was an advantage to carry the fertilized egg in the body. But the price was that the offspring was born more immature and needed a longer period of nurturing.

As the mammalian, or limbic, brain evolved, many mammals began to bond with their offspring instead of abandoning them or eating them. Simply put, we started to need each other. The limbic area is the centre of our emotions (in spite of the fact that emotions are spread more or less all over the brain). Caring, social communication, the ability to play, and dreaming are all located in the limbic brain. These are the capacities we use when we interact emotionally with each other, and if they are damaged, we cannot care for our offspring.

It is the limbic brain that "sees" other beings and is programmed to interpret and respond to signals from people and other mammals. The mammalian brain means that we can feel kinship with, for instance, a dog, and it also explains how the dog can sense how we feel. All mammals have a limbic brain that house emotions and interprets them in other beings. Aggressive signals like growling, showing the teeth and bristling up can be interpreted by all mammals, irrespective of species or race, and the same is true for positive signs, such as wagging the tail or gentle touching. We mammals need each other – we bond.

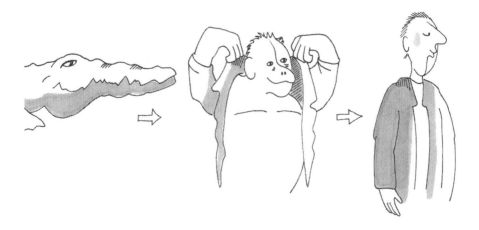

The Conscious Brain

The third step in brain development is what we call the *neocortex*, which is the part that makes us into the thinking, logical, and intelligent humans we are today (even if it's sometimes hard to believe we're so intelligent when you consider the state of the world). Our conscious will is situated here, as also our ability to plan and think ahead on an abstract level.

The neocortex is composed of six horizontal layers, each about one business card thick. According to Bonnie Badenoch, author of *The Brain-Savvy Therapist's Workbook,* the top layer carries representations built by experience, allowing us to anticipate what comes next. The bottom two layers take in new information, giving us the opportunity to attend to novelty. A creative neural event can unfold in the middle two layers as the expected and the novel meet. Moving from back to front, the frontal cortex contains regions for motor control of voluntary muscles and motor planning as well as for concentration, organization, reasoning, judgment, decision making, creativity, abstract thinking, emotion and relational abilities. If we move to the bottom-most area of the frontal cortex, we go to the highly integrative *prefrontal region,* a crucial area for healthy functioning in our relational lives [7]

The brain is of course much more complicated than this, and consists of a number of other parts with many special functions. One important part is the *hippocampus*, a seahorse-shaped mass that is situated in the middle of the brain close to the amygdala. It is our central organ for learning. The hippocampus handles memories of the when-where-how kind, and is incredibly important in the processes that create conscious memories. Since the hippocampus is so important to our memory I will return to it in another chapter.

---

7 Bonnie Badenoch, *The Brain - Savy Therapist's Workbook; A Companion to Being a Brain-Wise Therapist,* page 121

The Hand Model of the Brain

I'm not a brain researcher and this is not primarily a book about the brain--it's about relationships. There is now a huge body of knowledge about the brain, and new research continues to be published. So, be aware that I will report on only the most basic information that is relevant for this book.

During my childhood, due to dyslexia I sometimes didn't understand what "everyone else" grasped in school. Often, I used imagination and images to help. Many times this helped me understand. Let me show you an image of the brain that Dr Daniel Siegel cleverly uses in some of his books, including *Developing of the Mind* and *Mindsight.* It's a wonderfully simple and logical model.

Let's pretend that the hand is a model of the brain. (See Figure 1) The brain stem, or reptile brain, extends from the wrist up through the palm of the hand. Once again, this part of the brain contains the basic survival strategies: to flee, surrender, attack, and play dead. The brainstem also regulates sleep, blood pressure, breathing and other basic functions.

If we now place the thumb in the hand it makes the limbic area – the mammalian brain. Put both thumbs there, one from each side, since the limbic area covers the centre of the brain from both sides. The thumbs now represent the limbic system, the parts of the brain that control our emotions and our social life, and which was developed when we became mammals.

The Amygdala: Our Automatic Fire Alarm

At the bottom of the thumb, where thumb and hand meet, is now symbolically the area called *amygdala*. The amygdala consists of two almond-shaped groups of cells that convey emotional reactions, trigger the response to fight or flee in case of danger or makes us "play dead." The purpose of the amygdala is to warn us about direct or indirect threats. It quickly scans for dangers in the vicinity and sounds the alarm. It registers visual data of different kinds, for instance facial expressions and gestures – positive and negative – and then quickly takes over body, emotions, thoughts, and words. Our amygdala springs into action when we don't feel heard or understood.

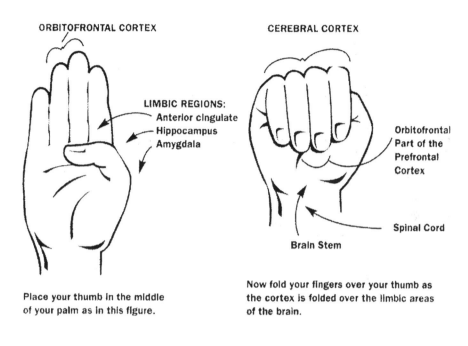

ORBITOFRONTAL CORTEX

CEREBRAL CORTEX

LIMBIC REGIONS:
Anterior cingulate
Hippocampus
Amygdala

Orbitofrontal
Part of the
Prefrontal
Cortex

Spinal Cord

Brain Stem

Place your thumb in the middle of your palm as in this figure.

Now fold your fingers over your thumb as the cortex is folded over the limbic areas of the brain.

FIGURE 1

The Brain in the Palm of Your Hand, Mindsight by Daniel J Siegel, page 15

Fear, anger and sadness can trigger this lightning-fast defence, but of all feelings, *fear* triggers the amygdala most strongly. When we are afraid, the amygdala forces us to act, with its excellent connections to important parts of the brain. The amygdala focuses our attention on what has scared us. A number of physical phenomena take place: Our pupils widen, the heartbeat increases and the blood vessels in less important parts of the body contract. Blood pressure rises and the blood is directed from the external limbs to the central parts of the body. We prepare to survive, by either fighting or fleeing. We instinctively become more attentive to our surroundings, such as the faces of people around us. We look for smiles or wrinkled foreheads that will help us interpret their intentions. The limbic system works with the reptile brain and the body when it comes to our most basic emotions.

But, you may be thinking, what does this have to do with my marriage?

I'll give you an example. If we have been criticized many times, that experience has been heavily impressed into our neuronal connections. Then, the amygdala will enlarge all signs of us being criticized. The amygdala focuses our attention on tone of voice, gestures, postures, words, yes, *everything* that we can perceive as criticism – in order to protect us. It makes us focus so keenly on potential criticism that, in the end, it's all we hear. It may even distort our eyesight and make us see the person's mouth as threateningly enlarged, so as not to miss the danger.

Imagine a person's face with a gigantic mouth, maybe even fangs. While I'm exaggerating a bit, this is actually how it works! When we're afraid, our brain turns the other person into something closer to a monster than a human being. If seeing things in images is not your thing, just read on.

Behind the Forehead

Cover your thumbs with the rest of your fingers and close your hand. The fingers bent over the thumb now represents the *neocortex.* Here lies the ability to do logical and structured thinking. The largest and most important part of this area is the prefrontal cerebral cortex, or prefrontal cortex. This part of the brain allows us to act with awareness, with reason and in a socially acceptable fashion, based on experience and the social rules obtained through life. Here also lies our ability to quickly and effectively scan situations that we are in.

In our trusty hand model, the prefrontal cortex is represented by the fingertips and nails, which now cover the thumbs. The two fingernails in the middle symbolise the middle of the prefrontal cortex. Just behind the forehead area, are several regions that are sometimes through to be the "higher part" of the limbic circuitry and a core aspect of the social circuit of the brain: the orbital frontal area behind the eyes, the medial prefrontal cortex behind the forehead, and the anterior cingulated just behind it. These more midline structures, along with a region called the insular cortex, serve important functions in linking body, affective state, and thought.[8]

With the aid of this "middle part" of the cerebral cortex, we can think abstractly, creating images of the future and dealing with questions of ethics and morality. It is primarily this part of the brain that makes us different from other mammals. The area behind the eyebrows is very important to our ability to consciously run our lives and calm our nervous system. It is also the centre for all communication, including the ability to listen and the sense of being heard.

When the Control Centre Doesn't Respond

If you now look at your middle fingers when your hand is closed, what do you see? Well, these two fingers (that represent the midsection of the prefrontal cortex) are in contact with all other parts of the hand. The prefrontal cortex is thus strategically situated, linked to both the limbic areas *and* the reptile brain – and, therefore, also the body. This middle part connects the three parts of our brain.

So let's take another look at the three areas again: *the reptile brain, the limbic brain,* and the *neocortex,* which includes *the prefrontal cortex.* When the hand is closed, the fingertips touch both the thumbs and the palm of the hand. The nails on the long finger and the ring finger here symbolise the *middle* prefrontal *cortex* that gives us access to very important abilities, including those that keep us mentally healthy, adult, aware, and in touch with each others. It's because of the prefrontal cortex that we can communicate, listen, and create loving relationships.[9]

Why is this so important to realize?

8 Daniel J Siegel, *The Mindful Brain*, page 32-39, Bonnie Badenoch, *Being a Brain-Wise Therapist*, 14-18
9 Daniel J Siegel, Lecture – CD: *The Neurobiology of We*, 2008

Well, look now: lift the fingers from the thumbs and see what happens: the prefrontal cortex no longer has any contact with the rest of the brain. In a simplified way, we can see that when the prefrontal cortex is disconnected; now, it is mainly just the limbic parts and the brain stem that govern our actions. This is how the human brain looks when we are terrified; perhaps when we meet a snake or a spider in the woods, sit in an airplane in turbulence, or get furious from a tackle when we play soccer. The prefrontal cortex is also disconnected when we are intoxicated.

But this is also how our brain looks when we stop being adult and aware in conflict with our partner. This is how the brain looks when we are involved in the dance of the power struggle. This is how my own brain, unfortunately, has looked a number of times with Sven and our children. The good news is that with knowledge and practice, we can begin to "close the hand" and act from compassion and wisdom.

Neurons that Fire Together, Wire Together-- and Survive Together

The hand model is a playful display of the basic structure of the brain. If we use both hands in our hand model, they can represent the left mode and the right mode of the brain. (See Figure 2) When the fingers are folded up (into a prefrontal cortex), they have contact with the rest of the hand (the limbic brain and the reptile brain). When the frontal cerebral cortex is disconnected, we often react violently, without thinking. You can say that we *react* rather than *respond*, and then things can go wrong – very quickly!

Let's try to understand more about how we are "wired", how the brain is connected.

The map of neuron connections is largely made up of experiences and results from contacts with other people) – especially our close ones. We are our relationships! Our experiences shape our brain and our mind. Nobody knows how the neuron connections end up as specific thoughts, feelings, or experiences – but that the brain cells send signals and are connected, that much we can see.

The expression "neurons that fire together, wire together and survive together" refers to the fact that neurons that fire at the same time bind together. This means that the chemical and electrical connection between neurons/nerve cells leads to the *forming of groups*. The nerve cells "discharge" signals, connect for a short moment and make traces that become a network map (think about lightning that strikes; if you look at it and then close your eyes you see "light tracks" for a while afterwards). Some of these connections are hereditary, and others we have learned. Since the brain works as it does, new experiences are "sucked" into old tracks, the same way as running water follows established lines. It's because of this that we have a tendency to experience what we already have experienced, see what we have seen, hear what we have heard, and so on, all according to our network map. This map becomes what we call our Ego, our "truth"--our mind.

With great curiosity, we can try to understand more about how these tracks operate (and sometimes go berserk) in the space between us. When we understand this, we can let go of unnecessary baggage such as guilt and blame.

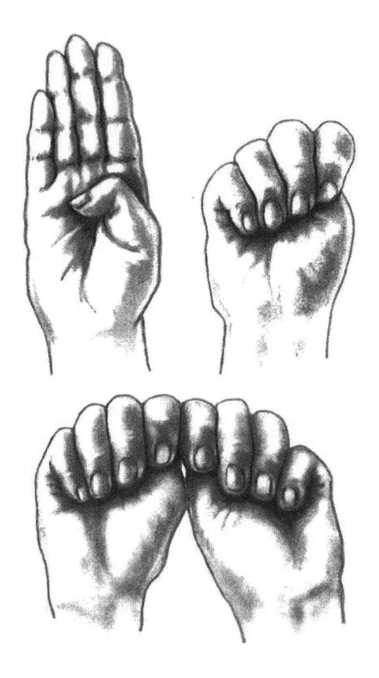

Figure 2
Being a Brain-Wise Therapist, Bonnie Badenoch, page 13

The Mind Alters the Brain

The mind cannot be placed in any specific part of the brain. *Relationships* create the mind. But, interestingly enough, we now know that the mind also changes the brain. This means that our mind is a constantly evolving process. Daniel Siegel describes the creation of the mind by three principles, like this:

1) The human mind involves two elements: *energy* and *information.*

2) The processes in the embodied brain (the connections of the neurons) create the mind. We know that our *relationships* can change the mind and the structure of the brain.

3) The mind is created through genetic programming and "responds" to our experiences. [10]

Siegel also states that regardless of the particular scientific outlook of researchers studying the brain, they seem to agree on these two elements: energy and information. Sometimes both are involved and sometimes just one. The information process flows not just within our own brain, but also between our brain and others' brains--for example, when we speak to each other.

I perceive the mind as something that slowly evolves during our climb along the ladder of development, via contacts and experiences. The mind is then mixed with our genes and, with time, creates our Ego. We shall experiment a bit with the flow of energy and information in our embodied brains and mind.

Disneyland

Notice what happens when you read the word "Disneyland."

Close your eyes. Notice if anything happens within you. Do you see an image in your mind? Many naturally see the image of an amusement park. Did you? How did it feel in your body? Let's take a look at what might have happened.

---

10 Daniel J Siegel, *Parenting from the inside out*, page 32, *The Developing Mind*, page 2

In the brain, there is a pattern of neuronal activity. This pattern or architectural structure we'll call Disneyland. When you hear (or read) the word "Disneyland," a number of neurons in your brain "discharge" and are connected to each other, especially on the left side of the brain where the centre for language is situated. If you have heard the word "Disneyland" before, the flow of energy has a symbolic value. It contains some information, and then you have access to an entire association bank of mental processes. Put simply, you can then *visualize* the amusement park Disneyland.

You may also experience an emotional sensation as your brain picks out the image of a particular ride. You want to shake hand with one of the characters. Can you hear the screams from people in the roller coaster? Maybe you have some unpleasant memory; maybe you got nauseous or even threw up, so that the word "Disneyland" triggers discomfort.

You may have heard stories about things that happened to other people in this amusement park, read a book or seen a film in which Disneyland appeared.

You may have other connections: some person that you dislike may have spoken very positively about it; some friend could go there and you could not; or something completely different. Or maybe the word "Disneyland" means nothing to you at all because you come from a different cultural background and have no association to the word.

Of course some words (or behaviours, smells, tastes, sounds, and so on) will affect you in one way, but affects your partner in a different way. Sometimes we confuse ourselves with each other because we don't quite grasp that we have different association banks. Under some circumstances, this can create major problems. For instance, the word "closer" can mean completely different things to two different people. (See Figure 3)

Figure 3
Picture of couple at the table..

(A woman, sitting at the far end of the table from her husband, may say to him: "Please honey, come closer," and she means she wants him to sit right next to her, so that they can touch and talk. He moves an inch or two closer, but continues to read his paper, thinking he is responding to her request. Of course, she is not happy!)

The example of Disneyland is a typical case of information and flow of energy that moving from one mind (the author's) to your mind as I asked you to think about Disneyland. Here we can see that the mind is not only something that happens in one brain, but also can be created between two or more brains. Our brains are "in each other" whether we like it or not.

This is one reason why the mind is not the same thing as a brain. This is also the basis for why it's possible for conscious, loving relationships to reshape, develop, integrate, and heal a mind. Some therapies that can help us to achieve these healing relationships are Imagotherapy, psychotherapy, body therapy, and cognitive therapy.

I repeat: our relationships and our way of communicating alters the structure in the brain.

Do it Again--and Again and Again!

All cells and networks in the brain just lie there, waiting for stimuli. Those that are confirmed are connected and activated. Those that are not confirmed regress. Simply, "use it or lose it!"

Scientists call the fact that our social contacts alter the brain *neuroplasticity*. This simply means that repeated experiences alter the shape and size of the nerve cells and their connections. By repeatedly activating a certain register of emotions in the brain, our most important relationships can gradually create some neutral circuits to tread these "tracks" so that we more easily find the path next time. When we repeat it frequently, it gets imprinted in our memory. The more times we take that route, the clearer the path is in the network.

In my hometown, there is a lawn where the kids take a shortcut to school. A path has been tread on the grass, and the authorities have long tried to block it and put new grass to discourage people from walking over the lawn. But one day when I passed, some workers where putting asphalt there. When I asked them why, one of them replied: "Oh, we gave up--people walk here anyway."

This is a good illustration of what I'm trying to say: what we do often deepens the tracks in the brain. Good makes good – and bad makes bad.

Treading a Highway

The latter, unfortunately, is more frequent in our relationships when we feel hurt, misunderstood, criticised, deserted, unseen, suffocated, or scared, and then we defend ourselves by yelling, fleeing, criticising, crying, or moping. But fortunately, we also create "good" tracks in the brain when we are loving, kind, and appreciative to others and ourselves!

This "track-making "ability of the brain offers a fantastic possibility for repair, healing, and integration. We can always *choose* positive reactions and behaviour that further our good neuron network. Since our brain is changeable we can actually tread new "lines," tracks, and yes, *highways* of good nerve pathways. It's so good that we are human beings with small, clever fingernails behind the forehead!

When you meet someone with empathy, you can experience the advantage of visiting another person's world, emotions and ideas – and understand that this person is not you. This is differentiation, connecting and integration: to see through the eyes of another person and *profoundly* understand that your world looks different than in mine.

When we can "take in" another person's world, it doesn't only lead to empathy, integration in the brain and creation of new nerve pathways – although this is great enough! It can also offer the wonderful experience of safe *attachment*. This is what we all are created for, what we all strive for from our first moments on earth.

We simply need each other.

Intimacy

— IN TO ME SEE

4

The Sociable Brain

Touch Me, Please

My colleague and friend, Hedy, steps into an elevator. The elevator, half full, is hot and crowded. Hedy stands in the middle and the doors close. The man next to her accidentally bumps into her and immediately says:

"Oh, excuse me."

Hedy smiles, turns to him and says: "Hmm, that's alright. I like it."

Not everyone may enjoy being bumped on an elevator, but the truth is, we *do* like contact. We are programmed for social contact on every level, and this is hardly news. But now neuroscience can prove that our brain is constructed in a way that makes it sociable. As soon as we meet and interact with another person, there is a connection between the brains.

As you may remember our centre for emotions and need to bond with other people is located in the *limbic brain,* the part that we have in common with all mammals and the site of our emotions. We desperately need what scientists call *limbic resonance*. I want to make it clear that when I continue to talk about limbic resonance, it's not only the limbic brain that is involved, but the entire brain.

Nonetheless, we can't achieve limbic resonance with a thing or being that does not also have a limbic brain – like a chair, a snake, or a fish. Limbic resonance can only be achieved with another mammal, such as a dog, a horse, or another human. What we want and need most is contact with other humans. When my limbic area gets in touch with your limbic area, exciting things occur: our nervous systems calm down! The stronger the emotional bonds we have to another person, the greater the mutual effect will be (like it or not).

Our nervous systems are constructed to be captured by the nervous system of others, so that we can experience others as if from within their skin, as well as from within our own. [11] We need each other and influence each other all the time. We are woven together in the web of the universe where we all are the fibres in the material, in constant interaction with each other, nature, and the whole.

Since our nervous systems are designed this way, humans need contact with other humans. When we have that, a map over our own Ego is made – a mind. Small children need adults around them, not only because children depend on adults to meet their physical needs, but also because the young ones need to mirror themselves in other people's brains and minds. The neuron links that exist in the grown person's brain are mirrored *directly* and *indirectly* to the child's brain. Simply put, in order for the child to develop a human mind, the child needs to be surrounded by other minds.

In our present world of high-tech, it is important to remind ourselves that human time together never can be replaced by telephone, texting, chat, Facebook, Twitter, Google +, blogging or any other kind of relationships on the web. Of course, Internet relationships can be positive in many ways – but we are meant to have strong bonding *in physical closeness* to other people.

---

11 Daniel N. Stern, *The Present Moment in Psychotherapy and Everyday Life*, page 76

We can only develop our language by hearing other people talk. We learn morals from other people's morals. The way that adults treat themselves and the child is integrated in the child's reality. That is, we are shaped by others close to us. We are simply sculptured from other people's minds and presences, and our self-image and self-awareness are cast on other people's minds. If we don't get this human contact and interaction, our brains start to wither and our mind starts to die. It's a chain reaction. Our experiences activate neurons that activate genes that activate proteins that change the structure of our brain.

Daniel Goleman is a doctor of psychology, a science journalist for *The New York Times,* and author of the books *Emotional Intelligence* and *Social Intelligence.* In the latter book, he describes thought- provoking research results from the new field of social neuroscience. According to Goleman, our social encounters are modulators, like a thermostat that constantly regulates important parts of the brain – especially emotions. The emotions that arise in our contact with others have far-reaching consequences when they spread like waves through the body and send out cascades of hormones that run our biological system, everything from the heart to the immune cells. [12]

Perhaps most amazing, social neuroscience now is beginning to chart a connection between our most stressful relationships and the function-ality in specific genes that regulate the immune system. It plainly means that in stressful situations, we are more prone to develop various kinds of illnesses – especially if we get stuck in our problems instead of using them as guides. Loneliness can also make us ill.

Hello, Hello, Hello

In order to feel alive, we need to be in touch with others. We depend on a larger context where we laugh, share thoughts and emotions and are in touch. We need a loving relationship to other people. We simply need

12 Daniel Goleman, *Social Intelligence; The New Science of Human Relationships*, page 4 and 5

limbic resonance, where our mammalian brains are in touch with other mammals--in our case, humans.

There is a tight connection from brain to brain when we interact with, another person. This "neural bridge" means that we can affect the brain (and thus the body) of everyone that we are in touch with, and they can affect us. This is especially true in our close relationships.

To a surprising degree, our relationships are affected not only by our experiences but also by our biological functions. It's important to understand that we need each other so much that, if deprived of human contact for a very, very long time, we go mad, nuts, crazy – and finally we may lose the zest for life and die. Children, of course, are at highest risk if they lack contact. As my friend and colleague Dr Pat Love says; "There is no such thing as a baby. There is only a baby and a caregiver."

A film that portrays this need for contact is *Cast Away,* in which Tom Hanks is stranded on a deserted island. In his desperate loneliness, he creates a friend: a volleyball he calls Wilson. When we don't have human contact, we wisely enough create a friend. It can be a fantastic friend, like in Cast Away. Children are particularly good at this: they readily create imaginary friends.

Once again: we simply need each other.

We are woven together in the web of the universe and we are very similar, but of course we are also different. At times, that difference creates incredible loneliness. I can recognize the longing both in myself and in many of those who have visited my clinic. Especially here in the Western world, we are becoming more and more isolated. Maybe it is more evident in big cities, where many people live alone in their apartments without much contact with neighbours, friends, or relatives. There is often a lack of natural meeting places for getting together.

Outside the Window Pane

The worst thing we humans experience is feeling left out--feeling that others are indifferent to us, and that we are alone. Contact and mirroring with others is of vital importance. We need to be part of a context and feel that we mean something to someone else. That is one reason it can be healing to have a pet if we live alone, and then preferably not a goldfish or a snake, but an animal with a limbic brain.

When we don't feel that we get any contact, or that the contact is threatening, we get scared. The automatic alarm in our brain (the amygdala) starts clanging. This alarm is activated whether we are actually outside of warm human contact or just feel like we are outside. To push someone out of a group is effective psychological torture, and bullying has been called the voodoo of our time.

It's interesting and scary that the feeling of being left out affects the brain in the same way that physical pain does. And it's so easy to feel outside.

Lost in a Small Town

I have a clear memory of feeling outside. I was a small girl of ten moving from Nigeria to a town in Sweden. I spoke both Swedish and English fluently, since my parents always used their mother tongue when they talked to me. So, language was not a problem. But I was small and thin and for a while I was bullied in my new school. Not all of the children left me out, but all the ones I thought were important did. I was different, the child that didn't fit in.

In Africa, I felt left out because I was white among all the black children. In Sweden, I became a black child among all the white ones. I was some kind of mix. My mother told me that when I was a small girl in Nigeria, I smeared myself in mud in order to be considered black. Hardly anyone was fooled.

Being outside was stuck on me. I was different. And I so wanted to be like everyone else! I have no problems understanding how it can feel to come to a new country with the "wrong" appearance and a strange language.

As a teenage girl I was skinny as a rake and felt that all the other girls had nice bodies, well-defined breasts and hips. I looked like a boy with my thin, rangy body. I so wanted to look "normal." In gym class I dressed in several layers of sweaters to hide my body. Those classes were painful. It didn't take long for the "cool" girls to expose my pathetic sweater-bluff.

In school, I wasn't only different. I was stupid, too. Since I'm dyslexic, I was often perceived as irresponsible, sloppy and lazy. Many times I studied like crazy for a test, only to realize with disappointment that I failed. To begin with I was enthusiastic, but after a while I just gave up. No matter how much I studied, the result was as bad. Failure became a reality. I didn't understand *anything*.

I will never forget at comment from a teacher in compulsory school: "Eva, you'll never amount to anything. You are completely hopeless and stupid."

Without my mother, her positive attitude and loving eyes, I would certainly have been stuck in the conviction that I was hopeless, stupid and powerless.

Dad on the Seven Seas

I felt outside at home, as well. Before my parents divorced and dad moved to Australia, we lived together for a while in Sweden. While other dads washed the car, renovated the house, or mowed the lawn, my dad sat drunk up on the roof because there, he, the artist, would find the best light. I was as much ashamed of my drinking father as I was proud that he could paint the most beautiful paintings.

Shortly after my dad moved to Australia, I invented a fantastic image of him. He became my idol. A dad who was fantastic and different but that I at the same time felt sorry for. I created an image of him that was easier to carry. In my imagination he was like Pippi Longstocking's father, out on the seven seas. He loved me more than anything and would soon come to visit me, the strongest girl in the world.

In my imagination, Dad was handsome, strong, healthy, always warm, sober, safe, and present – and only *right now* on the seven seas. You can imagine the demands I've made on men. It wasn't easy for anyone to live up to my naive fantasy of what a man should be.

Jeans from Wal-Mart

Many of us have had similar experiences of feeling outside in school. This feeling so easily appears. It's in our genes. Let's look at a few examples of how it may appear in everyday life.

At work, you notice that the others have gone for a coffee break, and no one told you.

A group of people are talking. As you approach, they go silent or change the subject.

You're an immigrant with a strange name and a strange accent and because of it; you have a hard time to find work.

You are a woman among men.

You are a man among women.

No one seems to listen when you say something at meetings.

Everybody laughs at something funny and you don't get the joke.

You don't understand the social codes of the country you live or spend time in.

You are homosexual in a heterosexual context – or the other way around.

You are fat, thin, tall, short, pale, knock-kneed, or have curly hair in a world where everybody else seems to be "normal."

You live with dyslexia, ADHD, cerebral palsy, Tourette syndrome, or some other variation on the structure of the brain and feel that people treat you differently.

Everybody is talking about the party yesterday that you weren't invited to.

Your parents drink while everybody else seems to have sober and tidy homes.

Everyone has designer jeans; yours are from Wal-Mart.

(And so on!)

Yes, there are many reasons to feel left out in daily life, in both small and serious ways. It's a natural feeling. Some of us have had very strong experiences connected to being outside, which make the brain more alert for similar signs. Things that for other people seem completely banal may trigger fear in us, and often we don't understand them ourselves. The brain reacts this way to *warn* us so that the terrible thing will not happen again. Others may have only been nudged to the edges of their social group once or twice, rather than completely and consistently rejected. Yet that kind of casual snubbing can also leave its mark.

It's a natural process that our brain warns us when we feel threatened by feeling left out. Once we have experienced it, the same feeling often appears in the space between us and our partner. In our most intimate relationship, we easily feel abandoned, unwanted and pushed out.

I Knew at Once that She Would...

You remember the *mirror neuron* that responds both to actions that another person performs, or is about to perform, and the feelings of this person. It immediately prepares us to imitate this action and feel with the person. A short repetition:

The mirror neuron quickly sees the purpose behind the movement of the other, and *what* it sees depends on the experiences that are stored in the individual's brain. The mirror neuron sees, copies, and takes in other signals. Not just what we see when we look at each other, but also the *purpose* of what we see – and the *emotion* behind the purpose. The mirror neuron helps us understand what is happening in another person.

For example: if I see you lift your hand with a cup of coffee in it, I think that the purpose must be to drink coffee. When you lift the arm, some of the mirror neurons in *my* brain discharge just as if I did it myself – in spite of the fact that I only watch your arm move the mug towards your mouth. My own desire for coffee awakens.

The brain registers, imitates, tunes in, learns, and this way builds a network of associations from experience which means that we *know* that next time someone lifts a cup of coffee that way, it means they will drink coffee.

The positive thing about this is that the brain saves energy. It doesn't have to learn anew every time. The negative is that our neurons quickly will discharge when we see certain actions, whether the actual intent is what we think or not. All perception--that is, what we see, hear, feel, smell and taste--can make the neurons discharge in the brain of the beholder. [13]

I think of the music in the movie *Jaws*. Hearing it immediately reminds me of the fear I felt when I saw it the first time at fifteen. Practically everyone has this kind of connections to music that trigger a memory that is bittersweet, fearful, painful, or wonderful. One of my friends has a song that makes her cry, every time. The same person immediately gets happy from a certain Brazilian accordion player! For a lot of people, music is a happy or sad button.

All of our experiences lie, as you know like small tracks in our brain. We all have a symbolic library with many shelves and on each shelf there are folders or albums As you remember, the albums contain images of things we have seen and see, things we have felt and feel, smells that we have smelt and smell, things we have heard and hear, and so on. We have images of *everything* that our senses have registered earlier, taken in or is taking in. And that which we take in NOW is based on the association bank in our library about THEN.

---

13 Joachim Bauer, *Varför jag känner som du känner* (Swedish title) page 22, Original title; *Warum ich fuhle, was du fuhlst, Intuitive Kommunikation und das Geheimnis der Spiegelneurone*, 2005

We interpret and read each other all the time... the words, tone of voice, what we see in the other persons face and all the signals that the other person's body send out. The left and the right sides of the brain interpret what it sees in different ways. Information is integrated and becomes what we experience.

Then, don't forget that the "images" really aren't stored as images, but are split up into components and are put together again or constructed *on demand*. But interestingly enough, we create the purpose that we *believe* exists, based on what we have experienced previously, regardless if this corresponds with the actual intention of the other person. We simply see what we believe that we see... and this goes like lightning! Our neurons will send signals, connect and *know* the purpose in the other person's head. This is especially so when it comes to negative events, since these are stored more deeply than the positive events – all for our survival.

...Hit Me

A simple example:

I lift my arm to wave at you. When you see my arm go up in the air, your mirror neurons will discharge signals in your brain – the same way as in my brain. Now the mirror neurons quickly read the *purpose* behind the movement of my arm. The result depends on what you carry along in your album and your network map. The result depends on the previous signals from your neurons.

Let's pretend that you have experienced this arm movement as something positive many times and thus have a track in the brain that makes this movement into something positive. When the arm goes up, your brain quickly and clearly reads the purpose: she is going to wave at me.

Now, let's instead say that you have stored a very negative experience: many times you've seen a hand go up in the air, not in order to wave but to hit you. When you see my arm rise in the air, your mirror neurons will interpret the *purpose* as that I will hit you, and you maybe flinch. The "I've been hit" tracks in your brain activate and you automatically go to defence. No matter that I don't hit you but actually wave; your neurons have already interpreted the signal that I'm going to hit you.

You are also "showered" internally with hormones that are automatically secreted at the feeling of threat and stress, including adrenaline and the stress hormone cortisol. Again, you are flooded this way whether my actual purpose corresponds to your image or not.

Intuition

When we meet other people, we always respond to the mood they display in different ways, for instance with body language. We unconsciously imitate each other and repeat certain emotional expressions. This mirror phenomena creates what we call *intuition,* which means that we can guess what is going to happen or how someone feels. [14]

Many experiments have been performed around this neutral dynamic. Daniel Goleman describes an example: When a woman that a man finds attractive looks straight at him, his brain starts to secrete the pleasure-arousing substance dopamine – but not when she looks the other way! [15] One would assume that this goes for women, too.

Each of these findings gives us a small glimpse of how our social brain works when we interact. This is a huge area that we have just started to study; more findings will soon be forthcoming.

The social brain is unique in its sensitivity to its surrounding. As soon as we have contact face-to-face or skin-to-skin or voice-to-voice, our social brains become linked. That we need each other and influence each other all the time is something we have in common. Our brain is

---

14 Joachim Bauer, *Varför jag känner som du känner* (Swedish title) page 11,26. Orginal title; *Warum ich fuhle, was du fuhlst, Intuitive Kommunikation und das Geheimnis der Spiegelneurone,* 2005
15 Daniel Goleman, *Social Intelligence; The New Science of Human Relationships,* page 9

our most social organ. We want to enjoy warm eyes, appreciative words, and human contact. We depend very much on it.

Together, Apart or Parallel

Quite naturally, we try to experience this warm contact all our lives, and when we experience it, we feel alive. It can be moments when cascades of substances, such as dopamine and endorphins, are pumped out into the body. Endorphins are substances similar to morphine or, i.e. painkillers that give a feeling of euphoria.

This longing to feel alive is the common denominator that makes so many people, both single and married, throw themselves into new relationships with such frenzy; to be in love is a way to feel alive. Sometimes I have been surprised by the incredible power behind the search for "true love." But I have been similarly impressed by the strength of our desire to be the best partner, parent, or friend that we can be.

Take relationships and marriages. How can anything that starts out so well (as it usually does when we fall in love) sometimes end so badly? How can the exhilaration of infatuation morph into constant quarrels, hostility, psychological torture, and even abuse? How can the shining promise of lifelong commitment end in bitter divorce?

Some people that separate or divorce do so after only a short time, while others leave each other later in life. Some choose to stay married, not because they feel good together, but for other reasons. They often live "parallel" – side-by-side but not together. I have the feeling that most of us live more-or-less parallel. It has become quite natural for many to live together without intimacy or closeness. However, it is important not to blame anyone for this, since there is an important reason why we so easily end up in this lonely place.

Many couples are very much aware of their lack of intimacy, but choose to continue living together for the children, economy, or comfort – or because of the uncertainty that life would present without a partner. We continue together, but we are not happy together. Still others choose to change partners again and again in their search for that vital feeling of intimacy and "true" love.

We are, as I mentioned earlier, brainwashed with images of eternal, passionate, and romantic love; we are told that love is about finding *the right person*. It's an image often presented in girls' magazines, TV series, films, and books. The media often invite us to believe in eternal, effortless happiness.

I know that many struggle, struggle, and struggle, but finally they find no other way out than divorce. This is especially likely to happen when they think that they are "out of love." But when the decision is made, it can be a difficult process. It's usually not so easy to divorce.

I want to make clear that I don't condemn other lifestyles that we adults may choose. In addition to those who choose to divorce, others believe that marriage and living as a couple is outdated, and don't want to try it in the first place. Instead, they want to live in extended families, generations together, choosing their housing on the basis of common interests or commitments. There are many ways to live your life.

Those that I attempt to inspire with this book are those who *want* to live as a couple. It is for individuals who want to live with the same person in deep love and intimacy for a long period of time, maybe all their lives. If this is the life you seek, read on.

We do not treat our patients for something that happened to them in the past. Rather, we try to cure them of what they are doing to themselves and others, to deal with what happened to them in the past.

JUDE CASSIDY

5

How We Become Who We Are

From Then to Now

Let's look a bit more at how the memory works, in order to understand how our brains are wired and how our experiences make us into what we are today.

Simply put, a memory is an experience from the past that shapes us and affects our actions, thoughts, and feelings in the future. So, a memory has three aspects: THEN, events in the past that affect us NOW and shape (and probably will continue to shape) our FUTURE.

Many people look at a memory as something we remember, but it is much more complicated than that. Researchers have discovered two layers of memories. The first layer is called *implicit* and the second, *explicit*.

Implicit Memory

Implicit memory involves our behavioural learning, emotional reactions, perceptions of the outer world, and likely also includes our bodily sensations. We can also generalize across experiences, integrating elements of lived moments into a schema or mental model of events. Further, implicit memory involves the readying ourselves for action or feeling called *priming*. [16]

Implicit memory doesn't have conscious focus and purpose. It isn't a conscious process. We do not perceive it as memory; it is all that which we take in and mentally "photograph" without registering it. Let me illustrate implicit memory by describing an experiment.

An experiment group wearing earphones listened to twenty names of animals in the right ear. They were told to listen as carefully as possible and, after a short while, to repeat the names they had heard (preferably in order). What the group didn't know was that at the same time as they heard the names of the animals, they would hear something completely different in the left ear – namely names of flowers.

The experiment showed that many individuals managed the task very well. They remembered something like 17 or 18 animals. But had they heard anything else in the other ear? Most said that they had, but they had been so focused on the animal names that they'd only heard mumbling in the left ear.

A while later, the participants were given a paper with some letters and spaces between, for instance T_ _ _P, D _ _ _ Y or A_ _ _ _ _E. They were then supposed to fit in letters in the empty spaces (here: tulip, daisy, and anemone). Most automatically wrote names of flowers – interestingly enough, exactly the flowers mentioned during the test. They did this without knowing why. They registered the names of the animals *explicitly* and the names of the flowers *implicitly*; that is, they

---

16 Daniel J Siegel, *The mindful therapist; A Clinician's Guide to Mindsight and neural Integration,* page 63

took in the information about the flowers unconsciously. *This is what implicit memory does all the time.* [17]

Throughout our lives, we take information in and store it internally. First, we do this implicitly in our emotions, our perceptions, our physical actions, and our bodily sensations, and then in explicit form (which I will address soon). As mentioned above, implicit memory has the ability to prepare us for what is coming. It is an automatic warning system that gives us signals without our knowing or remembering that we have been warned. This initial layer of memory is present already at birth (actually even *before* we're born, since the fetus registers sounds, such as the voices of the parents or song and music heard inside the womb).

Implicit memory is thus unconscious memory (though it is not what the psychoanalyst Sigmund Freud called "the subconscious;" that is a different entity.) An important and interesting factor in this initial layer of memory is that when we experience an implicit memory in the present, we respond in the here and now, but the associations come from the past. We don't respond to it as if it was a memory – we are convinced that it is about the present moment.

According to Daniel Stern, implicit knowledge is non symbolic and nonverbal. It is *procedure-oriented* and *unconscious*. A good example is the process of learning to talk. We learn to talk, but we don't remember how or when we did so. [18]

The Seahorse

Another example of implicit memory is a *motor* memory like riding a bicycle. We learn to ride a bike as children, and when we ride a bike as adults we don't think: "Oh, now I'm riding a bike!" – We just do it. We learnt it a long time ago, we know how to do it, but we don't remember *how* we know. We just know. We have a number of memories that allow

---

17 Daniel J Siegel, *The Neurobiology of We*, 2008, Cd 2
18 Daniel N. Stern, *The Present Moment in Psychotherapy and Everyday Life*, page 113

us to simply "know." This is important, because if we had to remember everything *consciously* in an active process, we would soon go mad. [19]

During the first year of life, the right mode of the brain is very active and it is primarily the body that takes in and register implicit memories. At approximately eighteen months, a part of the brain called the *hippocampus* is developed. When this part of the brain is mature, it starts to integrate the implicit memories with what we call explicit memories. "Integrate" here means to take separate parts and connect them. At this time our middle prefrontal region also comes on line and explicit memory becomes available. [20]

The Old Oak

In order for a memory to become explicit, it takes conscious focus *and* the involvement of hippocampus. The hippocampus takes the implicit associations and puts them together to form a whole.

Let's imagine that we are a small child (not yet eighteen months old) who experiences a tree in different ways. We see an old oak in our garden, hear the wind singing, and hear our parents read stories about trees. We listen to songs about trees, hugging, playing, and perhaps taking a nap under the tree, and so on. We experience and take in the phenomenon "tree" in different ways. We do this with the aid of the *implicit* memory.

Soon, our brain will make associations between all our implicit experiences of "tree." As long as the memories are only *implicit* they are outside our consciousness, stored in our emotions, in our body, and in how we act and perceive things. When the hippocampus is connected, it helps us to put all the implicit parts together to a whole that we, with the aid of language, will call "a tree" (and later on "an oak tree" instead

---

19 Daniel J Siegel and Mary Hartzell, DVD *Parenting From The Inside Out – A Ten-hour Seminar for Professionals*.

20 Bonnie Badenoch, *Being a Brain-Wise Therapist: A Practical Guide to Interpersonal Neurobiology*, page 28

of an elm tree, for instance). The memory has moved from the right mode of the brain to the left mode of the brain - from *implicit* to *explicit.*

Explicit Memory

Let's take a look at the second layer of coded memory, the one we call *explicit* memory. This memory demands conscious focus and purpose and it consists of two dimensions:

Factual memory:

A tree is a plant, larger than a bush with a wooden trunk… and so on.

Autobiographical memory:

Last week I lay in the shade of a tree sleeping (this includes a sensory experience).

With the aid of the *hippocampus,* the different impressions are integrated and put together into a common picture--a *factual memory,* and then perhaps an *autobiographical memory.* If we continue with the example "tree," our factual memory knows that a tree has a trunk, branches, needles or leaves, and that these look different depending on the sort of tree, and that the leaves usually fall in autumn, and so on. We know what a tree is and we know that we remember what a tree is.

The autobiographical memory contributes to our ability to not only know what a tree is, but also to put ourselves into a context with trees through time. Maybe we remember when we slept under the oak tree in the garden as a child, or we remember a tree house we built at the age of eight. Our emotions say: *"this comes from the past… I remember."*

Interestingly enough, there are two different kinds of autobiographical memory. In one kind, we remember ourselves from an observation point. We look at things from outside, "from a corner of the ceiling," so to speak, and we see ourselves as a child building a tree house. In the other type of autobiographical memory, we remember actions "through our own eyes," as we saw it when it occurred. We "see" the building of the tree house through our own eyes and from the perspective of then.

This we can do in spite of the fact that we *are very well aware* that it is just a memory that we "see."

Fear of Dogs

The memory is an association process. This means that events from different times are linked together. The brain creates "mental models" and when we have experienced something many times the brain will automatically *generalise* and quickly sort it into a pigeonhole. For instance, if you have been bitten or scared by a dog, you may experience all dogs as awful and dangerous; or your mother have been bitten by a dog and she communicates her fear to you in different ways. You have become scared by your mother's fear without even being aware that your mother had been bitten; this memory may only exist *implicitly* in you – and it may be implicit and unconscious in her, too!

Since implicit memory has the ability to prepare us for things ahead, you can in some situations be "warned" about a dog, by, for instance, feeling uneasy– but you have no idea why.

This phenomenon is called *priming* and means that certain elements around us affect our unconscious mind and our behaviour. Our brain apprehends many more messages then the ones we are aware of and works hard to sort the impressions and guide our behaviour. This system in the brain helps us to avoid experiencing – in this case -- an attack by a dog.

Let's continue with the dog example. You are on your way to see a friend that you haven't visited before. Already, when you enter the garden you feel uneasy. Somewhere in the garden, you have unconsciously observed dog things; you may have seen a bowl for food or water, smelled the odour or in some other way registered that a dog is in the vicinity – without any conscious thoughts about it on your behalf. You may feel uneasy and get the idea that you don't like her house, the area, or even the friend you're visiting. All of this happens because the brain is desperately trying to understand why you feel so badly. But it is actually your implicit memory that warns you of danger that may be close. All of this occurs unconsciously. But your body and your senses know and have *implicitly* responded to signs that here is a dangerous dog. You have an experience (priming) of going into an unpleasant house with a person who is not good for you, no matter whether it's the kindest dog in the world – or whether there is a dog at all!

Once again: *it is better for our survival if to believe that the stick is a snake than that the snake is a stick.*

With all of our senses, the brain has photographed and registered all of our lives, and these images are with us every moment in the present. Everything lies in the space between us. "Everything" includes all that we consciously (explicitly) *know* that we "put out" there, such as anger, tenderness, or friendliness. But, *and this is the important thing*, the interval between us also includes *implicit* memories, the ones we aren't aware of and thus *don't know exist* in the space between us.

The "Seahorse" Helps Us Find the Way

Every human has implicit memories. They can be positive as well as negative. The positive ones help us in everyday life; they are just "there" and we don't have to think about them.

But, terrible and traumatic memories have not been integrated with the aid of the *hippocampus* (the seahorse). In very stressful situations, the hippocampus becomes blocked. As you remember, the hippocampus is necessary for us to store new memories and for us to remember facts of various sorts like names, events, faces, and places. The hippocampus also allows us to orient ourselves in a room and not get lost in an unfamiliar environment, or in time. With illnesses like Alzheimer's, hippocampus functionality is dramatically reduced. The hippocampus is also blocked when we drink a lot of alcohol.

Put simply, the hippocampus integrates *implicit* memories and creates a carpet that then becomes a large image. It helps us make sense of our memories and transform the implicit to the *explicit.*

We Don't Get It

I will give you one more example of how implicit memories can be a problem for us. Let's say that you crashed and scraped yourself on the gravel when you just learnt to ride a bicycle, and get seriously hurt. Maybe you even end up at the hospital. You are afraid and it hurts very much.

But time passes. You forget about the accident. You ride your bike again.

Then, twenty or thirty years later, when you are going to teach your own child to ride a bike, you feel discomfort, but you don't know why. You simply feel resistance at the thought of your child riding a bike. You don't remember your childhood accident, but your body does. The memory is *implicit*. What you feel is perhaps anxiety or incomprehensible anger, and your child riding a bike triggers it. The memory is strong in you, but you don't consciously remember the incident.

But we can *transform* unconscious memories into conscious ones, with, among other things, the aid of hippocampus and integration between the brain domains. One key to achieving this consciousness is through communication.

I repeat: we *shall* not and we *cannot* remember everything that we register with our senses. We sort out and forget lots, and those that remain are the most important things--matters of survival. It is important to understand that we *do* forget! If you don't remember much of your childhood, it doesn't have to mean that it was difficult or traumatic.

I cannot emphasize enough that when we experience an implicit memory in the present, it doesn't feel like we are responding to a memory. *We are convinced it's all about here and now.* This confusion of present with past is often the essence of the "unsolvable" conflicts with our partner.

The Culprit

When our implicit memories play tricks on our relationship, what does it look like?

If we take the example of riding the bike again, it turns out that when your child (or your partner) is going to ride a bike, you get angry. You are actually afraid, but this can be manifested as unreasonable security-fervour or anger. You know that you're right! You know the truth: *riding a bicycle is dangerous*. It feels so real that you actually believe that this is correct and right – yes, it's your duty as a parent to prohibit the child from riding a bicycle! Such a conviction can give rise to conflict between you and your partner.

But, if your partner would be willing to "cross the bridge" to you in order to understand your "truth," then your partner (and you) will be able to understand why you are such an overly- protective parent and why you are so terrified of accidents and want to prohibit your child from riding a bicycle. As we engage in dialogue in a safe environment, telling and understanding our history, a remarkable number of implicit memories surface! Then we can integrate the implicit memories into the hippocampus and they become explicit. In the presence of a listening person, a feeling of resonance, attunement, harmony, and empathic vali-dation is created. With the aid of this "crossing the bridge" dialogue, we can step into each other's brains and "visit" each other's experiences. Suddenly, foolish reactions become understandable to us. But it's not just that; we can also begin to tenderness towards the very behaviour that annoyed us so much.

We often respond as in the example with the bicycle. We may believe that we make sensible and rational decisions, but quite often there are implicit memories behind our choices. Fear is such a strong emotion that it takes over. Because the fear is so strong, it "proves" to us that we are responding correctly. Or so we think.

The bicycle riding example above is a very simple one. We may have many much worse, traumatic memories related to sexual abuse, emotional abuse, physical abuse, being deserted, betrayal, and loss. In the intense stress of the traumatic event, our brain may choose to "spare" us from the memories by a process called *dissociation*, where we react to a traumatic event by disconnecting ourselves from that occurrence (for instance a rape) and focus on, for example, a light bulb in the ceiling. We temporarily close down the pain in body and soul and only see the light bulb. In this way we will have no explicit memory of the event. But we will probably experience *flashbacks* in which the traumatic event will flash by in symbolic images--perhaps a light bulb.

This seems to be a very intelligent defence – and it is. The catch is that the implicit memories remain, all the same. They send signals about how things really "are." But they are truths that sometimes lead us astray. The implicit memories can be the culprit in the drama of love and of life itself.

The good news is that everything can become comprehensible if we get the chance to tell, hear and understand the story behind the hair-trigger reactions.

I'm a Ruthless Bulldozer

I will tell you a story from my own life about what can happen when implicit memories run us. My colleague, Elsa, and I are at a conference called The Psychotherapy Networker Symposium. We are staying at a luxurious hotel in Washington DC. We have a double room on the eighth floor. It's our fourth night there and we feel well at home.

Then, at 3:30 a.m., we wake up to a shrill, deafening noise. *"This is the fire alarm, this is the fire alarm"* is heard from the loudspeakers.

The recorded female voice tells us to calmly get dressed and as quickly as possible get out of the building. My heart almost stops. I look desperately in the dark and start to frantically grab clothes to put on. I quickly jump into my jeans as I hear Elsa move calmly in the room.

From this moment on, I experience everything in a kind of mist. I know that I hysterically look for my handbag and the pictures of the children and Sven so they get out and don't get "burnt to death." At the spiral staircase, I rush down towards freedom and oxygen. I ruthlessly push my way past other people on their way out. My adrenaline is pumping, I have tunnel vision, I'm in a complete panic and am certain that I will die and never see my beloved family again. I sob, run, and push away everyone in my path. I have but one goal: to get out.

When I reach the foyer, my prefrontal cortex wakes up. Much to my surprise I smell no smoke, see no fire, and feel no panic. People are sitting on the stairs at the entrance. I breathe.

Suddenly I realise that people sitting there look calm. Well, not only calm – they actually look quite funny. Some are wrapped up in sheets and have curlers in their hair; others are dressed in bathrobes, floral nightgowns or checked pyjamas. Some men wear trousers and nothing more. A giggle bubbles up. What happened? How did I get here so quickly? And how funny everyone looks!

Suddenly it dawns on me that I can see everything clearly. I see everything around me. With increasing shame, I wonder how an intelligent woman like me could lose it so totally that I just rushed ahead without thinking about anyone else. And suddenly I realise: Elsa is not there!

The adrenaline rush returns and I hurry back. On my way back up the stairs I meet old, frail and handicapped people who are trying to reach the exit. I continue running up the stairs and offer excuses left and right for not stopping to help. The people I confront look at me, startled.

I only come a short way when I see Elsa, walking calmly down the stairs. She asks (and I'll never forget her surprised face):

"Eva, are you going back up again?"

"Yes, there is no fire. I was looking for you," I say, out of breath. And then: "Oh, I'm so ashamed, Elsa! I forgot you."

With soft and loving eyes, Elsa says: "Eva… it's alright, I realized that you were terrified."

"Weren't you afraid?" I ask, amazed.

"No, I couldn't smell any smoke, so I wasn't afraid," she says.

Then she tells me that her father, who was a fire-fighter, had taught her that whenever she heard a fire alarm, to immediately try to smell smoke so that you know where the fire comes from and where you can get out.

Elsa puts her arm undermine and says: "Now let's go out and see what is going on."

Together, we go to the foyer that minutes earlier I'd rushed down towards like a bulldozer gone out of control. This time I walked calmly with embarrassed steps.

So, what actually happened here? Well, my brain perceived DANGER (both implicit and explicit) and sounded the alarm: out, out, out! It did me a favour. The signals it sent out made me move quickly down to safety.

In my neuron tracks, I have experiences of disaster. As a child, I unfortunately woke many times in fear. It may have been an argument between my parents, my drunken father looking for more alcohol, lamps suddenly turned on, cries, screams, or furniture thrown in desperation. Sometimes I awoke to the drama surrounding my mother's illness; several times she was close to dying. There were also external factors linked to my fear, including leaving Africa in a panic due to the war in Biafra.

These are a part of my *implicit* memories. My internal alarm may have started up quicker than in many others. On top of that I also have experienced an actual fire – an *explicit* memory directly connected to the implicit memories of disaster, helplessness, and fear of death. At twenty-six, I experienced the physical pain of a burn injury when a sheet caught fire. Now, when the fire alarm sounded – more than twenty years later – the memories in the body powerfully reactivate. We are built that way for the sake of our survival.

Some of the *implicit* memories of disaster woke up within, quickly followed by *explicit* memories when I remembered the fire I'd actually experienced. Elsa, on the other hand, had no memories – neither implicit nor explicit – of a similar disaster. On top of that, her father had taught her how to behave rationally in case of fire.

When my alarm went off, I "lost my head"--at least the rational part. Remember the symbolic hand model of the brain? The fingers representing the prefrontal cortex (thinking brain) flew open and lost contact with the rest. I *reacted,* ignoring everyone and everything ran down the stairs, pushed old and handicapped, and behaves egotistically and terribly. I couldn't see anyone but myself since I was lost in my terror.

Elsa, by contrast, walked calmly down the stairs with her brain intact. She could consider the best response in this situation. She could choose to *act* instead of *reacting*.

With great compassion (and perhaps even love) for my terrible behaviour, and for everyone else who reacts instead of acting, we can realize that everything has a logical explanation. Part of the explanation is the natural instinct to flee from danger. Another part is our implicit luggage, which influences how we *experience* danger. The body reacts before we realize what is happening.

A Room with a View--or a Fire Escape

We can learn to understand our implicit reactions by making an expedition into our own mind and brain. We shall not look inwards to analyse, get stuck, or mush around in the past – but only to see the connection between NOW and THEN. This connection is an aid for us to feel empathy towards others and ourselves, and it offers an opportunity to integrate our implicit memories, create balance and harmony between our brain domains and make memories explicit. It gives us an opportunity to consciously choose something new.

Today, I can handle my fear of fire. When it comes to hotels I can, for instance, find the location of emergency exits and fires ladders, and if I need to, ask for a room on the first floor to calm myself. Above all, if my fear of fire would strike I have a better understanding of my impulses. Instead of spiralling out of control, I can calm my nervous system and focus on other things. This doesn't mean that I will sit down and read a book if there is a fire; I just don't have to get afraid without due cause.

As long as fear remains implicit, it can poison the *space* between you and your loved ones. Earlier, painful experiences that our brain "photographed" and designated DANGEROUS will pop up in the present as a *reaction*. We will perceive this reaction as if it has something to do with the present. But it doesn't have to be something as dramatic as a fire. It can be anything that may seem trivial on the outside, but that is still deeply traumatic for the individual. I have a friend who was criticized by her father when she as a young girl tried to put on makeup for the first time. As a result, for years afterward she was convinced that she was hopelessly ugly. An emotional memory can etch in that strongly.

Fortunately positive memories can also affect us in a similar way. It can be good to remember that.

Come On, Trim that Beard!

It's Friday evening, and I'm going to meet my husband in the food store to buy dinner. I can see him at a distance, his beard, his posture, and his distinctive way of walking. Without understanding why I am annoyed, I hear myself saying:

"You haven't shaved in a long while."

He sighs and leaves. We get our foodstuff in different places and meet up by the cash register.

I'm annoyed that there are so many people in the shop, pissed off by Sven being unshaved, and angry that he will not listen to my critique, which at that moment I feel is very justified. He doesn't realise that he looks like something the cat dragged in and that I'm *ashamed* of him! Interestingly enough, I'm also ashamed of myself that I'm so focused on externals and for a short while wonder if I'm really capable of loving. But my guilt quickly turns into renewed anger against Sven.

We go home in silence. Emptiness, guilt and irritation lie between us.

When we step in through the door, we are met by our happy children. They wonder what's for dinner and if it will be ready soon. Sven goes straight to the TV and I angrily start to take the food from the bags.

I can hear Sven opening a beer, hear him move in front of the TV, and I suddenly feel on the verge of collapse. I bang the pots and pans, whine, murmur, and finally I go in to him and yell:

"Will you be sitting here all night, or could you perhaps give me a hand?"

Sven gets angry and counter-attacks. He shouts at me about how frustrated, tired and overworked he is. The words keep coming. Slowly but steadily, I close the door into myself, teeth clenched in desperation, stomach like a hard knot, chest full of tears. The argument is in full swing.

I Go on the Slide

Let's take another look at this little incident, one that was commonplace in our house before we realized what was happening *implicitly* – in me, in him and between us.

What I *hear* myself doing in the shop is offering suggestions about how he can make himself look better for me and for others. I believe that I give constructive criticism to the man in my life. What I don't hear is the internal, *implicit* monologue going on at the same time in my brain; underneath all my irritated suggestions to Sven, a voice of fear and powerlessness is screaming.

The interesting part is that the instant Sven steps into the food store and I see his weary body language and his slightly unkempt beard, and hear his tired voice, a part of my brain called the amygdala (the "emotional brain") starts to register all of these details and my internal *implicit* dialogue starts. Who knows, my amygdala may have started to send warning signals even before Sven arrived? Maybe I had a negative expectation that I wasn't aware of?

My amygdala and the voice from my childhood screams: "Help, he is not well! He is intoxicated, drunk, or ill!" (Drunk like dad, ill like mum). Now it's chaos. Do something! Fix him so that he looks happy and sober, and if that doesn't work, get out, turn off the emotions and leave him quickly!"

My implicit response--*and in that moment, my truth*--tells me that I'm invisible again. Everything is about how he (they) is (are). I'm going into hyper-drive! I'm forced to deal with everything.

Explicitly, I'm just annoyed, angry, and completely convinced that Sven is the problem. If he just took care of his exterior, didn't rush, shaved, tucked in his shirt, and listened to me, everything would be fine. But because my implicit memory had also been triggered, in that instant he wasn't just unshaved, he was also irresponsible, lazy, boring, ugly and stupid.

That night could have been one of the worst in our power struggle. It could have continued with grumpy faces, angry attacks, crying, screaming, and finally … a door that slammed in my face. Fortunately, it didn't, because we were able to stop ourselves, calm down our nervous systems and realize what had started it all. What happened was that I *in a flash* read him and his body language, clothes, hair, beard, and so on. And I took the slide down to my worst implicit childhood memories.

When my dad was sober, he took very good care of his exterior. When he drank, he lost all interest in hygiene and clothing. His face got blotchy, he smelled bad, let his trousers hang at half-mast and didn't care one bit what people thought of him. He often felt powerless, sad, and lonely. I was ashamed and felt powerless myself in the face of Dad's despair.

My mother, who was often stressed and sad and sometimes very ill, also looked worn out in these situations. Usually a beautiful-looking woman, her eyes turned red from crying and her face collapsed under the weight of strong emotion. She, too, was helpless.

Back in the food store, I thought I was annoyed because of my husband and that I was entitled to criticize him. What I understood later was that the thing that really triggered my implicit memories was the sound of Sven opening his beer in front of the TV. He was angry and trying to calm his nervous system as he always did: by turning off, letting everything pour off, and being a rebel that didn't care what others thought of him. He was responding to all of his implicit memories (that weren't explicit yet) of being criticized and "not good enough" as a child. Part of his reaction was also completely normal and justified, considering the fact that his wife chose to criticise him on a Friday evening in the food store.

Others probably didn't perceive Sven as rude, sloppy, or unkempt. He was tired after a stressful day at work – it was evident in his voice and body language. But I only have to see his worried brow and feel the stress like a cloud around him. The trousers that hang a bit, the shirt that has slipped out a bit--I read CHAOS and I get scared. It is the speciality of the amygdala to interpret facial expressions and body language, and also read if there is danger. And as we now understand, the dangers are implicitly learned – but these dangers are not the same for you as for me.

So on this Friday evening, when I went on the slide down into my worst implicit memories, I once again became a small girl; a child affected by the surrounding chaos with no image of calm, limbic resonance. When the grownups were sad, I was sad, and when they were powerless, angry, and in despair, I felt powerless, angry, and in despair. The mirror neurons and resonance circuits fired away in my brain, and when they couldn't calm themselves down I couldn't calm myself down. My parents were not bad parents. They were a mother and a father that had their own implicit memories, responding to THEN as if it happened NOW. They, in turn, had parents who sometimes could not calm and regulate their nervous systems, and on and on it goes.

I'm not attempting to excuse us from responsibility for how we behave. We can choose to break our unhealthy patterns and change our behaviour, as we will learn later in the book.

So, it was a "small" and frightened parent that my children saw in me that Friday night. It's the mother they have seen many times during arguments between Sven and me. To interpret, control, fix, offer advice, criticize, sigh, be angry, and do everything else I can think of to try to *change and help* so that it won't all go to hell became a vital way for me to calm down. It became a defence – one of my Armani suites.

When I calmed down, I realized this. Sven could also see that he quite frequently loses interest in how he looks and is perceived. When he feels criticized, his own Armani suit is to rebel – to simply not care what others say and rather do the opposite. Sven has also (for generations back) carried along "the truth" that he isn't good enough, and that he thus must work hard, accomplish much, and generally push himself to the limit. He *implicitly* put this "truth" into the argument – into the space between us. It's an important observation, since the reaction of the one triggers the other.

We Cannot Trust our Emotions

What happens in our bodies when we, in a hundredth of a second, react and ignite a conflict that escalates and divides us until we feel like a couple of deserted and misunderstood poor sods that can't reach each other?

When we face stress, substances like adrenaline and cortisol are secreted into the blood and the hippocampus is turned off, the part of the brain that is necessary for integration between implicit and explicit memories (and, thus, also between left and right domain of the brain). When the hippocampus is disconnected, the memories are not linked to each other. We get stuck in a struggle.

We Can Change Our Brains

The good news--and the purpose of this book--is that we can learn to communicate in a way that creates integration between the brain domains in *contact* with someone else. This is the essence of the process "crossing the bridge." With this integration, the brain can make things that occur meaningful. The way we communicate alters the structure of the brain and the mind.

Armed with this knowledge, we can start to realize that the things that sometimes *feel strongly* within probably are not real today; they are simply an autobiographical (implicit) memory that pop up in the present – a memory that isn't integrated yet. We can start to see that even if something difficult really is happening, it usually feels much worse than it is.

Learning through Remembering

To a certain extent, our memories are reconstructions. Every time we remember something, *the brain rewrites* it a bit, updates the past according to our present concerns and understanding. [21] It's much the same way as a computer memory works: we collect a document from our "hard drive," work a little with it, and then save it again. Exactly *how* it is altered depends on what we learn when we remember it. If it's just the same fear flaring up again we will get more and more afraid by each time.

Jude Cassidy, professor of psychology at the university of Maryland and researcher in the field of attachment, says that we carry along two different aspects of the past:
- what actually occurred in the past.
- how we describe and remember the past. [22]

21 Daniel Goleman, *Social Intelligence, The New Science of Human Relationships*, page 78
22 Jude Cassidy, *Connection and Transformation*, Cd.

We know that experiences from the past affect and shape what we do now. We also know that much of what we think we remember today are *created* memories. And we know that when we see the red thread in what we carry along, it's easier for us to understand our behaviour and the behaviour of others and then choose how our future should look. We can choose how we want to be as parent, partner, friend, and fellow human being. We can put new images into our album for the future.

Let's take an empathic look at our close ones and ourselves. Or, as I often say: "Put a heart around yourself and others!" We are so prone to be negative towards our loved ones and ourselves.

The Jante Law

As I mentioned earlier, I like to describe concepts via images or metaphors. To respond strongly to something that we cannot remember, I usually call: "taking the slide down into the crater." Others may use other expressions, but they all refer to the same phenomena: to emotionally be thrown back to a difficult experience by something that we *perceive* to be happening in the present.

The trigger for our dive may come from the relationship we had with our grandparents, teachers or other persons to whom we have been close. Other reactions may stem from events and situations throughout life – in our childhood, last week or ten minutes ago.

Yet, other things can be a heritage that we carry with us implicitly and which *never* have had anything to do with us. It can be the state of our parents, including things that they haven't expressed or were even aware of. We also have been influenced by the emotional climate in the country and culture that surrounds us.

What is known as the "Jante Law" affects us in Scandinavia (and in many other cultures). According to this "law," first articulated in a novel by the Danish-Norwegian author Aksel Sandemose, you shall not think that you are someone special. You shall not think that you are as good as we are! [23] We believe that we shall not boast or otherwise call positive attention to ourselves because if we do, we will be punished by, for instance, suddenly finding ourselves ejected from the community. We shall not dream of great deeds.

But we *are* really something. We are fine, beautiful, unique, and amazing creatures. It's interesting to consider that this rule of unworthiness lies in our "collective brain" in the space between us all. Ponder for a while how this affects our life – if it does. Is the climate the same now as when Sandemose wrote his book about Jante in the 1930's? Has the mentality changed with immigration and increased exchange with the rest of the world?

Be that as it may, everything we carry along affects us positively and negatively. The fact that my mother always told me that I was fantastic indeed served as a counterweight to the Jante law to me.

Craters and Croatians

A few years ago, I participated in a lecture on human development, the brain – interpersonal neurobiology (IPNB), and psychotherapy. I filled myself up with new knowledge and was so enthusiastic about our human development that I almost screamed with joy.

So when I get home, I eagerly ask my husband to sit down in the kitchen to hear about everything new that I've learned. He is a kind man with great experience of my various whims, and now he sits down at the kitchen table. I pace around in the kitchen and talk, since I'm too excited to sit on a chair. I gesticulate and speak quickly, intensely. Sven listens and listens.

I tell him about the brain and how neurons are connected to other neurons and how we can always heal and make new tracks. I tell him what works and doesn't work in therapy and how fantastic our brain is.

---

23 Jante is his fiction name for his childhood town, Nykobing mother in Denmark, as depicted in his novel *Exile in search of a home,* from 1933

As usual, I'm eager to show the images I see in my head, to make it easier for him to grasp this thrilling new reality. So I retell a metaphor I just heard from a dear friend and colleague, Pat Love:

"Imagine a pile of sand. Someone pours a bucket of water over the pile, and the water creates rivulets in the sand as it pours down the sides. After a while another bucket is poured over the pile. The water of course runs mostly in the lines created by the first bucket. After one more bucket the lines are so deep that all the water runs in them. All other ways are sort of blocked. And now there are deep craters in the sand!"

All of this I almost scream to Sven, and continue out of breath: "In exactly the same way as in the brain when the neurons fire away, tie together and fire away again, and again and again! Then the tracks in the brain are so run in that no other way works. Craters are made that we don't get up from. We get *craters* in our brain! Do you understand?" I yell at Sven, my eyes gleaming with enthusiasm.

Or… that is what I think I say.

But as a dyslexic. I sometimes mix up words. I think that I say, hear or read a certain word or sentence, but to others this word means something completely different.

So in the middle of my ranting, Sven interrupts me with a twinkle in his eye:

"Eva… is it alright with Finnish people, Norwegians and British--or is it only Croatians?"

I don't understand what he's talking about, but I get quite annoyed by my husband, who has just interrupted me and seems so incredibly amused.

"What do you mean, Finnish people? I don't understand. Why do you say that?" I snap.

"Well… how many nationalities are there in the brain?"

"Which… what?" I now yell with rising anger. Why must he interrupt me now, when this is so important?

Sven laughs and says: "Excuse me Eva, I understand that this is some kind of dyslexic thing."

Now I stop and listen. Oh, a dyslexic thing. What have I said now? I know that I can mix up words and that we have laughed about it many times. In school, I suffered from feeling stupid. Now, as an adult with Sven, it usually ends up with laughter.

"You said Croatians, but I think you meant craters," says Sven.

We start to giggle. Suddenly we imagine a hoard of small Croatians digging tracks in our brains. We see before us how they run around with spades and buckets digging and digging – and interestingly enough, they dig a crater. I see a few Finnish people as well as some British run by with spades.

We have a good laugh. After that incident, the Croatians and the craters became a part of my lecture on the brain.

Sometimes, we need to resort to humour and images to see things from the outside. It is so easy to get stuck thinking in problems and solutions to problems. Unfortunately, my experience is that *all we focus on grows*. This goes for problems too. The more we dwell on them, the bigger they become. We have seen a lot of the problems from below, from our craters, and we don't gain anything by ranting around down there. We need to climb up and approach the problem from another vantage point.

Trauma

There is a lot of research on the subject of trauma--what it is, how it affects us, and how to deal with unresolved trauma. What I present here is just one way of looking at it.

A trauma can be a fatal and horrible incident that triggers a post-traumatic stress disorder (PTSD), but it can also be other experiences that the brain perceives as actual threats to our survival (for instance, the feeling of being left outside that I mentioned earlier). This can be experience from either childhood or adulthood. I heard about an old man who fought in the trenches during the Spanish Civil War. Once back home, he panicked whenever someone turned on a vacuum cleaner since the sound reminded him of enemy bombers. Many refugees from war scenes have a difficult New Year's Eve, since they associate fireworks with shelling and bombs. Others stiffen on the days that the public alarm system is tested.

To this day, many people in the United States cringe whenever they see and hear a plane in the air, because it triggers the memory of watching the planes crash into the World Trade Center and the Pentagon on September 11, 2001. These kinds of "national traumas" in a culture can grab hold of us and hang on hard. For instance, after the disaster involving the passenger boat in Estonia in 1994 a lot of people became afraid of traveling by boat, in spite of the fact that they were not involved in the disaster--they only read about it in the papers and saw it on TV.

Previously, we believed that trauma was only about very serious incidents like sexual abuse, severe assault, war, great losses, disasters and such. Now we *know* that it can also be caused by "minor" incidents, seemingly insignificant events that the brain associates with danger and that are terribly painful. We may have forgotten the reason for the pain long ago.

Fear is infectious. A state of fear immediately creates the same state in another person. When the son, daughter, or partner "sees" fear in a loved one (although we don't want to show it, or aren't aware of it) it is transmitted to us. Fortunately this process also occurs for joy and positive things that we carry with us. Who isn't affected by a smile? This is important to remember, because it means that we can create something new and positive.

We can try not to dwell on negative thoughts and realise that small, unresolved trauma is simply a part of life. Greater unresolved trauma, on the other hand, often manifests itself in flashbacks (remember the episode "the culprit"). PTSD is a difficult psychological condition that should be treated since it can cripple us. Separate implicit memories have been stored without integration and may continue to invade us without any control when we face something that is reminiscent in the present.

Even though it may not have been PTSD in my case, it did have a similar effect on me when Sven opened a can of beer. That little *sound*, the snap of a lid on a beer can, automatically activated fear in me.

Consider and old Native American saying: "If I have been bitten by a snake, I may become afraid of ropes."

Big T and Small t

Usually, we process unpleasant experiences spontaneously and can leave them behind. But in serious or repeated trauma, this ordinary healing process doesn't work.

Eye Movement Desensitization and Reprocessing, or EMDR, is a method of therapy often used in treating posttraumatic stress disorder. This method integrates the right and left brain modes and brings out implicit memories by, among other things, quick eye-movements in the patient (and also with certain soft touches or sounds). It is believed that the treatment activates the network of associated memories and the brain's ability to process them. Proven effective by neurological research, EMDR is now internationally recognised to be as efficient in treating trauma as certain cognitive behaviour therapies. Exactly what makes it work is not quite clear. Recent research tries to establish the significance of eye movements for activating memory functions and the effect in the central nervous system. [24]

EMDR was developed in the late 1980's by Francine Shapiro, a psychologist and researcher at the Mental Research Institute in Palo Alto, California. She defines trauma as a negative event that has had a continuing or long-lasting effect on the psyche. She refers to our traumas as either "Big T's" or "small t's." [25]

24 Swedish Medicine magazine, 6 /3 2007

25 Daniel J Siegel, Allan Schore, Michael Stone, Bessel Van der Kolk, Marion Solomon, Francine Shapiro and Joan Lang – *Cd Understanding & Treating Trauma*

Big T's are deep traumas such as abuse, great losses, abandonment, assault, or other events when we have experienced great fear, sadness or other strong feelings in a situation when we felt powerless.

Small t's can be less dramatic incidents with elements of humiliation, conflict, abandonment, feeling outside, or isolation occurring during our period of development, when we have experienced *less* fatal pain. Still, the pain may have felt very strong when we experienced it.

It can be difficult to precisely define trauma. The brain registers everything that is connected to pain much more quickly than things connected with joy and safety. It's an evolutionary heritage, for the sake of survival. We must also remember: it's not the event *in itself* that makes us experience it as a trauma. It's how what happened was *dealt with*--if we got help and calm contact with someone else after the traumatic event, and if we have been able to make the incident comprehensible to ourselves.

Unfortunately, a lot of people get stuck in the idea that trauma has to do with a good or bad childhood. I think that we need to play down this aspect, and understand that *everyone* (more or less) carries along some painful events and memories, generation after generation, which are then manifested in the space between us, especially in our most intimate relations.

A Poor Childhood?

As I see it, trauma is not primarily about a good or bad childhood. Most parents love their children and wish them well, and yet we transfer things to them that we don't want them to have. And we are not aware of it – we give them the things that "live" *implicitly* within us and in the space between us, things that we haven't understood and been able to make *explicit*.

A number of other factors have an effect. We may have grown up with the most loving parents, but in great poverty. War, unemployment, addiction, depression, loss, death, grief, and accidents also affect us. There may be problems in the relationships between parents or others in the family, suicide, inability to show emotions ("we don't talk about such things in our family") – or the contrary: the emotions of the parents "spill over" in the family and creates chaos. The point is that affects us. The more frequently an experience has been registered on our neuron map, the easier it is for the brain to pick it out. Most of us carry "little t's" with us. Who hasn't felt outside or humiliated some time?

Dr. Shapiro says that all memories are based on associations and everything we learn is based on new associations. When we are going to learn something new, the brain will automatically look for precious information on the current subject. In order to recognize a new object, we need to link it to previous experiences of the same object.

Our intellect needs to sort things into *categories* that give order and meaning to the incomprehensible world around us. Then we can assume that things we encounter in one category are similar to what we met in the same category previously. That is how we handle our complex, constantly evolving existence.

Daniel Goleman observes: "But once a negative bias begins, our lenses become clouded. We tend to seize on whatever seems to confirm the bias and ignore what does not. Prejudice, in this sense, is a hypothesis desperately trying to prove itself to us. And so when we encounter someone to whom the prejudice might apply, the bias skews our perception, making it impossible to test whether the stereotype actually fits". [26]

Thieves and Masks

Here is an example of Goleman's observation. Most of us have seen a mask, for instance on a dentist or people working in hazardous environments. We have learnt that you use a mask to avoid germs, dust

---

26 Daniel Goleman, *Social intelligence; The New Science of Human Relationships*, page 300

and dangerous substances like asbestos and such. This is what most people here have in their memory bank on masks.

A colleague and friend, Ditte Dunge, told me how surprised she was to see people with masks when she travelled to Singapore. She wondered if the air really was that bad, and asked a friend who lived there. The friend laughed and said:

"No, no, you carry a mask to protect other people against a cold that you have yourself!"

For Ditte, the word "mask" was immediately associated with protecting *yourself* against pollution, when it here was a question of protecting others. Ditte's brain made the connection it recognized.

Another example worth mentioning is an experiment done on a popular TV talk show. In the program, a bag-snatching was arranged; a woman was robbed in front of a group of people who witnessed the "the crime." The purpose of the experiment was to interview everyone who saw the robber take the bag and investigate how much of the event they registered. The interviewed (who didn't know they were participating in an experiment) got questions like "How did the robber look? Hat, cap, clothes? Colour hair? Gender and ethnicity?"

Many were dead certain that they'd seen a dark man, about forty, with baggy jeans, black hooded sweater, brown cap and dark, perhaps long hair. The witnesses differed a little about this man's clothes and the length of his hair, but *most* had seen a dark man with a brown cap and baggy jeans. After a number of interviews, the people responsible for the experiment decided to tell the truth, and let the "robber" come out. "He" was a Caucasian woman of about thirty-five with brown hair in a ponytail, dressed in blue jeans and blue-grey sweater. But most were convinced that they had seen a black or dark man snatch the bag.

This says a lot about prejudice, and also about our memory. We have a tendency to see what we *believe* we see. The result in this case is incredibly sad.

The experiment also tells us how hard it can be to be a witness. We can't really trust our memory. When we don't *know,* the left half of the brain quickly looks for information, and what it finds can be pure prejudice. It means that when the witnesses saw the robber, they actually *saw* this! Witnesses usually don't lie – but what they see may be wildly inaccurate.

The Smell of Africa

Our senses can also throw us back to something positive. It happens to me sometimes when I buy vegetables; the smell of an unripe tomato immediately brings me back to Nigeria. It smells of Africa, and a pleasant warmth flows through my body. The spicy smell of citrus fruits can give me the same delightful feeling.

Memories of taste and smell are very strong: a certain sort of candy brings us straight back to grandmother's kitchen. The plums from grandfather's garden turn us into five-year-olds in a second. Biscuits and apples bring out a beach picnic in childhood. And so on. Smells and tastes throw us back into our memories in fractions of a second and – BANG – an entire world returns to us.

Another such experience is rain. For me it's pure joy. Especially heavy rain pouring from a black sky in big drops! This memory also comes from West Africa. The rain meant that the dry season was over and people danced with joy in the streets.

For my husband, who is a bike rider, rain is frustration. He associates it with getting wet on his motorbike. So when we wake up on a summer morning and it is pouring down, I automatically get happy and peaceful, while Sven just as automatically gets frustrated, irritated and tired. This, of course, can be a breeding ground for misunderstanding and conflict, if you are not aware of it.

Take a moment to think about what connects your senses to previous experiences. What sights or smells make you happy and calm? What fills you with fear, nausea or frustration?

The nose can also help us judge if something is dangerous or not. Through thousands of years, we have learned to separate good smells from bad smells, rotten from fresh, and so on. Smell and taste are our oldest senses and they have been crucial for our survival.

We Prefer Tragedy

When capital T-traumas strike us, those images are much more strongly etched into our association-map than small t's or pleasant memories – so that our brain can warn us so that the same terrible thing shall not be repeated. This is a pure survival strategy. Our wise brain wants to save us from danger again.

Small-t traumas remain much stronger than positive memories, and this is also for our survival. That's why we always have to enlarge and enhance our positive memories; the negative ones press on us anyway.

The psychologist and author John Gottman filmed hundreds of couples in their everyday lives. He claims that for every negative incident that our brain registers, we need five positive ones to balance it and feel good.

Stefan Klein, considered one of the most influential science writers in Europe says: "The greater our prior experience of deprivation, the stronger is our subsequent pleasure. The first splash of water on a dry throat tastes the most delicious. With pleasure as its tool, nature seduces us into doing what benefits us most". [27]

Generally we experience negative feelings more strongly than positive ones, and the unpleasant emotions are also more easily triggered. If you show both happy and sad images to subjects in an experiment in neuropsychology, they will respond more strongly to the sad ones. We have a stronger tendency to avoid risks than to search for happiness. Bad news always gets the biggest headlines in the papers. Experiences of sorrow and dissatisfaction thus have a stronger impact than happy memories. This is an important reason why we should only make *brief* visits to our traumas, so that we don't get stuck there,

---

27 Stefan Klein, *The Science of Happiness; How Our Brains Make Us Happy – and What We Can Do to Get Happier*, page 27

going round and round and exaggerating what is there. Happiness is unfortunately something we have to strive for, while the opposite come automatically.

The encouraging news is that we have the capacity to retrain our brains. Our brain is flexible and plastic, and we now know that new nerve paths are made during all our lives. With new experiences and new awareness, we can make new tracks. The psychologist and TV personality Dr. Phil said something that touched me very strongly because it was so simple: "You cannot change what you cannot acknowledge." I think this is very important. First we have to see it and admit it. Then we can change.

Living in Denial

I associate this with the concept of "living in denial" that is key to Alcoholics Anonymous (AA). My beloved father could never make the decision to become sober. He denied his addiction until it killed him. In his own world, he didn't have any problems with alcohol. If he drank, it was because something had happened due to someone else so that he had to strengthen himself. *Someone else* or *something else* was the reason he had to drink. He never realized his addiction and therefore, he couldn't choose to be sober. He lived in complete denial.

Another example from my own life is that for a long time, I denied that I was a poor listener. I was completely convinced that when my husband and other people close to me said, "you don't listen, they were wrong. I defended myself angrily: "I work with this issue, for crying out loud! I teach couples to listen every day! Of course I can listen!" I yelled at others and myself. Again and again.

I didn't realise that I mixed my listening with "fixing," unsolicited support, and sometimes critique. I didn't realise that I had an *agenda* with the person I listened to, and that agenda was what I wanted them to feel and be.

So when my husband, in desperation, yelled at me that *"it's your way or the highway!"* I thought that it was his problem and he needed to get control of his emotions. I was completely convinced that I, who work with this issue, really could listen.

Finally, I mobilized enough courage, curiosity, and love for myself to honestly ask: "Could it be that I'm really not very good at listening? Don't I *hear* what he or she is saying? Am I only with myself when I listen?"

Yes, often. With this realization came enormous relief, as I understood that to listen means to only *visit, be attuned to* – not take care of, fix, solve the problem, or change the person.

In my awakening, recovering state from this denial, I was also bathed in self-contempt. If I'm such a bad listener when it comes to my close ones, how can I continue my work to help other people listen? I wallowed in guilt, felt wretched and was close to martyrdom.

With time, I could forget about myself and begin to imagine how it must be for Sven to have a wife who rarely could listen without fixing, mending, reprove, criticize or almost drown in her own negative feelings. To have a wife who could listen to other people, but not to him. In my profession I could listen better since the client wasn't close to me in the same way. But privately I couldn't.

I will never forget the feeling when I understood this. Neither will I forget the look on Sven's face when he realized that I had really *understood* that it wasn't easy to live with me. That I realized that sometimes I was very difficult for him and often didn't listen at all. I dared look inwards and listen to my own history and my own experience, and started to realize that there was something to what my close ones accused me of. With this I could let go of the defence that I so cleverly created as a child. Instead I could open up to the thought that I had been a bit blind. That I had been so busy *responding* to my inner alarm signals that I couldn't "step out" of myself and take in the signals from someone else – at least not from people close to me emotionally.

During this trying journey, my heart was also touched with sympathy for my parents, their parents, and other people's parents. When I looked inward and searched myself, I started to realise that I had a small girl inside who panicked when anyone close didn't feel well. An inner voice--one that I didn't hear--screamed. It was an existential scream: "Help him or he will be ruined. And if he is, you will die!" My father's anxiety became my anxiety.

The small girl within also had few experiences of really being heard. My father was lost in himself since he drank. My mother was sometimes lost in herself because of her own emotions. When they felt powerless, I felt powerless. And I realized that this was similar to my way of being with my close ones.

Since my father never left his denial, he couldn't "put a heart around himself" (that is, look at himself with understanding and love) and understand the genetic heritage that often plays a significant role in addiction of all kinds.

My mother experienced feelings of helplessness and guilt, and had difficulties asking for help and receiving it. Also, her inability to *differentiate* – in which she sometimes couldn't make a distinction between herself and me--has affected me a lot. When I write this, I can still feel sad for carrying this for so long. I feel sad that it felt this way to me, even though my parents wanted what was best for me.

As long as the experiences remained implicit, the result for me as an adult was that I couldn't listen. I put a lot of energy into the people close to me, and I wanted the best for them, but I didn't listen. I didn't take in the world of the other person, but became busy with my own. It manifested itself in the anger that I automatically felt when the feeling of being powerless hit me.

Now I understand that I didn't dare to listen because I didn't trust the adult world. I had been invaded so often by the feelings of my parents that I'd "gotten into my head" that they would not be able to cope if I didn't do anything, save them, interfere. Because they were weak,

I had to be strong. It got stuck in my head. Now, finally, I had become conscious of my feelings and was able to let them go.

Natural Narcissists

All children, especially small children, take the blame for any misery of their parents. The reason is that they are self-centred: their world is small and they think that EVERYTHING that happens in the world around them has to do with them. In psychological language, we say that children live in a narcissist world where they, quite naturally, are occupied with themselves. That's how it is because that's how the brain develops.

Just like all other children, I thought that I was responsible for the difficulties and power struggles between my parents. If I had not only needed them so much and been so demanding, they may have felt better! I wasn't even aware that I gotten this into my head. Since I wasn't aware of it, I continued into adulthood believing this. I got into my head that I was responsible for the misfortune of Sven and other people close to me. His anxiety became my anxiety.

I was implicitly swallowed up by my fear, and this resulted in criticism, control, manipulation, forced positivity, and difficulties listening. Sometimes, Sven didn't even have to be frustrated. I (that is my amygdala) interpreted a raised eyebrow or a wrinkle on his forehead – and I "knew" how he felt! I automatically was invaded with old, implicit emotions – and at the same time felt deserted.

Now I have started to see the difference between my own and his signals without feeling responsible for what he says or feels. Now when I'm aware of this, I can choose. I can choose to be present, curious, breath calmly, listen and visit someone else than me. I can be attuned and cross the bridge. And it's that – to create true mindful, intimate communication – that is the essence of this book. Soon, I will describe the dialogue process "Crossing the Bridge," which is a method of communicating mindfully, and how you can do this in your own relationship.

Look Who's Talking

To be able to listen and really take in the world of another person is very, very difficult for many of us. This is especially true when the other person says something that triggers our own pain. We so readily mix up ourselves with others and then stay on "our own side of the bridge." We stay with ourselves, and as a result, no contact is created.

How do we listen? In school, among friends, at work, in the store, in all kinds of places? How do we tend to communicate with each other? What I have seen and experienced is that we very often get busy with our own signals and then don't hear the other person. We simply stay on our side of the bridge, feeling frightened and threatened. We aren't aware that we are defending ourselves, however. In the situation, we are convinced that the problem lies with the other person – exactly as I was when I saw Sven in the food store. And when we get stuck in ourselves, we instinctively start to defend ourselves. Our own inner signals kidnap us--even from ourselves!

Which bad habits do we practice when we talk to someone else, then? We interrupt, we shout them down, repeat ourselves, criticise, ridicule, try to change them, turn away, do other things, read the paper at the same time, sigh, roll our eyes. Or we scream, threaten, or pretend not to hear. We can also twist everything the person says into "but I think…" or "well, I feel…" and so on. Another common way not to listen is to pretend to be empathic by constantly stealing the subject: "Yes, I understand! It was exactly the same for me when I…".

What happens to us during such a "conversation?" What is the likely result and what can we do instead?

Before we continue along the road of listening and finally arriving at the bridge, we first must become acquainted with the concept of *safe attachment*. The reason: In order to truly listen, we must feel safe with another person.

One wants to be loved, failing that admired,
failing that feared, failing that hated and despised.
We want to install some sort of feeling.
The soul shudders at the gap and want contact at
any price.

Hᴊᴀʟᴍᴀʀ Sᴏ̈ᴅᴇʀʙᴇʀɢ, ꜰʀᴏᴍ **DOKTOR GLAS 1905**

6

Attachment

The Initial Bonds

A number of people have conducted research on attachment. When Daniel N. Stern published his book, *The Interpersonal World of the Infant* in the mid-1980, a paradigm shift took place, and a new era in developmental psychology began. With the help of video recordings and other technology, he could, frame by frame, look at a previously unnoticed interplay between mother and child. From this research grew the image of a competent infant, constantly interacting with his or her surroundings.

A lot of people have heard the word "attachment," and, as always, we associate it with concepts we already know. If you ask people what attachment is, the answers can be:

"Everything that happens when we are very young is very important and established in the child as it grows up."

"It's about the relation between adults and children. If you had a tough time it will follow you forever."

"The ability of the parents to connect with their infant, respond to its signals and make it feel safe."

"The way we relate to each other in intimate, close relationships, where the development of someone depends on how they are treated."

What are your own associations?

Attachment theory is generally associated with the term *a safe base*. It is founded on observations made by the British psychoanalysis and researcher John Bowlby on the effect of the environment on children, especially their relationships with parents or other early guardians.

According to Bowlby, the human child is prepared to attach to the people taking care of it (usually the parents) since this serves the idea of the evolution to keep the child out of harm's way and help the child to survive.

During the first six months of life, the child is socially open, but then starts to clearly prefer the persons it has most contact with, usually the mother or the father.

At about one year of age, the attachment to the parents or others who have been present is almost complete. This manifests itself in the child's tendency to automatically look for their closeness, use them as "safe harbours" when they are worried and see them as safe bases when they explore their surroundings. If a strange person comes too close, the child automatically responds by keeping close to the parents.

Under certain circumstances, such as insufficient care, long separation or loss of parents, the child can develop an unsafe attachment that will affect close relations for the rest of their lives, according to Bowlby.

Alone in a Room

Bowlby's follower, Mary Ainsworth, contributed to attachment theory in the 1970's by starting to study the strategies that children use depending on the kind of relationship they have with their attachment person. That is, she studied the Armani suit they put on in relation to their guardian.

She described guiding principles for studying three types of attachment, depending on the child's behaviour toward the parents in a mildly stressful situation: *safe, avoidant* and *ambivalent*. She also showed that the different types were related to the response to the signals of the child during the first twelve months.

The tests were made by, among other things, letting a one- year-old child play with a parent in a room where they had never been before. After a while the parent left the room and the child was left alone with a stranger. The parent returned after a few minutes. Now the reaction towards the returning parent was studied. Some children got sad and a little worried as the parent left, but when mum or dad came back the child ran to hug them and quickly returned to the game that had caught their attention before the parent left. This response was defined as an expression of *safe attachment.*

Other children got worried when the parent left, and when the parent returned the child pretended not to see them or be affected by their return. The child avoided contact with the parent. This was defined as *avoidant attachment.*

The children in the third group also got worried as the parent left, and were inconsolable even when the parent returned after a couple of minutes. The child clung to the parent, cried and could not be comforted. This was defined as *ambivalent attachment.*

Another researcher, Mary Main defined yet another type of attachment, *disorganized;* we will return to that later.

It's Not All Lost

During the 1980's, Mary Main expanded the attachment research to include the attachment patterns of adults. She developed a form of interview, the *Adult Attachment Interview* (AAI), which with sufficient scientific security could predict how a person would attach to his or her own (yet unborn) children. Main's research found evidence for Bowlby's hypothesis that the type of early attachment we form follows us all our lives.

Susan Johnson, professor of clinical psychology at the University of Ottawa, Canada and the developer of Emotionally Focused Couple Therapy says: "The basis of EFT is seven conversations that are aimed at encouraging a special kind of emotional responsiveness that is the key to lasting love for couples. This emotional responsiveness has three main components:

- Accessibility: Can I reach you?
- Responsiveness: Can I rely on you to respond to me emotionally?
- Engagement: Do I know you will value me and stay close? [28]

We all need to know that there is someone for us out there. Someone that we can trust. Knowing that someone will listen to our signals is as important for mankind as breathing air. We need each other.

A lot of people dislike the term "attachment" since they are against the notion that "all is lost" if we didn't make a positive attachment in childhood, and that destiny would decide if we make a good or a bad job with our own children; that we are caught and sentenced by our past.

Fortunately, that notion is wrong. It's not all lost; quite the contrary. It can be of greatest importance to understand what happened to us as children, and understand how we attached to our guardians – but what is more important is how this experience became *emotionally understood* and *explicit* to us, and our attitude towards it. We must definitely understand that what happened THEN has shaped our way of looking at, perceiving and feeling NOW. While we need to understand this, we do not need to over-analyse and look at ourselves as victims, because that will make our past into our present and future. This is especially true for close relationships, to our children, our partner, and others who are dear to us.

---

28 Dr Sue Johnson, *Hold me Tight, Seven Conversations for a Lifetime of Love*, page 49, 50

Now we know that children can be emotionally healthy even though their parents carry great traumas. It's not about what we experienced, but how we emotionally have made sense of the *connection* between then and now, and how we behave in relation to what we have understood.

The Existential Scream

Let me give you an example how a type of event kept repeating itself in my life as a parent.

When I ask one of my teenage sons to do something--such as pick up the wet towel from the floor, arrange his shoes by the door or clean his plate after dinner (very simple things, in my world)--the response has usually been, "okay, mum." Then nothing happens. Nothing... and *nothing*. This occurred over and over again. After each "nothing" reaction my nagging became more and more angry--and annoying.

You may think: well, it's only normal that children don't listen and that parents nag! And it is. But when I calmed down I got curious as to why I continued to do something that so obviously didn't work. Nagging is the task of the parent... but screaming and turning into a complete lunatic? I did get *crazy* one day and heard my voice rise to a falsetto when I screamed my powerlessness and despair that they didn't listen (a bit interesting since that was exactly what my husband told me about myself, right?). Did they hear me when I screamed even louder? Well, they did what I asked them that time, but next time *nothing happened again*. Do you recognize yourself?

I got so incredibly tired and I felt so powerless by not being heard. Sven often told me: "But Eva, don't take it so seriously. Why do you get started so easily?"

Why, indeed, did I get so angry? Why couldn't I be calm and consistent? Why did I scrap all I knew in less than a second (concerning the fact that children are children and teenagers are tired and half deaf) and became an irascible person who didn't learn from her mistakes, who screamed at her children, treated them disrespectfully, and again and again concluded that it was all their fault?

Now you may think: Yes, but the fault is with them, since they actually don't pick up and don't listen. Children should obey their parents!

To some extent, that is true. But if we know how the brain works in children, *especially* teenagers, we can see that "not to listen" is part of their development. That's the way it's supposed to be. When the hormones rush through a teenager's body, they contribute to tiredness, cheekiness and need to liberate themselves. The brain actually looks a bit different during the teen years.

Teenagers have less access to the prefrontal cortex than adults, and their amygdala often run their lives and behaviour. You can almost see that when you wake them up in the morning. If I understand this as a parent, I don't have to explode every time this "disobedience" occurs.

It is, of course, natural and understandable that we as parents respond when children don't listen. Besides this, children need natural, warm and clear boundaries. But what I focus on here is not how they responded, but how *I* responded. When even my dog could trigger a rabid owner in me if she didn't come when I yelled, and when Sven over and over again triggered the same emotion, I finally realized that this probably said a lot about me (besides the dog, sons and husband, of course).

When we experience such strong negative energy and repeat the same behaviour again and again without the desired result, we can with great affection and empathy begin to look inwards at ourselves. Even better, we can think: How LUCKY I am to get stuck in this dance again and again! Now I have the opportunity to find out where this comes from and understand the wiring in my brain! Thinking like that is much more rewarding than only blaming the people around you – or walking around with a bad conscience for your uncontrolled behaviour.

I decided to visit myself. I did this by keeping a diary and with the aid of the dialogue process "Crossing the Bridge," together with my husband and some close friends.

I visited that crazy, irascible person within, the one who got so mad when the feeling of not being heard arose. I took a guided tour into myself and interestingly, I found that I got mad even when I just *talked* about it. I moved backward in time, reached through my anger, and arrived at a place of great sadness and powerlessness. Sentences of complete despair played inside me: *They don't hear me anyway. It's no use. I can't reach him anyway.* I moved back in time to a small girl who over and over again begged her father not to drink; begged, asked, yelled, manipulated, cried, whispered, joked and in any way I could tried to get him to pour out the wine, beer, and booze. I was again a little girl who begged a father kidnapped by alcohol and, when her father said, "Okay, I won't drink," he continued to drink as if my words never existed.

My father never perceived himself as a drunk. The bottle on the floor by the couch wasn't his; someone else put it there. According to him, it was sometimes my one-year-old brother who sucked it empty.

Not even during the nights when he rumbled around in search of alcohol did he realize his addiction. He just wanted a drink and to him, that was normal behaviour.

I remember lying in my bed, terrified by my father's anger, restlessness, and powerlessness. Above all, I was afraid of his tears when anxiety struck. I remember how my heart almost broke for the pain in my father when he felt sorry for himself; especially when he over and over again repeated, "poor me, nobody loves me!" I remember holding him hard with my thin arms, wiping the tears from his cheeks and assuring him that I would never, never leave him, I would always love him, and I would take care of him forever!

I remember how afraid and sad I was for my mother's sake. She really did have to take care of everything. I sympathized with her tears and with my little brother whom I loved. He was so small and I was his protector.

I remember the sadness and despair of that little girl as she slowly but steadily saw her father slide into misery and languish; a father who, without alcohol, might have listened to his daughter, read her a story, cleaned up in the hallway, put away his shoes, cleaned his plate or just been an adult. A responsible father who listened....

Your childhood may be completely different from mine. You may find it difficult to identify with if you didn't have an alcoholic parent – or you may know exactly what it is like to feel unsafe in this way. Whatever your situation was, I encourage you to be curious about yourself and your responses. Your irascible personality may occur at different times and in different ways. Or perhaps you are much softer in your energy – or perhaps much more violent in your response. Or, maybe you start to cry all the time. Your inherent anger my pop up with your children, an ex-partner, a current partner, a friend, a colleague, a politician, a TV host, or someone else who gets your unhappy energy going.

Sometimes, we don't express anger directly. When we turn the energy inwards and "turn off" by leaving the room, sulking, or making ourselves unreachable in some other way is simply an *inverted* strong reaction – it's just a bit less obvious and perhaps more difficult to discover. But it's no healthier. If you recognize yourself in this picture, get curious about when you turn off, and try to understand why certain situations and persons trigger you.

Whatever you do, I want to get you to put a heart around yourself. Put a *big* heart around yourself, make an expedition to understand how you respond in order to calm yourself and choose a new way with a better result.

Today, I can see that the "existential scream" my father expressed in various ways was about his own pain, about the small boy in his own story. It was about the terrible time he had at boarding school, and how his parents, in the name of love, did what they did, because they were crying their own "existential scream," which they inherited from their parents, and so on. For my father, alcohol was a way to calm down his nervous system. Unfortunately he didn't choose the constructive way – to acknowledge his dependency and to get free from it.

By looking inwards I could thus see that the "insight" that had carved the deep craters in my brain was *that I wasn't heard and didn't get through*. And I saw that this affected my behaviour towards my environment, for instance with my teenagers, very strongly. But with this knowledge, it was easier to change my behaviour as an adult. Part of the dejection I feel when my children don't listen goes away, and instead I can put a heart around myself and carry it with me. I can understand that "not being heard" is registered as a DISASTER in my brain – but it's just my teenagers who don't listen sometimes (which teenagers don't).

I don't have to become self-absorbed by dealing with these emergency signals. I can calm down, listen to my children and practice separating my implicit reactions from an adult mother's reactions. When I can hear the differences in my own and my children's signals, I can usually avoid getting lost in a feeling of powerlessness. I can regulate both my own and others' anxiety. I'm better at staying calm and clear, and the more often I manage to do this, the less violent are my responses. And if I overreact anyway, I can always cool down my nervous system and then go back and apologize.

My implicit memories have become explicit. I'm slowly making new tracks in my neuron map.

Safe Attachment

Are you there for me? Do I come first? Am I most important? Can you hear me? Do you care? I need to trust that you are there if I need you!

These are our initial signals to the world around us.

Dr. Sue Johnson is one of the leading researchers in attachment theory today. In her beautiful book, *Hold me tight- Seven conversations for a lifetime of love,* she describes how attachment problems can linger and mess up our relationships as adults. More about that soon, but first let's take a look at what happens in the different types of attachment. It helps us understand how we function together with our partner when we are adults.

Imagine a baby crying and screaming because it's hungry. Now a parent (or some other adult close to the child) must understand the scream and respond to it. The best thing for the child is that the parent:

- hears the scream.
- understands and make sense of the meaning of the scream.
- gives the child food and thus responds exactly to the needs of the child.

Everybody knows that it's not always so easy to understand the scream from an infant, and that we sometimes hear the scream but:

- we come with a blanket because we thought the child was cold.
- we hug it because we think it needs closeness.
- we put the child down because we think it needs to sleep.

We guess and try and usually we get it right in the end. We can do that since we are calm enough ourselves to hear the signals of the child. This is also a safe attachment, because our goal is to read the signals of the screams in order to offer the child what it wants. We try until the young one is satisfied.

When the child is so small that it can't yet talk, we need to *interpret* its signals in order to understand the needs.

Everything that the child experiences will be end up as the map of its mind. If the situation occurs frequently, the map drawn in the brain of the child in this case could mean:

"The world is safe."

"There is someone for me."

"I'm valuable."

"I'm understood."

"I can get what I need."

And so on.

With safe attachment, there is balance and harmony in the child. In addition to safe attachment, there are three other types of attachment.

Most of us experience a mix of attachment types. It is also important to remember that we can have one type of attachment with one parent, and a different type with the other.

Avoidant Attachment

Let's imagine the same situation again: the child is crying and is hungry. The parent might:

- hear the scream.
- not understand it, or not take it in for some reason. The parent might close his or her ears or the door to the child's room. The small one gets food later, when the parent decides to feed it. The signal "I'm hungry" doesn't get through quickly enough.
- make no response at all. Nothing happens.

In this case, the parent is busy with his or her own signals and may carry anxiety, insecurity, fear, sorrow, anger, or other strong feelings. But these feelings are turned inwards – the parent may be protecting him- or herself by turning them off. They may be so totally turned off that the parent doesn't experience them at all. The parent may become emotionally rigid and not be able to read the signals from the child. There is lack of integration in the brain.

The result for the child is, besides hunger, a feeling of powerlessness. The child will gradually turn off the feelings and give up. The child learns to avoid contact.

What the child experiences is "carved" in its mind. If the experience is frequently repeated, the map that is drawn in the brain of the child could be:

"There is no one for me."

"Contact isn't possible."

"I can't affect anyone and can't get what I need."

"I'm worthless."

"I don't need anyone."

With avoidant attachment, the child gets a feeling of unbalance.

Ambivalent Attachment

The child screams, cries and is hungry. The parent might:

- sometimes hear it, sometimes not.
- sometimes give the child food, and sometimes bring a blanket, without testing anything else.
- sometimes the parent responds to the needs of the child but mixes the response with exaggerated feelings (anxiety, crying, hopelessness, anger, etc.). The parent invades the child with his or her strong and unruly feeling.

In this case, the parent is busy with his or her own emotions and may carry a lot of pain in him- or herself. Worries, fear, sorrow, anger, and other strong emotions sometimes sweep over the child in a torrent. The map that is drawn in the mind of the child is a confused mix of safe response and an invasion of the emotions and needs of the parent. The result is that the child feels safe but also confused, powerless, and invaded by emotions in such a way that the child sometimes confuses itself with the parent. Again, there is lack of integration in the brain.

All of the experiences will end up in the child's consciousness. The map in the brain of this child could be:

"I don't know what I think, feel or want."

"Others know more about what I need than I do."

"I don't want you to decide! But what do you think?"

"I'm here for you, Mum/Dad!"

"Don't leave me!"

With such an ambivalent attachment, the child gets a feeling of unbalance. The main difference between avoidant and ambivalent attachment is that in the first case, the child is faced with disconnection and a lack of response, and in this second case the child sometimes get an exaggerated response and is thus invaded by the feelings of the parent. In both cases, the parent is kidnapped by his or her own signals, and the child is hurt. Neither of them can read the child's signals, especially not the nonverbal signals from the right domain of the brain.

Disorganised Attachment

This is the most difficult attachment and is accompanied by the greatest trauma for the child. This type of attachment was added to Mary Ainsworth's research by Mary Main's research group. In this type of attachment, the child is screaming, crying and hungry, and the parent:

- doesn't register the needs of the child, but only experiences his or her own response to the screams of the child.
- responds to his or her own internal response and becomes irascible, hysterical, and often even dangerous.
- responds violently, becoming the child's the worst nightmare. The parent almost scares the child to death in various ways, and may physically hurt the child.

Here, the parent is completely overwhelmed by his or her own signals and the consequence is that the child becomes terrified. The inborn behaviour makes the child seek closeness to the parents when it experiences fear. But when the parent is the threat, there is a short circuit between the impulse to avoid danger and to seek safety. The child doesn't know how to behave, and thus the behaviour is called disorganized. In order to survive this traumatic situation, the child closes down its emotions, and the map in the little brain loses context. The child lives in complete fear and powerlessness and, in worst cases, can only develop fragments of its ego. The degree of damage depends on how badly the child is treated.

In these cases, the parent carries an extreme amount of pain that is manifested in violence, panic, abuse and uncontrolled anger towards the child. In disorganized attachment, the child gets a feeling of severe imbalance.

Nobody is Perfect

At this point, you may have started to become dizzy with questions about your own family. How was it when you grew up and how have you been (or are you) as a parent? As soon as we hear about such results from research, we want to put ourselves into categories and find out what "kind" we are: "I'm like that," "my mother did exactly so," "my father always let me down." Or perhaps: "help, I've treated my children so badly, I'm a lousy mum," or "help, I've turned into my father."

But, make an effort to let go of that! Imagine a beautiful bowl, maybe brilliant blue, in top of a shelf. Now take all the guilt, shame or anger you may feel and put all of it into the symbolic bowl. Let it contain all that is negative.

Instead, I want you to look at this from a larger perspective. We usually bring a bit of everything with us from the different types of attachment (especially the safe attachment), and I encourage you to once again "put a heart around" yourself and what you see.

I think that we as parents and adults often convey the three first kinds of attachment (safe, ambivalent, and avoidant), although we want the best for our children and love them more than anything else. Then why isn't it "perfect?" There are a number of explanations:

- You never learnt to show feelings or talk about them yourself.
- You have not learned how to read nonverbal signals
- You may be depressed, sad, or in despair and let these emotion invade the space of the family.
- You may have had difficulties as a parent in seeing and tolerating differences between "me" and "you" – *differentiating.*
- You close down your emotions and maybe perform work or exercise instead.

- You have irascible outbursts (like I had) and feel more-or- less violated when your children don't respond as expected.
- You may have great difficulties listening (like I had).
- You may be a control freak and get nervous when things don't turn out as you planned.
- External factors like losses, accidents, and illness occur and you don't know how to deal with the situation.
- You may be overwhelmed by feelings of betrayal, or in a conflict with your partner, so that your children get obscured.

Yes, lack of attunement with our children can be manifested in many different ways. What they all have in common is that when we are kidnapped and busy with our inner, implicit signals, we don't automatically hear the other ones. Actually we don't even hear our own essential signals! Let's take a loving and humble look at each other. Most of us do the best we can. Very few (if any) of us *choose* to hurt our child. Part of our behaviour may be connected to our own attachment history, and other aspects may have genetic roots.

And, of course, we inherit what the people close to us carry along in their brains. Quite a lot of what we bring with us is due to external factors and lack of knowledge. It wasn't so long ago that we in the West believed that hospitalized children should be visited only one hour a week by their parents – at the most. Or that it was good for children to cry themselves to sleep otherwise they would get spoiled. Or that infants should get only so much to eat every four hours, or they would get fat and spoiled. It wasn't so long ago that we simply didn't understand what children needed to thrive.

I think that we still haven't taken attachment seriously enough. We still don't understand the magnitude of a child's need to be seen, heard and understood seriously. How else can we accept larger groups of children in day-care classes with fewer adults caring for them, although most researchers now agree that small children shouldn't be in groups of more than ten to twelve? How else can the US job culture dictate that mothers should go back to work after only 6 weeks at home after her child is born?

Our ability to attach is developed all through life, but the first period in life is etched especially clearly into our consciousness. The more harmony and safe attachment we have, the greater is our ability to calm ourselves in stressful situations, regulate our own emotions, turn outwards for contact, see appropriate difference between you and me, feel empathy for other people's views and to *listen* – both to others and ourselves.

Everything occurs in the space "in between." The encounters we have make us into what we are (though our genes also have a part in this process). We are very vulnerable if nobody comes when we call, whether our signal is quiet or loud. But when somebody hears us and we get a response that is coherent with our needs, harmony and balance is created inside us. This goes for children but it also goes for adults in loving relationships.

Harmony and consistency are needed in order for us to develop our ability to listen, respond to the signals of our own and others and learn to differentiate – that is, to see the difference between you and me.

Finally, it's not "all lost" if we don't get all this as children! There are ways to heal. We can draw new maps and make new tracks in our brains. One way to create a safe attachment and integration is to listen actively, with presence and attunement, to another person, and to listen to yourself and create new neuron-tracks *together.* We can actually learn as adults to hear, understand and integrate our own signals and those of others, in order to securely and empathically respond to our own needs and the needs of others. The dialogue process "Crossing the Bridge" is a powerful way to practice this.

But now, let's follow the path of thorns and rose petals to the beginning of everything.

Falling in Love

It's a quite short period in history that we have chosen to build marriages on romantic love. It's a cultural phenomenon that is actually not the dominant one. Most people in the world still marry for other reasons. It wasn't until the Reformation in Europe in the 16th Century that the current idea of a strong, loving and emotionally engaged relationship between man and woman first arose. This contradicted the medieval ideal of chastity, which sees marriage as a necessary evil. It wasn't until the Industrial Revolution and the rise of the middle class, that romantic love became such a firmly accepted ideal in the West that it was enough for a man and a woman to be in love for them to marry.

For centuries, marriages in the European aristocracy were mainly a question of keeping property within the clan, or to form alliances for political purposes. This went for farmers and merchants as well, that is everyone with some kind of property. Almost all marriages were arranged, although stealing brides and eloping did occur when young persons were "afflicted" by passion.

But there was a practical system operating beneath this official reality: while waiting for a financially or politically suitable consort, the nobleman, prince or king could choose to take a kind of "pre wife" or concubine. When a "suitable" wife was found, the concubine was usually given away to some other nobleman. The children of these "pre-wives" were always accepted by the biological father and taken care of, raised according to the father's standing and with the right to inherit (unlike the children of "whores") [29]

For poor people, marriage was a question of finding someone who was healthy and capable to work and could contribute to the support of the craft or farm. In fact, modern-day arranged marriages where lust and love are not the driving forces still dominate in many parts of the world.

Drugged--and a Little Bit Brain-Damaged

The anthropologist Helen Fisher has scanned the brain of people who have fallen in love. The scan shows that three areas in the brain are active and "light up" in both men and women. These areas are part of

---

29 Pia Gadd, Swedish book: *Frillor, Fruar och herrar* (and many other places)

the brain's reward system; the main "player" is the signal-substance *dopamine*. This substance creates a feeling of happiness and at that same time promotes a drug-like addiction; you want to have this pleasant feeling again and again.

The person in love often experiences heaven and hell at the same time. It is difficult to focus on irrelevant things like work, duties and agreements. Moods can swing between exhilaration and despair. In many ways, falling in love is some kind of insanity, a mania spiced with illusions, obsessions and a pinch of paranoia. If you didn't know better, you might suspect that the person in love had sustained slight brain damage. [30] But it is a brain damage that usually feels quite wonderful.

Love and Sex

Marianne J. Legato, professor of clinical medicine at Columbia University, also writes about falling in love, faithfulness and differences between the sexes. She observes: "Lust is the spark that ignites between two people, and romantic love is the kindling." [31] The signal substances that are believed to have an important role in falling in love are not lasting. The level of testosterone is genetically individual, but when we fall in love the couple attunes to each other's needs, and the need for sex and closeness is usually equally strong.

When the love moves into the next phase, the levels return to what was "normal" to them before. For many this is a great disappointment, as "normal" for some can be a very high level of testosterone and a greater lust for sex, while for others the level is low, which means a smaller desire for sex. (And it's not necessarily the man who feels the greater lust). Of course a number of other factors, both external and internal, are significant when lust ends. But the fact of the matter is that many marriages fail because partners have different needs when it comes to sex. It becomes a stumbling block in part because we don't understand

---

30 Swedish Science magazine: *Illustrerad Vetenskap*, Number 3, 2005
31 Marianne J. Legato, *Why Men never remember and woman never forget*, page 103

how this works! We also charge eroticism with strange values, guilt, shame, and martyrdom. On top of all this, we often have difficulties talking about sex. Three books about sex that I really can recommend are: *Mating in Captivity –Unlocking Erotic Intelligence,* by Esther Perel and *Getting the sex you want* by Tammy Nelson and finally Pat Loves *Hot monogamy.* All of them wonderful couple and family therapists.

The Love Hormone

Following the falling-in-love stage is what anthropologist Helen Fisher calls the *attachment phase.* Now that the "love cocktail" (a mix of dopamine, phenyethylamine, and norepinephrine) is accompanied by an increase in other chemicals, which work to strengthen the couple's bond, as well as the feeling of contentment and comfort that we have in the relationship. While these may not give us the speed like rush of infatuation chemicals, they are happy drugs in their own right. [32] The primary signal substances secreted during this phase are endorphins and oxytocin.

Endorphins are lust-creating signal substances and have a great impact on our mood. We secrete them when we laugh and the endorphins help us to be kind, sociable and relaxed. They are also created when we have an orgasm; together with oxytocin they are behind the wonderful feeling of euphoria after good intercourse. These natural painkillers also kill the pain of social isolation, separation and loneliness.

Oxytocin is a hormone that stimulates sexual lust in both men and women, and that is secreted more during intercourse and orgasm. The hormone is not only active when we have sex but is also connected to contractions of smooth muscle tissue. For instance, the drug that starts the contractions of childbirth is a synthetic form of oxytocin. The word oxytocin comes from the Greek term for "quick childbirth." Oxytocin also stimulates milk production in breastfeeding mothers and is always secreted when we are under stress, in order to calm down our nervous

---

32 Marianne J. Legato, *Why men never remember and woman never forget,* page 104

system and deal better with the stress. The oxytocin helps us to *attach and create relationships* to other people, making it easier to achieve affinity and contact. Since oxytocin helps new mothers to attach to their child, this may be the reason why breastfeeding mothers are less likely to suffer from postpartum depression than those who don't. Just like endorphin, oxytocin creates a feeling of wellbeing and is often called "the love hormone."

It's important to be aware of this because then we can help each other and ourselves get more "attachment hormones" flowing in the space between us. It helps us to understand why couples that are easily sexual and sensual together attach to each other in a way that non-physical couples don't. Caressing, touch and sex binds us together.

During the next phase of intimate relationship, the level of love hormones goes down and the lovely, narcotic love-cocktail leaves the body. Some couples can still remain in contact and closeness. Others fall down into a crater of power struggle: constant arguments, difficulties and perhaps a complete loss of loving feelings. Some stay happy and continue to experience intimacy and contact while others lose lust for each other quite swiftly. Why are there such differences?

I have had the privilege of working with many couples who lost the lust for each other but still found a way back from the conflicts and feelings of despair because the love "ended." Today, we know that falling in love and being in love belong to different parts of the brain. So maybe the old saying is right: "If you can't get the one that you love, love the one you get."

We can learn to attach. We can learn to differentiate and in that way create integration between us as a couple. New research suggests that love actually can *be taught*. With effort and a bit of luck, our hormones and our smart brains can turn the recurring frog back into a prince--if a prince is, indeed, what we want.

"Darling, your shoelaces are untied."
"Stop controlling my life!"

UNKNOWN

7

The Power Struggle

It Looks Like a Dance

To quarrel, keep silent, misunderstand, criticize, turn off … our power struggles have many ugly faces.

But we don't wake up one day thinking: "What can I do to make life miserable for my partner today?" Nor do we wake up and discover that the love we knew had disappeared during the night. The power struggle usually creeps in slowly. When the infatuation bubble bursts, hormones calm down and everyday life knocks on the door, sneaking up on us with small treacherous steps.

For some, this power struggle is very discreet and hardly noticeable. For others it hits them in the gut, the quarrels and the strange new vision of the partner:

Suddenly we say things like:

"I don't recognize him!"

"She fooled me; she wasn't like this when we met!"

"I can't believe he said that!"

"Shit, she nags just like my previous wife!"

Now we start to negotiate about chores and practicalities, we close down, attack, scream and yell, nag, leave, follow, hide, become workaholics, weeps, criticize openly or behind each other's back, fight, threaten. We get a new house, mock, repaint the bedroom, pretend not to hear, play martyr, flirt with others, wash the car, belittle, ridicule, are unfaithful, redecorate, sulk, over-focus on the children, dole out shame, guilt, play golf, go to therapy, play computer games, surf porn sites. We drink, sneak away by sleeping, talk things apart, take evening courses, joke, quarrel and make up, clean like a maniac, fall in love with someone else, give up, get divorced.

We now place all of this in *the space* – the place where we'd earlier put so much tenderness and acknowledgment. Consciously or unconsciously, we do what we *think* will work and make us feel good again. We try to calm our nervous system and ourselves and, wisely enough, we try to ease our pain and loosen up the knots in every possible way. The power struggle gets out of hand and we rush to defend ourselves – by putting on our safe Armani suits.

Unfortunately, our attempts to deal with the power struggle often fail and the distance between us increases. But we can't see any winner in this struggle, just losers.

You could compare it to a dance. Some of us dance the dance of power struggle with great passion, like the tango. We pour petrol on the flames and have grand and stormy rows so that we then can enjoy a passionate reunion – and thus get dependent on these negative emotions. For some couples, this can be the *essence*, the very definition of love.

Others dance without contact, "alone together" on a blinking disco floor, slowly sliding into parallel lives where both live their own life and the children, the house, the boat, or the summerhouse is what keeps them together. If your partner takes one step forward, you take one step back, and the two of you never meet. This contact-free dance can go on for years, until passion strikes and one of you finds a new partner.

A lot of people who get stuck in power struggles give up any idea of creating a lasting working relationship. There are also couples, of course, who find the way back from the power struggle to a loving and genuinely intimate relation. Still other couples seem quite well off. They are good friends and not lovers, and feel that their friendship is sufficient for them.

What is nearly inevitable is that at some point, in some way, the power struggle will knock on a couple's door. Remember that this is normal. It's *supposed* to happen! The love will change, just as sunshine is followed by a period of rain. This does not have to mean the end of the relationship.

But no matter how aware we are, this shift is likely to come as a shock. During the drugged period of falling in love, we have nourished the feeling that *this time* we finally found the right partner. Now, everything that had felt so hopeless in previous relationships is gone forever! The tough things will never occur with this partner, because he or she really *sees* us and understands us. We know that this *right* partner will make us feel good forever. The illusion is often well anchored, for we *want to* fool ourselves.

Do you recognize yourself here?

In my groups for singles, I have heard a lot of people say that they don't believe in love any longer and that it's too difficult to live together with someone. They may be dispirited but deep inside they retain a small hope that maybe, just maybe, there is someone for them as well – that's why they are there. Some have decided that their intimate relations shall be with close friends, or that they can have some short sexual adventures with someone they met net-dating or in a bar. Short, intense, passionate and then goodbye!

Some singles really want to live like this. Once again, I am not judging these decisions. There are many ways to live your life and anything is possible, as long as it goes on between consenting adults. No, I'm talking about when the feeling of hopelessness has gotten a grip on us and *because of that* we avoid an intimate and lasting relationship.

But do remember: in any important relationship, *the power struggle shall come*. Difficulties and conflict *will* turn up – and may also appear not just between us as a couple but everyone who is close to us. Conflicts are a natural and important part of life. Conflicts are actually our friends.

Now you may think: "But I don't live in a struggle with my partner and we have a good life together. I just feel a bit empty inside… and maybe it's my boring job that makes me feel bad. Is anything wrong then?"

No, there is nothing wrong. If you both feel that you have a good relationship, then that's wonderful! But it may also be so that your conflicts manifest themselves in different ways; or you are simply a person with few conflicts in your life. We are all different.

What I want to say is that when conflict knocks on the door, no matter how or when, it is good to remember that it's natural and normal. We can *practice* looking at them from the outside, from a different angle. Thanks to our conflicts, we get the chance to evolve and understand more about ourselves. We can give ourselves some free therapy and excellent guidance! We can play both electrician and pioneer in our own brain; put in new cables and find new ways. In short, we can rewire!

The Simple, Beautiful Life

We have a natural tendency to avoid painful things. Whether the pain is physical or mental we want to avoid it, for the sake of survival. And conflicts can be very painful.

In the modern world we also have a notion that difficulties, hindrances, conflicts, wrinkles – yes, even death –shouldn't exist at all. We think that we shall be physically perfect and live in perfect relationships without pain. If a relationship is very difficult we think that it's *wrong*; we have been tricked to fall in love with the wrong person! We think that when we get stuck in pain it must be removed in some magical way, and if the relationship gets difficult and painful we should leave.

We all know that it sometimes can be difficult to live in a close relationship. Yet it's somewhat taboo to talk openly about difficulties in the relationship and look for help from the outside. Some go to family counselling, or some other kind of therapy, but most do it secretly. We may tell a friend that our partner is difficult – but to openly try to get help and admit that we are stuck in a power struggle is much more shameful. It seems as though we are expected to either "fix" our relationships ourselves or else realize that the love has ended and it's time for a divorce.

Sometimes, it *is* better to get a divorce if the relationship is very difficult – especially if you are not both curious and prepared to see what lies behind the problems. For some couples that agree to separate it can be a simple process, but most times it's a very difficult decision, especially when children are involved. Sometimes a divorce is necessary. Sometimes it may be unnecessary.

I have followed individuals that divorced and have a good, loving life today, either alone or with a new partner. I have talked with people who say that it was the best thing they'd ever done – to leave and go on. I have also followed many, many couples that saved their marriage and found the way back to love. These couples chose to face the difficulties, learnt to communicate and create a loving and exciting life together.

A lot of people who are in difficult relationships, but don't know how to face the difficulties, meet someone new and fall in love again. When the cocktail of hormones flow in the blood again it's very hard to resist falling in love. It becomes a drug – a love-drug that makes us feel that we're really *alive*. We experience limbic resonance for first time in perhaps many, many years! But the drug makes us mix up *falling in love* with love itself.

For many of the couples that come to me, infidelity has occurred. In some cases it has been a question of casual sex; in other cases one partner has fallen in love with someone else.

Let's go back to our couple, Lisa and Michael Johnson, who could be any of hundreds of couples that stepped into my clinic.

Michael and Lisa

"Nothing Helps with Her"

Michael threw the heavy door shut with a thud. His brain was boiling and his heart was beating furiously as he marched down the gravel-path with crunching footsteps.

It was a cool night in November, with a stiff wind and pouring rain. The cosy evening had degenerated when Lisa started to criticize, as always, what he did and didn't do and what he should have done.

It felt like Michael's head was going to pieces when he strode towards the gate with hands clasped hard and his knuckles turning white. She always won their verbal fights with her torrent of words, and finally there was nothing left to do but to leave. He really felt like hitting--hitting and then running. Not hitting her, he could never do that, but hitting and crushing something with his bare hands, and then leaving.

Because nothing helped. Nothing helped with her.

Before his eyes, Michael saw Lisa's grumpy face, the disapproving frown between her eyebrows, and her tense, thin lips. Her face always looked like that now! Whatever he said, she was disappointed and always found something to complain about.

Since he had a glass of wine, he knew he couldn't take the car – or perhaps he could anyway and drive into a tree and finish it off? Or he could take the spade and chop her rhododendron to pieces or cut down the new pear tree. Or why not demolish the entire house that he wore himself out building, just to sit there and listen to a lot of nagging!

He threw the gate shut with a bang and strode along the road in the residential area. He must by all means get rid of the terrible feeling of powerlessness churning in his stomach. Just then he understood how seemingly inexplicable violent crimes could occur. Michael wasn't a violent person and he knew the he could never hit anyone unless in panic or self-defence – but the impulse he could understand.

After a while, Michael turned onto the path among the trees. He strode with decisive steps but didn't have any idea where he was going. He just wanted to get away, far away. "She thinks she knows who I am, what I feel and what I think," he mumbled between panting breaths. Then he took a deep breath and roared into the darkness:

"But she hasn't got a damn clue!"

The rain fell hard against his face. He didn't have any plan for his angry march but was drawn towards the sea, where he'd walked so many times with Lisa and the dog, then, before, when they were still… lovers.

He walked and walked with his aching head. It felt good to be alone in the dark, to be enclosed, to disappear. His stomach felt calmer now. The solitude made him relax. Since childhood, he'd always felt calmer in isolation, especially when he was under stress. When he was apart from others, he always felt free and light. But the difference was that before, he always longed to be home with Lisa before too long.

When they met twenty-one years ago, he felt whole for the first time, and the hours he spent apart from her were unbearably long. During the first intoxicating months, when he thought he'd found a soul mate, it was almost physically painful to be separated from Lisa, even for a couple of days. He had been in his conference hotel thinking of her sleek body, long dark hair and brown eyes; he had made long phone calls to her and had only her in mind when he satisfied himself.

The first two years had been wonderful. They talked about everything, laughed a lot, done a lot of things together--hiking, camping, sailing, horseback riding, playing squash, going to the movies, travelling. And made love, made love, made love! Now it must be a couple of months since they'd had sex, at least. He couldn't actually remember – perhaps because their uninspired intercourse wasn't worth remembering. It was joyless routine in the dark. She was a body to rub against in the absence of some other body.

Someone else's body.

It wasn't any use to count the sexless weeks any longer, they were only depressing. He had turned off his desire for Lisa a long time ago, actually for sex at all. He had turned it off and become a non-sensual work machine. That was especially evident after that week in June, when... Michael cut the thought short. There was no use tormenting himself again; he had gone over and over it the last six months and it didn't change anything.

He could see a faint light ahead among the trees and when he stopped he could hear the rush from the sea. He was cold and his feet were wet in the thin-soled shoes he'd slipped on as he rushed out of the house. He started to walk again in his squishing shoes.

Sure, he had been away a lot. Sure, he withdrew; sure, he spent a lot of time in the gym; sure, he preferred to be at work or the golf course; sure, he turned off and kept silent when he was at home. Just as well not to wake the sleeping bear. In a way, he could understand Lisa's frustration. He knew that she disliked being alone. But what could he do?

All these damn demands! When he came home, she usually complained that he'd been away. She seemed under stress, angry and displeased with everything. She wrote her to-do lists, cleaned and picked up while complaining that all of them just dropped everything on the floor. She nagged at the kids, nagged at him, and was generally boring and morose. If she could just relax a bit, chill, as the kids said.

Lisa didn't put as much effort into looking nice any longer. A few years ago, she'd even cut her hair very short so that it would be easy to clean. He was shocked when he saw her, and felt both angry and disappointed. But she claimed that her hair was too grey to keep long.

"What are you complaining about?" she snapped. "You simply have to choose: a witch with long grey hair or a witch with short dark hair."

The truth was that there wasn't much resemblance between the dark-eyed sensual beauty with hair to her waist that he fell in love with twenty-one years ago, and the short-haired, bitter women she was now. Sure, she still looked good, and other men looked at her when they were at parties, but... she seldom dressed up now. She seemed to expect that *he* would be "present," sexy and courting after ten to twelve hours at work. But she wasn't willing to make the same effort. That was crazy. He almost worked himself to death so that his family could have a good life, and she didn't seem to understand it. Demands, demands, demands, and even more demands. No, it wasn't strange that he stayed late at work.

Yet, sometimes he missed her. It could be when she talked to someone on the phone and laughed that ringing, bubbling laugh he'd fallen in love with... that laugh that was never meant for him anymore.

Sometimes he missed their three teenagers. It was easy to love them.

Suddenly it felt wonderful to walk, just let his strong legs carry him forward along the path down to the sea. The darkness felt safe as the cool rain washed over his face. For a short while, he almost felt harmonious.

"I Don't Deserve This!"

Lisa sat on the bathroom floor crying, her face pressed into a silencing terrycloth towel and the water running in the shower so that the kids wouldn't hear. Her face was red, the mascara smeared over her cheeks, and she was literally shaking with tears. She cried because she was angry. She cried because she couldn't take it anymore. She cried because she couldn't reach Michael. She cried for her children who didn't understand that their parents would divorce.

The mascara made big stains on the towel, and just the thought that it had been washed clean this morning made her cry even more. All this damn WASHING that never ended! How much could you wash for five persons? It was Sisyphus work that no one thanked her for but simply took for granted. She cried over her loveless, boring life, filled with control and nagging and vain struggle and meaningless work that had to be done over and over again and which only made her irritating to her family, not at all loved. Damn! She ought to go, just *go* and leave them there to wade in odd socks and breadcrumbs and dust and be drowned in their own dirt. They wouldn't understand what she did for them until they got salmonella from the cutting board or mite-allergy from the sheets.

But it was probably her fault. She had spoilt them all, wanted to be a perfect mother and create a perfect home. Somehow, she had turned into a bitter, whining, nagging machine. But was that so strange, when she had to take so much responsibility? Nobody understood.

Another wave of sobbing tore through her body. Aaaah! She must be nuts. How could she be thinking about washing and cleaning when Michael just left her?

She lay down on the heated bathroom floor and cuddled up like a small baby, hugging herself, letting the tears silently run. In some strange way, it felt good. It felt like the heated floor was the only thing that could make her warm and soothe her despair. She grew numb and forgot about time and space for a while, forgot the children, and forgot the water in the shower.

"I can't take it anymore," she mumbled. "Can't carry everything any longer, *I can't take it anymore!*"

In despair, she rocked back and forth. For how long had she felt this lonely and thirsting for contact? Maybe always.

The worst thing was that they were so different, she and Michael. He seemed to be happier without her. "I don't understand him," she often thought. "Sometimes he says he loves me, at least when I ask. But that can't be true because he never wants to be with me anymore, and never really close. Sure, I'm nagging and horrible sometimes, but it's not that bad all the time!"

The tears had ebbed. She angrily straightened her back, unfolded her body and stood up. "I fight and I fight but nevertheless I get treated like an old piece of furniture that is always there but nobody sees," she thought. "An old worn couch that no one has needed for a hundred years. It's time to change that now. I'm worthy of something better than that!"

Filled with rebellious thoughts she turned around and faced her gaze in the mirror. But she hardly recognized the ugly, bloated face that looked back at her. The hair stood on end. The eyes were swollen slits with something red in the middle. Her green linen dress was shrivelled like a dishcloth and there was mascara on the bodice.

"My God, I look awful," she whispered aloud. "I'm ugly… ugly and broken down." The power and resolution just drained from her and the discouragement returned. Nobody would want her the way she looked now.

"You're so pretty my little girl, you got the brown squirrel eyes of your grandfather!" She could still hear the soft voice of her mother. So many times he mother had told her she was beautiful! Her father maybe said it too. In weekends when he drank he could sometimes become loving and wanting to hug her, but then he smelt bad and his exaggerated feelings felt hollow. When Dad was like that she didn't listen, and just wanted to get away from there since she guessed that the Friday evening that started so well would end in a row between her parents. Lisa then found it best to disappear into her room, not be seen, and play with her dolls.

The evening usually ended with her father leaving the house to the sound of her mother crying in despair, and Lisa taking care of her mother and comforting her. She comforted her all morning, all night, every day.

Back to the present: Most of the time, Lisa felt pretty; she felt that she looked quite good in spite of greying hair and some insidious pounds in strange places, in spite of the fact that her breasts had nourished three children. She felt quite all right that she was close to fifty.

But now her eyes were swollen and she felt like she would never be beautiful and happy again.

"I'm not going to take this," she whispered to her reflection. She had thought this many times, but now she felt the need to say it out loud. She cleared her throat and raised her voice a bit. "I deserve to have a husband who wants to be with me. Not someone who leaves as soon as the shoes don't fit."

There was a knock on the door and she started.

"Mum? Who are you talking to? How long are you going to stand in the shower, really?" It was John, his deep, nineteen-year-old voice still coming as a bit of a shock to her. It sounded so much like Michael's.

"I'll be right out, I just felt like a nice long shower. I'm almost ready!" She called out in a surprisingly steady and cheerful voice.

"Okay."

Shit, how am I going to hide this? Lisa wondered. She turned off the shower and turned on cold water from the tap, where she started to wash her face.

What she wanted to do most of all was to emerge from the bathroom and tell John and Anna what their father was really like. That he wasn't quite as wonderful as they thought. Explain that it was easy to seem like a good guy when you didn't have to run a household and nag everybody to get the simplest things done. It was easy to be nice and take the kids to amusement parks and then leave again as soon as the work week starts! And they didn't seem to notice how cold an insensitive he was towards her.

She wanted to tell them about all the times their father ignored her and how much that hurt. But she wouldn't do it. Not yet anyway. But if they got divorced, she would tell the children everything. Then she would tell them about all Michael's betrayals!

She swallowed her anger, washed her face, brought out the foundation cream and put on a new layer that covered the red marks on her face. Then, powder on. With the eyeliner, she drew skilled lines close to the lids. New mascara was brushed on and, finally, she rubbed out the sharp lines with eye shadow. She was so used to applying makeup that she could probably do it in her sleep. Last of all, she put in a discreet lipstick and rubbed the lips against each other. Then she tried with a smile in the mirror. It was a little better, but not much. The makeup did nothing to disguise her sad, swollen eyes.

Michael had been gone for almost two hours now. Was he… with someone else? The thought touched her brain, but she quickly warded it off. It was no use calling, either; he never answered when he left the house upset. Lisa sighed deeply, pulled herself together, opened the bathroom door and went down to John and Anna with a tense, stiff posture. The snack bowl was empty and the glasses were smudged with greasy fingerprints. Lisa fetched a new bottle of soda for the kids before she sat down on the couch. They were still watching "American Idol," and seemed not to even notice her.

"How are things going here, then?" she asked with strained light-heartedness.

"Everybody sucks but the dark girl," John said.

"Bullshit! I'm going to vote for Kevin! Can I use your iPhone?" Anna asked Lisa, her eyes shining.

"Okay," Lisa said, and just then she thought she heard a car in the driveway. She ran up the stairs to the kitchen and got there in time to see a car driving away. Who was it? Sometimes people used the spacious driveway for a turnabout. But when she went out to look, Michael's car was gone.

No Room for Little Lisa

Lisa woke up with a start and a thumping heart. From the clock radio by the bed, the digits 1:07 blinked red in the darkness. She must have slept a while, perhaps a half hour of forgetfulness. Then she remembered.

The other side of the bed was empty, cold and untouched. She closed her eyes again and moved her body closer to the middle of the bed, closer to him, overwhelmed by a painful longing for his warm body. Would he ever lie there next to her again? Her heart thumped. Had he left her for real this time? He had left in anger many times before, but had always returned after a couple of hours of walking. Was this the end? He had returned – *but left again in the car*! Could he have gone to another woman, one who was smiling, welcoming, warm, and sexy, who looked at him with gleaming eyes and had long hair that reached down to her pointed breasts, a beautiful woman who opened her arms to him and… NO!

The tears welled up again and she pushed her down into the pillow, which smelt of his shaving lotion and soap, and she whimpered softly into it so that the children wouldn't hear. Since it was Friday night, they might be still sitting and chatting or playing some mindless computer game. Earlier that evening, at about 11:30 p.m., Johnny had come home and asked, "Where is Dad?" Lisa answered vaguely, "at a conference." Strangely enough, none of the children asked any more, in spite of the fact that it would have been very strange for Dad to have gone to a conference a Friday evening after first having dinner at home. But maybe they were so used to him vanishing that it didn't feel strange anymore. Or maybe they heard the argument in spite of the TV and didn't want to interfere. Anyway, Lisa was glad she didn't have to explain.

Now she was as completely alone as she always had been, since she was born. Those first years with Michael, the good years of falling in love and believing in the future, had only been a break in the loneliness, and now the respite was over.

As a small girl, she'd felt that there was no room for her, with the quarrels storming between the parents, mum wallowing in self-pity and dad in alcohol-fuelled anger. Their strong emotions filled the house and made her shrink herself to a small ant who could barely be seen in her corner, an ant-girl who didn't take up any space or have any needs. When Dad finally got so mad that he left the house, Lisa had one more task: comforting her mother. She had to listen to her mother's self-pitying tirades about Lisa's horrible father, casting herself as an innocent victim of his drinking and infidelity.

"That's it now," her mother would sob. "We're getting a divorce!" This *divorce word*, Lisa realized was the worst thing that could happen to a woman. Divorce was a word filled with tragedy, degradation, and disaster.

Early on, she learnt more about the intimate life of adults than she wanted; things that made her feel stained and dirty. At the same time, she was very proud that her mother wanted her for a friend and confidant. And she fixed things for her mother! She made tea, made sandwiches, answered the phone – she was a clever girl! She did everything without nagging, because she was so *clever*. It was her responsibility to see to that mother didn't collapse and fall to pieces. And she succeeded!

"What would I do without you, Lisa?" mother used to say. "I would probably just lie down and die."

Pride swelled in little Lisa. Fear did, too.

But when Dad came back home again (usually in time for Saturday lunch), Lisa was instantly forgotten. All of her mother's attention turned to Dad, cooing and flattering. Either they made up with kisses and disappeared into the bedroom, or they behaved as though nothing had happened. Dad sat down at the table with a closed face, and everything was as usual again.

Faking It

When Lisa once again inhaled the smell from Michael's pillow, she lost it completely. The sobs pushed past her throat and the tears streamed. She loved him and missed him. She had been missing him for so long! She pushed her face into the pillow. She wanted to reduce herself to a piece of dust and disappear.

Finally, she must have fallen asleep.

Hours later, she faintly heard a monotonous beep. Lisa opened her eyes in the glom and realized that she was lying across the bed with the cover rolled up over her. Shivering, she looked at the clock radio--10.30 a.m. Oh my God, that late! The last time she looked it had been 5:30. It must be Jimmy's alarm beeping now. She faintly remembered that he had a soccer match today and would be going there with another boy on the team. She must go up to the kitchen and make brunch.

Michael still wasn't there.

To everyone else it was an ordinary Saturday, a cosy morning in bed with breakfast and the weekend sections of the paper. Saturday with the family and excursions or cinema, cleaning the house together, perhaps guests, or a movie. But not for little Lisa--the little Lisa she now felt herself to be. She had failed.

This was a family starting to disintegrate--something she must not let happen. She took a couple of deep breaths and tried to find her safe "inner room" as she'd learned at the meditation course, but it didn't work very well. At least she managed to ward off the tears for the moment and slowly crawl out of bed. She pulled her dressing gown tight and shuffled out to the kitchen on heavy legs. Must put coffee on, make scrambled eggs, heat up leftovers, make juice, empty the dishwasher… get every-thing back into order. Must think about something else. Michael will be back soon.

But if he was gone forever?

Divorce.

The word hung over her like a thundercloud. Of course she would get her share of the company, the house, the boat and everything else they owned… bought with money he'd made. She would get her share, but what then? She'd been such a fool! Now that she'd given him three children and done her service, he would trade her in for someone younger, and perhaps have some second-marriage kids! Or they would stay together and she would quietly wither away like so many women did, plagued by the infidelity of her husband but choosing silent mar-tyrdom in order to cling on to her little piece of the whole, of Michael. No, never! Quiet she would never be. She would fight hard to keep him!

She turned on the kettle and it quickly started to sing. The children expected a "super-brunch" on a day like this--all the regular breakfast stuff plus omelettes and leftovers from the past week. The boys usually ate colossal amounts before their sports activities.

Lisa cracked eight eggs and whisked them into a frying pan. She mechanically started to move between the refrigerator and the table and put butter, cheese, milk, marmalade and muesli on the table. The package of muesli was empty; someone had taken the last bit and hadn't bothered to put it on the shopping list.

A burst of anger grabbed hold of her. Michael could calmly lean back and enjoy the honour of being the *breadwinner*, and let the kids grow up in a nice house in a nice area close to the sea, let them buy all the right computer games and skateboards and go to all the right trips abroad. All of that was his doing – while her work was like writing in water! Who remembered the folded washing and the repaired jeans a couple of years later? Who took pictures of the cleaned kitchen, the home-cooked dinners? Who blogged about Mom's pancakes? A trap for women, that's what it was.

But…she had to admit it: she'd chosen it herself. She had *chosen* to stay at home with the children and then she had *chosen* to work part time as a nurse. She couldn't blame anyone. She had been a present mother, a *good* mother, and it had been worth it. She had loved the years at home when the children were small! Many times, she'd felt gratitude for Michael's income that made it possible for her to be a fulltime mother, and later to work half time. Maybe she hadn't shown her gratitude enough? Maybe she had been whining too much, making too many demands on closeness and social life?

Yes, of course she'd chosen her life as a homemaker and mother. But… the whole plan was built on the premise that she and Michael would continue to live together! That he would take care of her when they grew old. It would be worth the fact that her pension was lousy, since it didn't matter, his would suffice. And they would be a couple forever. Was that just a lifelong lie?

Lisa's anger changed into a deep sorrow when the memories pressed on, images of Michael's naked, sweating, muscular back on their first hike, his strong brown hand in hers when they took the evening walk with their first dog. There was also the clear memory of how, during their first night together, Michael was in such a hurry to get out of his underwear that he jumped around on one leg, fell and sprained his finger while she lay laughing in the bed. Then he whined: "Aoaoao, it hurts! But it's worth it." That had become a loving figurative speech between them.

There was the memory of Michael's green eyes, shining with tears of joy when he looked at her, just before he put the ring on her finger in church. That image she had saved inside as the most beautiful, the one that would always be there. His warm eyes when he loved her. All of these images were pressed together into a ball of pain in her stomach, a physical cramp that made her bend over double by the counter.

Anna came into the kitchen.

"Mum, do you have a stomach pain?"

"Just a little…pinch," Lisa replied. She rose with effort and managed a small smile.

"Shall I give you a massage? Or a hug?" her daughter asked, and put her warm arms around Lisa.

Nononono, no more crying now.

"Thank you darling, but I just think that I need to go to the bathroom," Lisa said in a small voice and ran to the bathroom. There, she put her forehead towards the mirror and took deep breaths until the glass fogged completely.

When she returned to the kitchen a while later, Jimmy was at the table too, fully dressed and with his dark hair waxed in spikes. His soccer trunk was already packed and stood in the hallway. Jimmy was always quick and dynamic whatever he did – as long as it wasn't a question of cleaning or doing some other housework. This was probably also Lisa fault. She had been a typical over-ambitious mother.

"Better now, Mum?" Anna asked and poked her lovingly in the stomach.

"Yes, it's fine. Good morning Jimmy," she greeted her son, who replied with an "mmm" but didn't look at her because he was busy filling his face with omelette with his right hand while texting with his left. His thumb moved like a sewing machine over the phone. She felt slow and stupid whenever she tried to text; it took forever and usually turned out wrong. The other day the phone chose "beer" when she tried to write "bye" – and then sent it to a parent of one of Anna's school friends. That was so embarrassing! Lisa put three spoonful's of instant coffee in the cup; she needed to wake up.

"Is Dad still asleep?" Anna asked with surprise.

"He's at a conference," Lisa stated as she opened the massive weekend paper.

"Oh, yeah. But… wasn't that last weekend?"

"Mmm," said Lisa and pretended to focus on something in the paper.

Coming Alive Again

Michael's fingers moved more slowly than usually over the keyboard. The beginning of a headache sat like a tight band around his forehead. The clothes he'd worn to work on Friday morning had hung on him for more than twenty-four hours. They smelled of sweat, and the shirt was wrinkled and stuck to his back. He turned queasily and looked at the screen. Numbers soothed him because he didn't have to think or feel. The overview looked good, and he started to go through the quotations of this month.

His architecture business had done well. He often felt a deep satisfaction when he thought about all the alarmists who had told him that it wouldn't work, that you can't start a business of your own in this field, or that he should at least start it with someone else. But he wanted to be his own boss, make his own decisions, and take responsibility himself. So, in spite of the risks, he bought his colleagues' shares in the business, using some of his father-in-law's savings as collateral. He hired two of his former colleagues and he also found three young (and therefore still inexpensive) architects. And they went full speed ahead.

Now, sixteen years later, he had employed fourteen people. They were a strong team, and together they created something new. New ideas and, eventually, ecologically-sustainable design had become the speciality and trademark of his business. In this tough profession, his company was one of the most renowned in the country. He had every reason to be pleased.

He also knew that none of it would have worked without Lisa. His wife had taken care of everything at home; he himself had only taken some time off with the kids in the summer. In the early days he often sat alone in the office, for hours, weekdays and weekends, drawing suggestions and solid ideas, and if he said so himself, he inspired in his customers some new ways of looking at things– but it took a lot of Zantac.

His stomach still gnawed. His thoughts, as they did so often, fled to Cecilia with the blond curly hair, Cecilia, whom he kissed under the trees by the lake at the conference hotel, and to whom he made love for two long, wonderful nights. She had seen him! Someone finally saw who he was deep down, and with her he felt wonderful and attractive and alive. Yes exactly so! She made him feel alive again.

Cecilia worked at a company in another city. After the conference, they had an intensive contact by e-mail and text-messages for a couple of months. He had almost been consumed with guilt towards Lisa, but the feeling of a passionate life had been stronger than the guilt, and he had been hopelessly lost. Cecilia was his chance for life and love.

If it had been up to him, he would have filed for a divorce already in July, never mind the consequences! But Cecilia was also married with two small kids, and couldn't or didn't want to make this decision. Then, in September, she broke off all contact--on account of both their families, she said. But since then Michael felt even more cut off from the living, and he worked even more than before, if possible.

For how many years had he had felt dead inside? For a long time, he'd managed to feel alive through his work. Then the golf, and the jogging, where his efforts increased constantly and he could get an endorphin rush. It had become almost like a drug. But after a couple of years it wasn't enough, and so he tried mountain climbing. The adrenaline and dopamine rush had been really something when he hung over the cliffs! But in later years, not even that danger made him feel alive. Everything was... dead.

Until he kissed Cecilia, there under the trees.

For a short while, he felt a lust for life and a hope that he would once again be the person he was meant to be. And then he lost everything. His life, and Lisa's, kept moving in parallel tracks.

But during the fall he had slowly realized that it couldn't continue like this. He had to be true to the feelings that Cecilia had awakened in him. Even though she wouldn't leave her husband, he had to free himself. It was more honest to Lisa, to himself, to everyone.

The wintry dawn light fell in through the louvers and created melancholy stripes of shadows over the empty desks in the office. He ought to eat breakfast. But not yet. His fingers kept running over the computer keyboard and his eyes swept over the screen as he continued to go through the bookkeeping of last month. Sure, he had people who took care of that, but it was never wrong to check to make sure it looked good yourself. With your own company, you could never quite relax. There was always something in the distance, a worry that the market would go down or that some employee or other would mess things up.

Michael wasn't really a computer person and wasn't quite comfortable with the new technology. He loved the drawing board and the pens, the handicraft, the feeling of paper against the hand. Entering figures and results into the computer he liked. Numbers, structures and order made him feel safe. The piles was like a beautiful building, like pillars in his own temple, and he could see clearly how things where connected. The world was understandable. It soothed his stomach, just like playing with Legos and drawing in his room had calmed him when he was a boy.

A few years ago, during one of their rows, Lisa had yelled at him: "Damn it, you're just like your father!"

Maybe there was something to that; maybe he was turning into his father. But he wouldn't admit that to her, it was too painful. Not that his father had been that bad… it was just that he wasn't *there*. Actually, his father had been a complete stranger. He worked, worked, and worked. When he was home, he isolated himself in an unreachable bubble, reading the paper, sorting through the mail. Or he'd be sitting in his armchair in the living room and listening to reports from the stock exchange, leafing through the business papers or (most important of all) looking at the news. During this half hour he wanted complete silence in the house and mother would hush the children. Once, he'd even hit his fist on the table and yelled, "*No, enough of this!*" and the kids had scuttled into their rooms like frightened mice. Since Dad seldom showed any feelings, this event was etched with fear in Michael's mind. Afterwards, he felt a twinge of anxiety each time he heard the signature tune of the news.

When Michael was eight, a disaster occurred that devastated his family. His younger sister, Carina, died. She was five and run over by a drunk driver. She died a couple of hours later in hospital, and his mother sunk into a grief so deep that she was catatonic for a period of time. And his father became even more remote. What he remembered from that time was his father's rejecting back and his mother's tears.

He quickly became mother's little boy, now that he was the youngest. It would be an understatement to say that he was over-protected. After the accident, his mother was always worried and almost never happy. But she didn't complain openly--you didn't do that in Michael's family. You didn't complain when you were so well off. But many, many times he found her sitting by the kitchen window, staring at something that no one else could see, lost in a silent, joyless world where he couldn't reach her. It wasn't until he tugged at her arm that she came to and, at best, put up a weak smile. Sometimes when he came from school he could hear her crying behind the bedroom door.

Afterwards, Michael realized that his mother was deeply depressed and probably took pills of various kinds. But they never talked about what happened in the family. They never cried together. His mother who used to be so full of love was sad all the time, and nothing he did helped. Dad was busy and seemed vaguely disappointed all the time.

So Michael stayed at home as little as possible. He spent a lot of time at school, where he felt more secure. He studied and got good grades. When he was at home, he tried to be as good a son as he could so as to avoid complaints. He played soccer, handball and table tennis and was good at all of them. But no one came to watch. But he felt that this hadn't hurt him very much; in fact, it had strengthened him. He became independent. He became capable, strong, and needed little.

And now, he was good at providing for his family. Because of his income, they lived in a beautiful house in a nice area, the kids got just about everything that they pointed at, and he neither drank nor beat his wife and kids. He was everything that he'd learnt that a real man should be. But no matter what he did, it wasn't enough. Both Lisa and the kids sometimes said:

"You're only interested in your work!"

"Well, well," he used to defend himself jokingly, "if it weren't for my work, we wouldn't be able to send you on that skiing trip. So try to be a bit grateful that I work hard and earn this money!"

But inside, it hurt more than he wanted to admit. Especially when his own enthusiasm for the work had cooled off a bit. Interestingly, he seemed to have lost the spark when the company started to go very well. It was as though the fight to get to the top was what spurred him to struggle against the wind, to succeed! Like when he climbed mountains. To fight upwards and stand alone on the top in the cold wind with the world at your feet – that was wonderful. It cleared his head of a lot of shit.

But it didn't clear his head of Cecilia. He had a terribly bad conscience. Once, he had felt like that for Lisa. The betrayal consumed him from inside and poisoned everything.

Something must be done.

Michael was so consumed by his thoughts that he managed to forget both the bookkeeping and his rumbling stomach. But now it sounded like a cat in the silence of the empty office. In spite of the fact that he didn't feel like any food, he knew his body needed nourishment, He put on his coat and went to the hamburger bar close by and ordered an egg burger, coffee and a donut. With the depressing breakfast in a bag, he went back to the office.

All These Damn Emotions

"Thanks, Mum, that was really good!"

Jimmy, who was on his way to a match, had thrown down the brunch with gusto. Without being asked, he'd said thanks, rose and cleared away his plate. If Lisa had not been so depressed, she would have been overjoyed by this small gesture. Jimmy had become more mature during the summer.

Lisa was grateful for that, but she was still worried about John. Her oldest son had become stuck in a sulky silence where he was completely unreachable. Sure, she could get mad at Michael being inaccessible, but their son was actually worse.

Lisa couldn't understand the thing with silence. She herself was always close to all kinds of emotions, and verbal she had always been. Even as a child, she'd felt at home with anger, tears and laughter. The emotions had welled tempestuously between her mother and father as they waged a struggle that no one could win. Yet the quarrels, in some strange way, felt safer than this damn silence that she couldn't understand.

Anna rose and left the table after picking at the food. She wasn't on a diet, was she? If Anna got an eating disorder that would probably be Lisa's fault, too. She should have been able to give her daughter more confidence and self-esteem.

Lisa sighed and looked at John, who in his slow tempo still sat eating leftovers. "Do you want some coffee, John?" she asked as she rose to pour some for herself.

"No thanks," he replied shortly. Small talk wasn't at home in John's mouth.

"Okay. Are you going out later?"

"Mmm, to Otto's to check out the new version of Butterfield he bought."

"Is that a computer game?"

"Mmm."

"Okay. But please just walk the dog first."

"Sure."

The old golden retriever rose from her place in the basket by the fridge and expectantly followed John out into the hallway. She seemed to understand what they'd been talking about.

Lisa took her coffee and went into the living room where she sank down into the white leather couch. John was so closed that it worried her. She'd mentioned it to Michael once.

"Bah," he'd said. "John is the model of a man."

"A man in the Fifties, yes! Silent, closed, keeps on working, never talks about feelings..."

"Men don't want to talk about feelings, Lisa."

"No, but... look at Jimmy, for instance. He talks about everything!"

"Relax. Give John some time; there is nothing strange about the kid."

No, perhaps there wasn't anything strange at all with John. But in Lisa's world, silence meant that something was very wrong; it was the calm before the storm. Lisa herself realized that her anxiety was exaggerated, so she usually tried to keep it to herself. Michael dismissed her fears as ridiculous.

"It's nothing to worry about, Lisa, it's his personality. He is like that! I was also quiet and reserved as a kid," Michael said, zapping between the TV channels.

Was? Lisa thought sarcastically. And at the same time: How wonderful it would be to be like Michael and not worry all the time.

Running feet rambled down the stairs. "Bye," Jimmy's voice called from the hallway.

"Good luck!!" Lisa shouted as the front door shut close.

One gone.

Lisa's coffee was cold. She went out into the kitchen, put it in the microwave and watched as the cup rotated in the light within.

The dog came pattering in.

"She pooed once," John reported. "I'll go now, be back for dinner, okay?" He stood in front of her with his black cap pulled down his forehead.

"Okay."

The front door closed again.

Two gone.

She was incredibly tired. Last night, she'd managed to sleep three, four hours at the most, and now it felt like the entire world was rocking.

The microwave beeped and she took the warm cup out and carried it into the couch by the open fire. Tomorrow was Advent Sunday and she really ought to get started with the Christmas decorations. At least for the kids, she ought to pretend that everything was as usual, that she didn't sit in the shambles of a wrecked home, a wrecked marriage, a wrecked life. *A life where she wasn't loved.*

When the kids were small, they always decorated together. The heart-warming little results of their pottering at day-care covered all the windowsills in the house--Santas, angels and snowmen. But now the kids seemed offended if she brought out the things that they once were so proud of.

Christmas decorations. Maybe she should make another attempt with Anna? Anna always used to want some "cosy-time with mom." Maybe they could do some Christmas decorations together.

Lisa rose from the couch and was on her way up the stairs when Anna emerged from her room in a very short skirt, neon-pink stockings and a small sleeveless top.

"But… where are you going? Is there some… party going on, or?"

Her daughter sniffed at her. "Huh! Today? *Mom!* I'm going to meet my friends and we're going shopping for clothes for the Christmas party."

"You are? You haven't said anything about that!"

"No, we just decided. Is that a problem?" Anna gave her mother an innocent look, eyes framed by thick black lines.

"No… but… what… why… " Lisa hesitated. Whatever she said it would be wrong and probably cause a fit of anger. She braced herself. "Shouldn't you have something a little warmer on if you are going shopping? You could get a urinary infection!"

"Oh please, Mom." Once again, her daughter used that patronizing tone as if Lisa was an idiot, a dinosaur, that didn't understand anything. "We'll be indoors at the mall, mostly. No problem, promise!" She leaned forward to give her mom a kiss, but a combination of anger and feeling abandoned welled up in Lisa and before she could stop herself she said:

"But you look like some kind of *hooker*! What kind of signals do you think you give people around you dressed like that? And I don't understand why you have to put on so much makeup to go shopping! It doesn't look very pretty, especially not in daylight…"

"Oh, you're such a nuisance! No other mom interferes as much as you do! Everyone else can wear any skirt they want and put on makeup however they want to! I'm fifteen, not twelve!" Her daughter hissed before she pushed her way past Lisa on the stairs and marched out into the hallway.

What alternative did Lisa have? Say, okay, it's your problem if you get cold? Threaten her with suspended allowance? Just let it pass?

The tears seeped up in the corners of her eyes and once again she felt the deadly tiredness overwhelm her. She couldn't say anything today. Simply didn't have the energy.

"I may go home with a friend if that's okay," Anna said from the hallway. "Mom? Bye? Is that okay?" testing in a tone of reconciliation.

"Oh yes, darling," said Lisa. "That's okay, I guess. Just give me a call. You've got your cell phone with you, don't you?"

"Of course, kiss!" The door closed behind Anna.

Three gone.

Four, if you count Michael. Yes, four.

Claws clicked against quietly the floor as the dog came in and lay by Lisa's feet with a satisfied sigh. The dog seemed to be the only one who cared about her. It started to seem like *ten little Indians*. One by one, they disappeared. Once she felt so incredibly rich, with her family around her. Now her worst nightmare seemed to be becoming true. To be completely alone, abandoned, unnecessary and unloved by everyone but an old dog. The children were moving away from her and now it seemed like she would be without a husband, too. A deep pain cut through her chest and made it difficult to breathe. If you invested everything in the family and had your work only as a pastime, then it might go like this, she thought. Then you become a pathetic, aging woman who desperately clings to her children. Shit, shit, shit, I must pull myself together! I do have a job and friends and especially I have Petra. She decided to call her friend later.

Lisa took her cup out to the kitchen, cleared away the brunch dishes and filled the dishwasher. Then she went with heavy steps to collect the box labelled "Christmas Decorations." It would soon be Christmas, whether she like it or not. And she was obliged to do her best with this gloomy reality. She had always decorated the house for Christmas and she would do it now.

Home Alone

Michael drove the car south with the sun in his eyes. The traffic was not too dense. He brought out his sunglasses and put them on, thumping the steering wheel to the happy music on the car radio. For a moment, he forgot the uneasy feeling in his stomach.

At a pedestrian crossing, he saw a dark-haired woman with a pram waiting for a green light. He felt a stab in the gut. She could have been a younger Lisa.

He had a bad taste in the mouth because he hadn't brushed his teeth, and after a night in the couch in the office, his clothes had a musty smell. Michael had always been careful with his hygiene, took showers every day and used deodorant, and the smell from his armpits made him feel somehow depraved, like an old drunk. It smelled worse than usual today, and he thought that it was sweat of anguish, simply.

There were no simple choices for him now. He must take the bull by the horns. He must be honest with Lisa. Honest with himself. Honest! It was his father's voice echoing from his childhood. He'd had a good upbringing and learnt what is right is right and what is wrong is wrong. He'd learnt to take care of himself. After the disaster, when the silence fell over them like a wet blanket, his parents seemed to stiffen in themselves.

Still, he thought his parents had done a good job. All these damn emotions were overrated. How much fun could it be to grow up like Lisa, in a family with constant yelling and shouting? You could just look at what became of Lisa, dependent and over-sensitive, constantly interpreting every gesture and facial expression, clinging, terrified of being abandoned. By contrast, he had become strong. Independent. He had learnt to work hard and achieve, doing sports, selling papers, distributing ads, making his own money, saving. Yes, his parents had done a good job! A good, honest job.

Honesty. What was that, really? Was it honest to say things that could make your wife lose the will to live? Or was that just cruel?

It didn't matter any longer; he had to put the cards on the table. If Cecilia did change her mind and wanted him, he had to be free. And even if she didn't, he couldn't continue as a member of the living dead. He must *live* – with Cecilia, alone or together with someone else.

Michael pulled the car up alongside his house and approached his front door. But when he pressed down the door handle, to his surprise it was locked. It was very rare that no one was home when he came. He couldn't remember the last time he came home to an empty house! Often the kids had a crowd of friends there. And Lisa was usually home.

He unlocked the door and stepped into complete silence. His surprise was mixed with relief. If nobody was home, the execution could be postponed, at least for a while. He took off his shoes and stood in the hall with them in his hand, listening. It was an eerie silence; he could hear the clock ticking in the kitchen. This house that always used to be filled with life--music from the kids' rooms, laughing from the TV, loud voices, welcoming barks, banging pots and sizzling pans in the kitchen.

Now, there was a difference in the atmosphere. It was almost a bit scary. The home felt like an exhibition and he couldn't quite say why. The house shouldn't be empty! He was proud that so many other kids chose their house for a meeting point. He guessed that many teenagers were hanging around in the city, making their parents worried. But their kids were safe.

Of course, it was a bit too lively sometimes – and astronomical amounts of bread, cheese, milk and other drinks disappeared in a no time. But of course it wasn't he who brought the food home. It was Lisa who created this generous home, and he admired her for it. In spite of the fact that she was often under stress, she always welcomed the kids' friends and tirelessly filled up the fridge with constant trips to the food store. What a difference from his childhood home, with its niggardly, silent atmosphere where nothing was allowed to disturb the peace! He was proud that they had created such an open and generous home for their children.

But sometimes, he felt that everything in their life was about the children and their needs. Work, food, driving. Michael and Lisa never spent intimate time together, except for the occasional afternoons when Lisa had had a hard time at the hospital; maybe someone had died in the ward as she sat at their bedside. At such times, she came home crying desperately that so many old people had to die alone and forgotten, without a single relative to hold their hand.

Then, Michael would cuddle her up in his arms and caress her hair. Since he wasn't the reason for her tears, he didn't feel threatened by them – and then he could step into the role as strong, calm and protecting husband. Then he could comfort her and dare to feel closeness for a while… like before.

But except for these moments, their entire life was one great treadmill that went around, and around without ever stopping. Where did they as a couple fit into all of this? When would they satisfy their needs for relaxation, play, and sex? How could things become so dead between them that he felt like a zombie and she felt like a complete stranger – no, like an enemy.

He brought everything to the family, but no one seemed to appreciate what he did. It wasn't so strange that he fell for another woman who could praise, appreciate and see him for what he was. See, see, and see that he *existed!* His wife of twenty-one years did not see him anymore.

A feeling of guilt twisted his stomach--guilt for his own self-centeredness. After all, Lisa had been there, faithfully by his side all these years. The nausea increased when he went up the small staircase to the living room and looked at the bedroom door that was strangely closed.

He called the dog in that special tone of voice he reserved for her. Could it be that Lisa and the dog were resting in the bedroom? He went up the stairs and opened the door. Empty. Bed made, furniture dusted, sterile clean. Suddenly he saw that a star hung in the window, filling the space with warm light. Lisa had put up the Christmas decorations! That's why it was different. He went downstairs again and saw that she had decorated every room. The Christmas curtains were up in the kitchen. Why didn't he see that at once! He must be blind, damn it. How often did he miss what she did?

Just then, he thought of looking for Lisa's car in the garage. Her yellow Toyota was gone.

He felt a stab of fear. She hadn't done something stupid because he hadn't come home last night? No... then she wouldn't have put up the Christmas decorations? Or was that exactly what she would do? Go in style: first put up the Christmas decorations and then jump off a bridge. That would be typical of Lisa--the perfect housewife until the bitter end. But no, she wouldn't do that to the kids. He was sure of that. Or? She had been unusually under the water lately, much quieter than usual. At one point, she'd actually said that she had lost the will to live. Oh my God, what the hell would he say to the kids in that case?

A terror-image pushed for attention and Michael's whole body went cold. He saw his wife at the bottom of the sea, her hair swaying like seaweed. Then he saw her lying helpless in the woods with a broken leg and the dog nervously yelping beside her, without being able to call for help. Then he saw her with her head smashed on a cliff by the sea. Whatever had happened, it would be his fault. He pulled his cell phone from his pocket and dialed her number. Only her answering service. He left no message.

Restless and brooding, he paced the house. He had been preparing himself all day for his confession. What would he do now? He ought to take a shower and change clothes, but... he called again and heard Lisa happy voice: "Hi this is automatic Lisa, I can't take your call right now, but leave a message and I'll get back to you!" Michael cleared his voice.

"Hi it's me," he said in a rough voice and realized that he had not spoken to a single person since he'd left the kitchen table last night. That was fourteen hours ago and his vocal cords seemed to have rusted. He cleared his throat.

"Where are you? Please call me, I'm at home."

He hesitated for a moment. Should he finish with "kiss," as usual? It felt unreasonable. At the same time, he knew that this was what Lisa wanted to hear. If he didn't say it, she would be even more upset. A left-out "kiss" would be a declaration of war.

"Kiss," he said in a dull voice.

Now he was even more confused. Lisa *always* answered the telephone. She had an almost manic need to be in touch, always wanted to be reachable if something happened. He called Anna.

"Hi, darling. Ahh... do you know where Mom is?"

Anna seemed to be in a noisy place, maybe a coffee shop; he could hear Christmas songs and rattling in the background.

"Isn't she at home?"

"No." He tried to keep his voice calm.

"Well, I don't know. She was at home when I left. Maybe she's out with the dog? Call her! Or try Petra."

He called Petra and John's home number, but no one picked up the phone. He didn't have the number for Petra's mobile. What to do now?

A vague thought started to form: if he could have his "honest talk" with Lisa someplace in the city, there would be less risk that she would make a scene, and none of the kids would hear it. But where could she be? He knew his wife well and knew that she would be relaxed by noise, hubbub, people, and crowded places, talk and laughter. In spite of the fact that they lived just by the sea, she usually went into the city to become calm. She preferred to have Petra or someone else with her so that she could talk, talk, talk. If there wasn't anyone to talk to, at least she wanted to be in a lively place.

Michael himself loved the ocean--the silence, solitude, and force of nature. His entire system wound down when he went running in the woods or near water, and of course that was an important reason why they lived by the sea. Lisa wanted to live in the city, but Michael argued that it was much better for the kids to grow up outside the city. He was a bit ashamed of his sly egotism, but he comforted himself with the fact that it was better for the kids to grow up outside the city, with all its traffic, pollution, and other hazards.

In the beginning, he was attracted by Lisa because she was so different from him--so lively, sociable, energetic and emotional. When he was in love, he had actually felt reborn. It was as though Lisa lifted him out of his solitude and made him feel a part in life! Now the differences were mainly a source of irritation and arguments.

He walked around in the house and scratched his neck, unable to calm down. Lisa was probably walking the dog in the park or the botanical garden. They both loved dogs and it felt natural to them both to have a dog. But walking the dog was another one of those things that they'd stopped doing together.

Michael glanced at his watch. It would start to get dark in a couple of hours. He put on his coat, hat and boots, went to the car and drove into the city again.

He wasn't quite sure if he wanted to find her.

In the Botanical Garden

Lisa had been walking so fast that she was sweating in her down jacket and her hair was sticky under her cap. She'd kept a lively pace uphill; now that she was going down, she began to walk more slowly.

Back when she and Michael were in love, they often walked here. Lisa recalled one early summer day when they had made love under the spreading trees. They had been so happy, it was *the two of them against the world*, and they believed they would never, ever lose interest in having sex with each other.

That time felt so distant, now! It was as if she couldn't remember it with her brain – but she could with her body. Unexpectedly, she felt a rush of lust in her genitals when thought about how Michael had torn his clothes off that time and had thrown himself on the ground behind some bushes and beckoned her. He had lain there naked while the sun shone down through the leaves and danced on his beautiful muscular body.

Then she rode him, forgetting where she was, carefree, horny like a siren in the woods, happy, strong and young, and it was wonderful! They had giggled at the possibility of being caught red-handed by some near-sighted botanist. Michael had gotten lots of splinters in his buttocks that she had to pull out, and it made them giggle even more. And when she lay on his arm afterwards, he looked at her with the tenderest eyes in the world and said that he would always love her. Always, always.

The wind was cold on this side of the hill, and she pulled the scarf tighter. The dog moved along with jerky steps and Lisa took off the leash; it wasn't necessary when there were no people around. She picked up the mobile from her pocket and pushed the short-code to Petra, who was number five – just after Michael and the kids. This reflected Petra's significance in Lisa's life. They had found each other as soccer moms with sons the same age. After a short while they started to meet outside of soccer practice, and later their husbands found each other and became friends.

Petra and John were harmonious, calm, and collected. Some would say boring. Sometimes Lisa actually thought that, and when she did she felt a bit ashamed. They were wonderful people and fantastic friends, but they were a bit like two turtles moving around in a terrarium without raising much sand. They were safe, slow and unglamorous, in a marriage that was everything but passionate. But Petra explained that she was "so happy" with her old man and declared that she had finished messy relationships for good. She said she would *never* go "out on the market" again. She had found her way home.

So, Lisa thought, what's wrong with me?

The phone rang three times before Petra answered. "Hi dear! Where are you?"

"In the botanical garden with the dog."

"In this weather?" No!

"Yes... I... I think that Michael left me."

"Oh, not again?"

If anyone else had said that Lisa would have been furious and even offended. She knew her friend's dry sense of humour and it *wasn't* the first time she called with this news. She also knew that Petra was loyal and that she could trust her.

"Yes, you can joke... but this time I think he left for real."

"*What*? Are you serious? Why, what happened?"

"We argued and he left and he didn't come back tonight."

"But, he must have slept in the office? Did you call him there?"

"No, he never answers when he's gone. And why should I call him? He behaved like shit, insensitive and cold and detached as usual and... well, he has a tendency to rush away like that, so I thought that he would come back in a few hours. But he didn't, and this has never happened before... that he has been gone overnight."

Lisa was puffing from the exertion of walking and talking at the same time, and she stopped to breathe. The wind was blowing cold in the trees. The dog sat down beside her and looked patiently at her, waiting for a treat, game, or an order.

"But, do you think he's unfaithful?" Petra asked.

"Yes, I'm actually starting to believe that. I have never done that before, but now I really wonder."

"Has he been behaving differently? Smelling differently, got strange calls, fussed with his looks, bought new clothes, going on a diet, working late...?" Petra bombarded Lisa with the classic questions that you could find in a ladies magazine.

"Wait, calm down, let me think," said Lisa. "Yes, he has been unusually quiet all autumn; he *has been* working more than usual – if that is possible – and a couple of times he has been sitting in front of the computer at home and he closed it when I entered the room, as if he was doing something forbidden."

"Okay. And smells?"

"I haven't smelt anything in particular. I haven't found any lipstick marks either, but that must be a cliché. Nobody can be that stupid."

"Have you asked him?"

"Yes I did that last night, and then he got so mad he left. Besides he wouldn't admit that... or... I have felt insecure some time before. But this is different, I can feel that."

"Do you have sex?"

"It has been a while. I'm not so keen anymore and now he hasn't been either, and then nothing happens, sort of... I mean we hardly have any contact! He comes home from work is tired, takes a shower, and goes zapping on the TV, I cook... or he goes jogging first and..."

"What, he takes a *shower* when he comes home? How long has he been doing that?"

"I think he always has... sometimes at least. Why?"

"Well, that *could* be a sign that he wants to wash away some smell, perfume perhaps. Like George, you know, that's how I found out."

"Don't say that."

"Put him up against the wall!"

"But what if he admits? Then it's over. I don't know if I could cope with that."

"You *can* cope with that. Look at me, I managed, and I got something much better. John is the best man possible, not because he's Mr. Gorgeous, but you know where you are with him and he's *kind*, Lisa, that's the most important thing. He wants what's best for me. He's my best friend."

"Well, but I'm not like you, Petra... I want some passion, some excitement, a little extra... I want to feel that I mean something, that he wants me, that he loves me..."

"Love can be many different things, I always say. It's also love to look at John's big belly on the couch and know that it's my old man, only for me."

"If that's the case, yeah," Lisa puffed. "You're sure about John, but Michael..."

"Try a seductive dinner then some champagne, candles, sexy underwear..."

"Ah, that just about what I did yesterday. He looks right through me and I feel like the most insignificant creature on earth. Even the dog is sexier!"

"Maybe you're asking for too..."

"Maybe you're asking for too much, blah blah blah," Lisa mimicked. "Yeah yeah, I've heard that before. But I won't accept that we have to live like two... two...", she was looking for the right word, "damn *zombies* who've lost contact!" Her voice had turned despairing.

"I get it, Lisa," Petra said soothingly. "If he really is so cold and distant as you say, then something may have happened. And then you must leave him. Infidelity – no way! Put him up against the wall and get the truth out of him! You will not take this kind of shit, Lisa."

"Yes, yes I will. Tonight. If he doesn't come home tonight, I'll hang myself."

"He will come, Lisa. He will come."

"I'll call you and cry otherwise. Can I do that?"

"Of course, and come by my house before you hang yourself, darling. Promise me that." Lisa nodded numbly. "Okay, I promise."

She sighed and put her cell phone back in her pocket.

The Confrontation

A quarter hour later, Lisa put the leash on the dog and walked through the entrance to the botanical garden. The sun was setting. On the path a bit further on, she saw a man with his back to her. He looked as though he were searching for something. She hadn't met anyone for an hour and no one else was in sight. The dog got tense and growled. Suddenly, Lisa recognised his body language.

It was Michael.

The dog must have seen him too, because she started to whine and wag her tail. Michael heard it and turned around just as Lisa sidestepped in panic and pulled the dog with her into some evergreen bushes. The dog tugged at the leash and whined and Lisa's heart beat furiously. She felt like a fool hiding in the bushes from her husband. But what if he was there with another woman? In the botanical garden, their special place? She must calm down, think.

"Lisa?" came Michael's voice. The dog started to bark.

Lisa had no choice but to step out and let go of the dog, which ran to her master like a hairy, galloping yellow streak.

To see Michael's familiar face was a punch in the stomach, a punch of equal parts joy and panic.

He had seen her car in the parking lot outside the botanical garden. He parked next to it so that Lisa couldn't miss it if she was leaving. Quite naturally, there were only two other cars there. Who really wanted to walk around in a botanical garden on a leaden, windy day in December when there was nothing to see? Well, of course, Lisa, his garden-loving wife who loved this botanical garden in every season.

During their first summer together, he and Lisa actually had sex in the bushes, not far from the path. So long ago that it was like thinking about two strangers. He tried to imagine them doing something like that again. The icy wind made the fantasy even more absurd. That Lisa actually was the same person as the warm, beautiful and willing girl he embraced on the lawn that day was just about unthinkable.

But how different was he, really? Was he an old boring man? Not really; in his mind, he was still fit, active, healthy, and potent. The same Mike as always. He was definitely not the cold fish that Lisa said he was. If nothing else, his adventure with Cecilia had proven that. His passion was still there.

He had been walking around at random but finally decided to find shelter by the greenhouses. Sooner or later, she must come to the exit. If she didn't arrive soon, he would go sit in the car and wait.

While he stood there, stamping his feet to keep them warm, his thoughts wandered further.

Lisa. He simply wasn't in love with her anymore. Love had sort of... passed. Been worn down, withered, and died from lack of nourishment while they'd been busy running on the treadmill. The same thing had happened to many of his friends. Love died. These things happened.

Still, it didn't give a person the right to be unfaithful! You have an obligation to fight and try, and if it absolutely didn't work you should get a divorce. Not do like a few of his male colleagues, who went around flirting with every woman that came to the office. They made fools of themselves. Others went further, and had affairs.

Roger, who had been in the company from the start, had gone behind his wife's back and had affairs with numerous women over the last ten years. Roger was on his third marriage, now with a woman who was 23 years younger – same age as his daughter! Michael despised Roger's behaviour. Michael looked pretty good himself and several female colleagues had made passes – but he'd never liked one-night stands. Although his sexual experience wasn't enormous when he met Lisa, he had been with other women before then. But he wasn't even very curious. Sometimes he'd wondered if he wasn't normal, wanting no one but Lisa, and believing that no affair was worth the effort, risks, possible breakup and pain. He would never have an affair, he thought – until he fell into the trap himself!

The difference was that he had only one affair and suffered such a bad conscience that he couldn't take it anymore. He would confess to Lisa. But how would he manage that? This self-pity immediately gave way to self-reproach: How could he be such an egotist? How would *she* manage it, he ought to ask himself. She would be broken.

"Shitshitshit," he mumbled with frozen lips and wished that the icy wind would blow all the painful thoughts out of his head. It was too cold, time to go to the car and sit there and wait before he got stiff as a corpse. But what if she didn't come? What if she was there with another… man? And were having sex in the bushes? They must be Eskimos, in that case. He managed a brief laugh and shook his head. In a way, it was a pity that she wasn't having an affair. Maybe that would have been the solution; then they could have shared the guilt.

Just then, he thought that he heard a dog yelping somewhere close by. He turned around in time to see a red down jacket and something yellow vanish behind a shrub.

"Lisa?" he called out.

No reply, but the dog continued to whine and bark behind the shrub. He was not sure if it was their dog. Half a minute passed and then Lisa stepped out from behind the shrub with a stiff, inscrutable expression.

"Hi," he said while he patted the dog, who was delighted to see her master. "What… are you doing behind the shrub?"

"Hi," she said, expressionless.

"So this is where you've been."

"Yes. And where were *you* and what have *you* been doing?" she said almost without moving her lips.

"I was at home."

"I don't mean now!" she snapped. "I mean last night!"

"I slept at the office. Or I didn't sleep really, I sat…"

"And you want me to believe that? That you were at the office?"

"I was there. You could have called me to find out."

"So you run away and then I'm supposed to call and humiliate myself? You never answer anyway. You could have called me!"

She was starting to build up a fury. And he understood, in a way. It wasn't fair of him to disappear when he knew how hard it was on her. She must have had one hell of a night.

"Lisa… I really needed to think. On my own."

"Yes, I know that you want to be on your own. Rather than to be with me."

"But you were so damn aggressive last night, just a lot of accusations, one after the other, finally I couldn't take it, I just…"

"You, you everything is about you! *I* have to take it! I haven't slept all night!"

"Lisa, I didn't have any choice."

"You always have a choice, Michael!"

He looked down at his shoes. "No, I didn't."

She looked at him searchingly, her brown eyes narrowed, as if she was testing his truthfulness.

"I mean it," he said. "It can't continue like this, Lisa. We must talk."

"Oh, so now you need to talk? After all these years of me trying to get you to talk? It must be very serious, Michael."

"Do you have to be so aggressive?"

"I'm not aggressive, I'm just whacked out after a sleepless night thinking about what my husband was doing and with whom."

Michael let out a heavy sigh. "Okay, maybe we had better talk in the car...."

"In your car or mine? Shall we call a tow-truck for the other one?" she snapped.

"Lisa, now you are completely impossible."

His wife looked at him, her brown eyes turned black. Then she sighed and tore off her cap with a tired gesture. Her dark curly hair was blown around by the wind.

She looked past him, refusing to meet his gaze.

"Okay. Sorry. I was so angry," she finally said with a toneless voice, still not looking at him.

"You're always angry."

"I *said* sorry," she said hotly.

"Come, let's walk to the parking lot," he said.

Shit, he thought. This conversation would end in disaster whether they were here, in the food store, on the street or at home.

"So you came after me anyway," she said with a tinge of reconciliation in her voice.

"Yes," he said, relieved that she didn't know his full motive--yet, anyway. They walked stiffly towards the parking lot with some distance between them. Once or twice, the sleeves of their jackets brushed against each other. When they reached their cars they parted, wordlessly, for the drive home.

It's Christmas, After All

The Advent star glittered in the window and threw a pleasant light on Lisa, who sat by the kitchen table cuddled up in a chair with one leg close to her body and the other stretched out on the chair next to it. That's how she used to sit in just this chair. The kitchen was her favourite place in the house. The kitchen represented warmth, safety, community and family happiness. Usually. But this was not a usual day. It was not a usual Christmas.

Lisa's face was motionless and her eyes dry, but inside she was weeping. Her breathing was locked in a cramp high up in her chest. The night before had been terrible, the worst time in her life. It probably meant the end of everything. But she had to, had to, *had* to stay in one piece! She couldn't afford to crack. Not yet, not in front of the children. Then all would be lost.

From John's room a guitar was heard – he was practising. Anna had a friend down in the rec room. Jimmy was out somewhere. No, she couldn't just lie down and give up. Maybe there was a final, microscopic chance.

The days that had passed since her meeting with Michael at the botanical garden had been one long torment. Both had been tiptoeing around. She had not dared pose the crucial question out of fear of getting the wrong answer. As long as she didn't pose that ultimate question, she could pretend that all was normal. Then there was still hope. He, in turn, had more or less been sliding around the house like a ghost, probably out of fear of provoking one of her tantrums.

And the damn Christmas. It was closing in, mercilessly. The sound of Christmas carols nauseated her. She would prefer to crawl into bed a week before Christmas and not come out again until it was over. But you couldn't do that, not when you were a mother and the children expected Christmas pottering, presents, gingerbread, tree, and everything else that had sneaked into a tradition. It was so often that way: first you did something to make someone happy, and suddenly it was expected and then, before you knew it, it had become a *demand*. If you stopped doing it, everyone would be terribly disappointed. And you would be to blame.

Damn Christmas!

When she was growing up, Christmas was a drinking holiday for her father and the day usually ended in drunkenness and fighting. The worst disaster occurred when she was twelve and Dad fell down the stairs to the cellar and had to be rushed to the emergency room, where they spent all of Christmas evening. Strangely enough, she didn't remember anything in particular from the years before she was twelve. It was as though all of it had been erased from her mind.

With Michael and the kids, there was no drinking, no arguing over Christmas lunch, no drunken Santa throwing up in his beard, shouting "go to hell" to her mother and stumbling down the stairs and breaking his arms and legs.

She'd read in an article recently that the body remembered everything; that there is a memory outside one's conscious awareness. This interested her, although it sounded a bit fuzzy. As a trained nurse, she was more comfortable with things that could be proved under a microscope and in a test tube. But maybe this article could be right? How else to explain that she could smell an addict from fifty yards? With a hundred percent accuracy, she could determine if a patient was an addict or not, long before tests and reports showed her to be right. It was a mystery, and sometimes her colleagues joked about it – but Lisa kept the reason for this sixth sense to herself. Only Michael and Petra knew about the nightmare of her childhood.

She turned anxiously in the chair, swallowed the lump in her throat and longed for company, someone to talk to. But Petra was away for a couple of days and Michael… yes, Michael would be at work for several more hours. Besides… he was the last person who could comfort her. It was he who crushed her.

She drank the cold coffee – cup number six today – but it tasted terrible and couldn't chase away her tiredness. She dashed up from the chair, poured the coffee in the sink and started to walk around in the kitchen, opening cupboards at random. Maybe she should have some rum-spiked cider instead? Warm her inside with some alcohol to feel better? Light a fire in the fireplace, take a blanket and sit in her favourite armchair with her hands around the warm drink?

No.

Not alone. That was her big fear, that she would become someone who sat alone drinking, smelling of alcohol and getting all sloppy and blurry. As a nurse--and as a daughter--she well knew the enormous problems that alcohol created. All of those children who had alcoholic parents, children whom no one protected or helped.

She sat down at the kitchen table and listened to the sounds from her children's rooms. They had a good life. Didn't they? You couldn't take responsibility for all the children in the world. It was good enough if you could take care of your own without harming them.

The guitar in John's room grew silent. Maybe she should put on a record, but which one? She hadn't bought a record for ages; it must have been a year at least. Usually she just used iTunes. Suddenly she rose. She would go into the city and buy herself a new record! Perhaps something nice to wear for Christmas, a dress or a nice sweater – a red one! She would smell the perfumes, try on clothes, divert her thoughts, and chase the anxiety away. She would go into the city and be among people. She wouldn't give up, lie down and die – not yet!

Caught by this sudden urge, she ran into the hallway, pulled on a thick sweater, her jacket and boots and shouted:

"Bye, kids, I'm going into the city for a while!"

Anna said something from the rec room, but Lisa was already gone.

Decision Time

Twenty-one years.

Twenty-one years of up and down, downswings and peaks, happiness and gloom. An entire life together! And now he was about to wreck it all.

Michael opened the door to the car and sank down into the driver's seat that still smelled like new. He closed the door, wiped the sweat from his forehead and sat still, staring straight ahead. The anxiety tore at his intestines while crazy thoughts invaded every corner of his brain and went around and around and around.

"What the hell am I doing?" he shouted. The interior of the car muffled the sound. "What the hell am I doing?" he said again and suddenly he just roared: "*Aaaaahhh!!*" The sound was scary but no one could hear him alone in his private sphere. The hands moved to the wheel and the familiar feeling under his fingers calmed him for a moment.

"Lisa, this has nothing to do with you," he said again and again, trying to keep his voice steady. "It's about me; there is something wrong with me."

He turned the ignition key and the vibrations from the strong engine quieted his nerves. He drove out of the parking and continued on the familiar road home.

In a way, he was glad to feel this anxiety. He had felt empty and indifferent for so long that anxiety was almost a gift in the barren landscape that was his emotional life. Strange images popped up in his head. His passion for Cecilia had been like a rare, tropical flower that had mistakenly turned up in the middle of a desert landscape, looked around in fear and quickly lay down to die. The flower had been pale yellow, like Cecilia's hair. O my God, where did he get these poetic images? Could a life crisis suddenly call forth a poet in every middle-aged man? He continued on the familiar road.

What if everyone really walked around dead inside? He thought gloomily. Time moves faster and faster, suddenly you realize that life has passed! That you only have eaten, slept, and worked, but not lived. Maybe he was ill? Or depressed? Was it really healthy to not be able to feel joy – or even remember how joy feels? No he couldn't continue like this, life was too short.

He felt a sharp pain in the neck and Michael suddenly realized how tense he was. His shoulders were drawn up towards his neck; his hands were clutching the wheel tightly as if he was afraid he would drive into the abyss if he relaxed ever so slightly. Aloud, he said:

"Breathe... take a deep breath and hold it and clasp the left hand... and exhale... relax..."

As an athlete, he'd spent a lot of time on mental exercises and some of the relaxation tapes were etched into his mind, word by word. That had saved him many times when the stress was overwhelming.

He exhaled, inhaled, and felt how his body quickly got heavier while he listened to the voice in his head, where he also could hear the music that was on the familiar relaxation tapes. It was fascinating; it almost always worked.

Continuing on, he took a detour to delay his arrival, but told himself it was a nicer route.

Then he got stuck behind an old car driving at eighteen miles per hour. His anger awoke in a fraction of a second and all relaxation was gone. "What the hell," he shouted aloud in the car and then mumbled, "Bloody old lady driver."

He tailgated the old car for a while, his hot foot nervously pumping the accelerator. When he finally got a chance, he pushed the pedal to the metal and the engine roared and flew passed the old car. He took a quick glance at the driver. It wasn't an "old lady" but an elderly, shrunken man.

"A man in a cap," he mumbled. "Probably both blind and deaf. Shouldn't be allowed to keep his license."

But... the old man had reminded him of someone. Grandpa... behind the wheel in his old blue car with the deafening noise, and a cap on his head with white hair sticking out by the ears. He drove that car until, early one morning, he died in the barn. Grandpa who all of his life toiled at his farm. Grandpa who took care of him that summer of chaos when his little sister died, and also on holidays and summer vacations. Michael sighed with a shiver. He had loved his grandpa and now he was gone.

His family never talked about Carina's death or about difficult things at all, and he was grateful for that. *What you don't talk about doesn't exist.* It was actually better that way, there is no use in going over things again and again; it solves nothing, he thought. And whom could he talk to about Cecilia and the feelings she woke in him? Certainly not his friend John – even if he hadn't known Lisa. John was meek and satisfied with his life. He had never been unfaithful to Petra, ever! He wouldn't understand the notion of feeling *dead* inside.

This was the worst. He was dead, his feelings for the woman he shared so many years with were over and he was about to crush her and the children's world. Their marriage couldn't be saved because he *was* nothing, a cold bastard who had been living a lie for many years. The only one who could save his life was Cecilia.

He was closing in on home and knew that it was a question of minutes until he would face Lisa accusations. He started to sweat again.

The scene the day before had been horrible. Crazy, devastated, mad with despair, Lisa had screamed, yelled and beaten him with feeble fists, her face twisted in despair. Then she heaped guilt on him, saddling him with a bad conscience that would burden him for the rest of his life. It had been even worse than he'd anticipated.

But he didn't have any other choice than to tell. One week had passed since his nocturnal escape, and for an entire week he had been living in a limbo. He couldn't sleep close to Lisa anymore, feel her smell, listen to her voice, pretend to love her and pretend to be normal. A piece of ice was wrapped around his heart and it felt as though it would never thaw.

When he stepped out of the car he longed to be back at work, protected by the safety of his desk, the stacks, the statistics. He walked along the gravel path up to the front door, looked at the well-kept garden, and he thought about Lisa's sorrow when she would have to leave this garden and everything she planted and cared for there.

He opened the front door. Just inside, he almost stumbled over a pair of gigantic shoes, and for a minute he wondered who was visiting – until he realized that they were Jimmy's trainers. His youngest son had bigger feet than he did! Oh my God, it was only a couple of years ago that he took pictures of all the kids in the little pool at the back, naked, happy, pink little fellows.

The dog came by lazily, but she didn't have the energy for a welcoming bark today. He bent down and petted the yellow fur.

"Hello?" he yelled when he closed the door behind himself.

"Hi, Dad!" yelled Anna as she swept passed and bumped down the stairs to the rec room in two steps.

"Where's Mom?" he shouted after her.

"In the city, I think!" Anna shouted back.

Was Lisa in the city? Late last night, when her tears had turned into pale bitterness and thin lips, they agreed to sit down and talk when he came home tonight. Not that he was sorry to get some respite, but not showing up was so unlike Lisa. She used to be on to him constantly if they had a problem; she was the one who insisted on talking, talking, and talking until his head practically exploded. What was she doing in the city, what was she up to now? His stomach was churning.

Dramatic sound from a computer game was heard from Jimmy's room. Michael popped in his head and said hi.

"Hi," said his son without taking his eyes from the screen where two muscular creatures beat each other up with bludgeons. He looked into John's room, too, but it was empty.

Michael went to the bathroom to empty his bladder. By the bathtub, he saw a bra hanging to dry. It was light blue with cotton lace on the cups. Anna. His little girl, who just a while ago had sat in pink pyjamas on his lap, feeding from a bottle. Now she had breasts and was almost a grown woman. A woman he didn't know very well, he realized with pain. Time and the children had run away from him! He loved his kids, they loved him, but… he wished he'd spent more time with them.

What would things be like if he and Lisa got divorced? Would the kids want to see him at all when they realized that he was the one who did wrong, that he had cheated on their mother? Lisa wouldn't mince words about his betrayal, as bitter and despairing as she was.

He went to the fridge and opened a beer before he sank down into the couch and started zapping the TV channels.

Taking a Chance

They sat at the kitchen table with a glass of red each.

In a worrisome way, it looked like a rerun of the evening that ended with him running away a week ago. But the difference was that now they weren't sitting there as a married couple, but as a divorcing couple. Now it was serious business. Michael was sweating and thought he smelled bad, although he'd taken a shower, put on deodorant and changed into a clean shirt.

Lisa came home from the city laden with bags. Michael's irritation blossomed for a moment: why must she always shop herself to death? Was she aware of what things cost? Heating, maintenance on the house, insurance, the cars? Now, what was all this?

"Christmas presents," she said shortly, as if she could hear his thoughts. "For the kids."

And with that, she collected all the do-gooder points this time too. He himself had not bought a single present for the kids yet. Come to think of it, he didn't have a clue what they wanted. It was Lisa who took care of lists and presents. Sometimes he would be ordered to go and buy something like a computer game, a specific mp3-player, or maybe an iPad, but Lisa took care of the planning and coordination. Always.

Lisa had steeled herself before she entered the door at eight-thirty – long after dinner time. It would be interesting to see if they had eaten any dinner, and if so, what. She had been rejected, dumped, stuffed in the trash. Should she stand there and cook for them all? No. She'd had a sushi in the city and finished off her shopping with a big latte. While shopping, she'd decided to keep the cell phone off even though it was hard, since it made her feel that she'd lost control. When she turned it on going home there were three missed calls and three messages:

Anna: "Hi, Mom, when are you coming home? I'm going to Laura's to watch 'Dancing with the Stars.' Can I stay over there? Call me later, kiss!"

Jimmy: "Hi, Mom, me and a couple of friends are going to play Fifa 12 and play online. Can I stay over with them? Call me on my cell phone, hug!"

John: "I'm going out… I'll be back around twelve. Bye."

Nothing from Michael. No, he would probably just be glad if she didn't return… so he could call or chat undisturbed with his mistress! Oooh! She really wanted him to wonder, to try to reach her. To feel some regret. But no! He was busy with someone else.

She cried a little in the car. But then she calmed down and dried the mascara from her cheeks. After all, the kids had called her. They came to her for everything. They wouldn't like what Mike had done, and they would be on her side. Didn't he realise that? Or didn't he care?

When she returned home he sat like a zombie on the couch watching the History Channel with a can of beer in front of him. There were three empty pizza boxes in the kitchen. So, that's how they fixed dinner. They couldn't even take care of the boxes. She had been breathing deeply in the bathroom for a while before she went out to him and said:

"Weren't we going to talk?"

Now, they sat on each side of the big table, wine glasses in front of them. The Christmas decorations shone cosily, and Lisa had lit a candle. She always lit candles; it was practically a mania – Michael used to jokingly call her a "cosiness fiend." But now it seemed very strange, he thought. Like they were going to enjoy some kind of intimate evening. They were going to talk about their divorce!

The house was empty except for the dog in her basket by the kitchen door. She was watching them with unblinking dog's eyes. She could probably feel the tension.

Michael was sweating.

"So what do you say, Mike?" Lisa said.

"About what?" he said stupidly.

"I have been crying rivers, and I'm so damn sad, Mike. I'm so angry with you, so disappointed. But I don't want to divorce!"

"But... I... I don't think it's possible to continue, Lisa. I have no feelings for you anymore. I'm completely dead, as I said yesterday."

"You can't have been that dead when you jumped into bed with that Ce..."

"Lisa! I told you that I'm sorry about that, but I couldn't help it! She made me feel like I was alive for a while! I have never done it before... but this is serious. Even if she never will divorce, I can't continue with you, I can't. I can't do it any other way."

"But I've never been unfaithful, Mike!" Lisa hissed. Her eyes were black; furious and despairing at the same time.

He looked at the floor while the knife of guilt shredded his intestines slowly. He knew that it was true.

"Look at me, damn it!" she yelled. "You can't just leave me now!" Lisa stopped herself. No, no, no. Now they were heading in the same direction as they had last Friday. It would just end with furious, fruitless arguing and him leaving the house again. All her plans would be ruined. She must swallow her pride.

"Okay Mike, sorry, I understand. I really do. It has been so bad, you have withdrawn, I have been angry all the time, and then you have withdrawn even more... we haven't been able to meet each other. But has it really been *that* bad? It has been good, too, hasn't it? Or do you mean it has been shit all the time?"

Michael kept quiet and looked out the window. Suddenly, he jumped up from the chair and paced back and forth in the kitchen like a tiger in a cage. He scratched his neck and looked at her with a dark gaze.

"I must go out for a while. I can't talk more right now. I'm going for a walk. I'll be back later."

Lisa sat staring for a long time after the door slammed shut. Tears were streaming and makeup was running down her face. Then she rose, with a jerk, as if someone pinched her, and ran to the study and turned on the computer.

What was the name again? She ran back to the hallway and scrambled in her bag for her calendar. She did write it down there! With the calendar in her hand, she rushed back to the computer and spent the next hour researching and reading on the Internet.

Michael stood in the doorway.

"What are you doing?" he asked suspiciously.

"Michael," she said and rose. She made her voice as calm and steady as she could. She looked into his eyes. "I don't want to give this up, not so easily."

"Do you think I give up easily when we have been married for twenty years?"

"Twenty one."

"Yeah, I know it's twenty one," he said in a tired voice. "I was just rounding off."

"Listen. A girl at work has been to a kind of couple's workshop. They were going to get divorced, but after that they almost fell in love again. She said it was the best they ever did."

"Yeah."

"Mike, I want us to go there."

"But…"

"I know that you hate that kind of things, but give us a chance. Give the kids a chance! I'm prepared to forgive that you were… unfaithful, if you go there with me."

Her husband looked at her with something like panic in his eyes. To reveal oneself, talk about emotions, expose oneself… she knew that he hated it. But if he would only do this, maybe there was a chance that disaster could be prevented.

"Please Mike," she said and felt the tears pressing against her eyelids. "I am worth a chance after twenty-one years, am I not? Please."

He saw his wife sitting in front of him, begging for another chance. She was so… pitiful, and yet so strong-willed! Lisa hade pulled a heavy load all these years. He really didn't want to make her crack. If it would calm her down, make her stop crying, stop her accusations, rid him of his bad conscience, give him peace and quiet for a couple of days… then he would agree to anything. He didn't want to crush her, after all. He just wanted to get out in one piece and be able to move on.

"Okay," he said. She looked at him with clear eyes.

"Do you mean that?"

"Yes. We'll go there. I agree to that, *one* workshop. But don't have any high hopes, Lisa. You know I don't believe in that kind of thing. And I have already decided."

"But it's worth a try," Lisa whispered. "Twenty one years is worth a try. I love you, you know."

He couldn't answer, but he took her hand.

A ship is safe in the harbour
but that is not what ships are made for

WILLIAM SHED

8

Conflicts are Natural

Finding the Tools

Like Lisa and Michael, all couples that get stuck in the swamp of the power struggle feel powerless to reach each other. Then we often (and naturally enough) want to escape and seek happiness elsewhere. Others of us cling to the struggle and hope that by talking and talking about the problem, we will finally be able to reach each other. When this doesn't work--and it usually doesn't--we may decide to end the relationship, believing that by doing so we'll get rid of the difficulties.

Another way to "leave" is to stay in the relationship but in various ways sweep the conflicts under the carpet and pretending they don't exist. We leave *our selves*, turning off our painful feelings or using various forms of escapism and drugs to distract us from them. Seldom do we focus our attention, even for a brief moment, on the pain in order to understand *what lies behind it*. We actually ought to cry out, "hooray, now we have a chance to change!" But we need more information in order to see our conflicts from a new perspective.

I do repeat: *This does not mean that it is wrong to divorce.* To leave a relationship is sometimes both necessary and wise.

When powerlessness strikes, we usually don't lack the will but rather the knowledge and tools to reach each other. I want to inspire you to scrutinize your arguments and difficulties from a new perspective, and let the energy in the conflict lead you to a new place.

Life in itself offers the possibility to grow, even though the current situation can be seen as an argument, crisis or complete disaster. No matter in what disguise the conflict appears, we can choose to watch our own response with curious eyes and pose the questions to ourselves: Why do I "get started" in this way with him/her? Or: Why have I turned off all emotions toward this person? What does this feeling remind me of?

This does not mean that everything that the other person does or says is acceptable; it only means that we now have the opportunity to get familiar with our implicit memories. And how do we know that our response in the moment is linked to our implicit memories? Well, we often notice this by an increase in energy; we may lose our temper, feel *incredibly* hurt, or become deeply offended and "go cold." This is especially evident if we return to the same emotion over and over again. Perhaps our partner also responds this way, and so together we dance the hopeless dance of the power struggle.

Again, while we cannot--and should not--take responsibility for the behaviour of the other, we can with curious eyes study our own actions, our part in creating the situation, and the feelings and behaviours that the "hopeless" party trigger in us. It sounds simple, but can be very difficult. Often we get the idea that if we stop and look at what we do, then we become responsible for both our self *and* the other. But that is not the case. Each of us is responsible for our own behaviour only. We can learn to see ourselves as fundamentally separate from the other--to "differentiate"-- in order to re-establish ourselves as a healthier couple.

Damn Fool! Hmm, Very Interesting....

We can also practice not taking the reactions of the other so *personally*. We can chose to look at the conflict from the outside instead, so that we get the chance to put an extra spotlight on those topics or emotions that we often get stuck in. The same basic conflict may continue to occur, but in different form. When it rears its ugly face, we can call out:

"How interesting! Here we go again!"

This is probably the last thing that we want to call out. Conflicts hurt. We *shall* not stay in the dance of the conflict – we shall only make use of it, like a treasure map. Beneath the conflict, you may find gold.

I'm not suggesting that we celebrate our conflicts to the extent that we fill our lives with struggle. Not at all. I just want us to take a loving look at the places where we get chronically stuck, where our energy automatically goes, our implicit memories. But just *look*, don't over-analyze or become overwhelmed. (or take a swim in the craters. - Chapter 5) Instead, we can learn to differentiate ourselves from our problems.

If we are exposed to something that we experience as very, very difficult or dangerous in a relationship, it is vital to quickly leave that relationship. We must remove ourselves from conflicts that lead to violence or threats of violence. I primarily think of physical abuse, in which someone takes out his or her powerlessness on others and endangers them in the process. In this kind of conflict, it's very important to leave or get help, in order to protect yourself and/or your children. Such situations are usually too difficult to handle on your own. But you can learn even from these relationships – afterwards.

I want to make it clear that not *everything* is about our implicit memories.But when our reactions have to do with hurts from our past, we can actually change those patterns. We can get a bit curious. We have a choice. The more often we choose the new way to act, the deeper the new neuron tracks get until, finally, they become a natural path (recall the bucket of water and the pile of sand).

If we look at our arguments with our partner (or our sulking, silence, freezing out, or however we choose to disconnect), we usually get stuck on two or three subjects. Subjects that constantly reoccur and make us scream our existential screams, the ones that plead, "It hurts! Understand the need behind my scream!"

Discovering the Wish

Beneath the defence of the Armani suit is a wish. There is a wish behind every frustration. Do we take the time to see and understand the wish? Not usually. Typically, we get stuck in the dance of power struggle where we only use our defence--a defence that doesn't help us get what we need, but that gives us a false, external sense of power when we *make up* that we don't have any inner power of our own.

Many, many times, Sven and I have "bathed" in our defences until we've almost drowned in them. I have chased him around the house, criticizing, nagging, arguing, crying, screaming, manipulating, complaining, enticing, coaxing, begging, tiptoeing, analysing, and anything else I can think of to try to make contact with him.

Sven, in turn, withdraws and "turtles" himself, goes downstairs and sits in front of the TV or the computer – or takes the car and drives away with wheels spinning. Often, he has gone to work or driven around for hours, just to be left in peace. I wanted contact. He wanted space.

I cried. I felt angry, abandoned, rejected, dejected, hurt, and lonely.

Sven went cold. He felt angry, smothered, invaded, abandoned, rejected, hurt, and alone.

Loneliness was painful to me. Loneliness was safety to him – in the moment. But within, loneliness paralyzed him as much as it did me.

The Hailstorm and the Turtle

When we're embroiled in a relationship struggle, we are seldom in touch with the well-developed part of our brain behind the forehead, the central part of our *prefrontal cortex*. Instead, our emotional brain gets activated and we send out energy one of two ways--by screaming and pursuing or by pulling back and turning off. Either way, we are signalling an existential scream because we are *experiencing danger* –implicit or/and explicit. Harville Hendrix and Helen LaKelly (the founders of Imago Relationship Therapy) call these two fundamental types of responses "the hailstorm and the turtle."

In the relationship between Lisa and Michael, Lisa is the hailstorm, the one who turns the energy outwards. In heterosexual relationships, the woman is usually –though not always – the hailstorm. Lisa turns her energy outwards and pours out her feelings, pursues, criticizes, and throws hailstones of emotions and words at Michael. She longs for contact and does whatever she can to try to get it.

Michael, in turn, is a typical turtle. He gathers in his energy, hides under his shell and tries to protect himself. He turns off, "plays dead" and waits until he feels safe enough to cautiously stick out his head from his shell. The turtle also longs for contact, but it must feel calm and safe.

Maybe we all have both hailstorm and turtle inside us. Some of us alternate between the two, behaving like a hailstorm in one relationship and a turtle in another. Others vary little from their usual mode. We become chaotic or rigid. We must remember that the one way of behaving is not worse than the other. It's only a question of whether we turn our energy outwards or inwards when we feel unsecure and are trying to calm down our nervous system. In some cultures, self-control is seen as the nobler quality; it is better to keep your feelings to yourself and clench your fist in your pocket. Perhaps it is valued more because it is

190

men who typically respond this way. Yet, this mode is just as unproductive as shrieking and pleading when it comes to getting what human beings need: safe contact, intimacy and love.

Interestingly enough, these different types of people often marry each other. A common dynamic is that when they feel insecure, one partner hurls hailstones while the other one withdraws into a shell. But some relationships are comprised of two hailstorms. A well-known example is Richard Burton and Elizabeth Taylor, who for years engaged in a passionate, sometimes chaotic dance of arguing and reconciliation. Sometimes, two turtles get together--and nothing much happens at all. They live a quiet life in which no one "wants" very much or, if they do, they avoid making scenes about it.

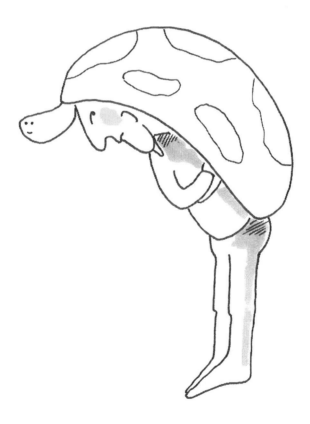

As I described above, I've been a classic hailstorm, while Sven has been a typical turtle. It isn't difficult to figure out that the more I chased and screamed, the more he turned off and hid. Interestingly enough, though, we sometimes changed roles. If I had been a hailstorm for a long period of time, suddenly our dance would shift. Sven would explode, turn his energy outward and become a hailstorm, while I would seek cover and become a turtle, vanishing into my body. Regardless of who played what role, our dance was frustrating and seemingly endless. It failed to give either of us what we truly needed: positive contact.

Disconnected

If we for a moment go back to the "hand model of the brain" by Daniel Siegel (see Chapter 3), we can see what happens in the brain when we "lose it." When the fingertips are lifted away from the thumbs, the prefrontal cortex behind the forehead--the rational brain--is disconnected from the rest of the brain. It is out of order, *just then.*

This is exactly what happens when we lose our temper and become scared – or furious. The central prefrontal cortex is disconnected and doesn't integrate body and mind into the unit it should be. Becoming furious and/or scared often occurs in intense emotional situations, whether we turn our energy inward or outward.

When the central part of prefrontal cortex is disconnected, we lose important abilities, namely:

1) regulating the body;
2) attuning to others;
3) regulating and balancing emotions;
4) being flexible in our responses;
5) soothing fear;
6) creating empathy (the "you map");
7) creating insight (the "me map");

8) creating moral awareness (the "we map");

9) intuition. [33]

Anger Breeds Anger

The Danish psychologist, Imago therapist and author Jette Simon writes:

"To 'lose ones head' can also be congenital, meaning that you have a hereditary genetic disposition or a prenatal experience like stress as a foetus or a difficult birth. These constitutional traits can mean that the prefrontal area has a short fuse and that you quickly lose the integrated abilities at a quite small provocation." [34]

When it comes to anger, we now know that the more we *feel* our anger, the angrier we become. This occurs because the body responds to anger by producing more of the stress-hormone cortisol. Too much cortisol can also contribute to depression. So we need to be careful, because what a lot of people believed in previously – that it's healthy to get the anger out of the system--is not always the case. Each time we swim in the crater of our anger, the easier it is to slip down into it again – and more difficult to get up. Here, I am talking about the hazards of chronically expressing anger. I am most definitely not talking about those people that never dare to feel the anger they feel inside. For such people, it can be really good to "get it out." If handled with care, anger can be a very healthy source of energy.

Whether we inherited our temper or learnt it over the years (naturally, it's a mix of both), we can learn how to access more energy in the prefrontal cortex that integrates the various parts of the brain. This is the region of the brain that helps us repair the contact when we have broken it (with others or with ourselves). The prefrontal cortex gives us access to the nine abilities that calms our nervous system. (See page above)

---

33 Daniel J Siegel, *Mindful brain, Reflection and Attunement in the Cultivation of Well-Being*, Page 26

34 Jette Simon, Swedish: Imago – *Kärlekens terapi,* page 91. The book is out in English as well: *Imago - The Therapy of Love*

What if all adults could learn to own their responsibility, repair what is broken and re-establish contact? Think about it. Can you even imagine how the world would work? Might we be able to build genuine peace instead of endure chronic war, conflict and chaos?

It is worth repeating that defences in themselves are neither right nor wrong. They are simply survival tactics we use to deal with experiences we perceive as painful or dangerous. Some defences--which I've earlier referred to as "Armani suits"-- we learnt to put on as children when we witnessed pain or danger or experienced it ourselves (and not necessarily a serious trauma). In order to be able to deal with what happened, we instinctively learnt how to protect ourselves with the aid of a particular kind of behaviour--striking back, running away, or freezing. In this way we got the experience of power, or at least a bit of control, instead of a sense of utter powerlessness.

The Courage to Look Inward

Our Armani suit drapes itself around us with the speed of lightning, usually without our awareness. Dressed for protection, we march into battle. So perfect is the fit of this suit that when we step into it, it *feels* right; we don't experience that we've just put on some kind of defence. (Interesting--yes.) However, our partner and others close to us usually notice when we dress up in the suit. The telltale signs include getting stuck in the same old quarrels with the same old behaviours and outbursts: "Don't raise your voice again!" or "Now, you're not listening again!" or "I've asked you a thousand times to not just walk away!"

Let's once again try to put a heart around that suit and learn to notice when we put it on. If we can recognize and accept it, we will be free to choose to behave another way.

Sometimes, we try to "talk about problems" while wearing our Armani suits. That usually doesn't work too well. When we're in our defence gear, we tend to focus on being *right*--winning the discussion/ fight/quarrel--rather than on connecting. The discussion often takes the form of stating "truths" about the other: "you never listen" or "you're so aggressive" or "look who's talking," and so on.

Ironically, when we engage in this kind of struggle we become completely powerless. We feel as though we're trying to maintain our power, and in the process we become increasingly helpless to change anything. But if we gather courage to focus on ourselves and look soberly at our own role in the conflict, something different will emerge. We will gain power and choice.

You and I are one – and I am the one.

HARVILLE HENDRIX

9

Separate and Together--A Delicate Balance

The Challenge of Differentiation

"Oh, what a wonderful movie!" Maggie exclaims happily. "We should really go to the movies more often!" The music from her youth wrapped itself around her heart like soft cotton.

"Wonderful? Are you out of your mind?" Johnny responds disdainfully. "It was silly and ridiculous. How the hell can you like this?"

She turns around, and meets his eyes with a surprised, bitter gaze.

"Are you serious?" she asks, trying to keep her voice even.

"Yes, it was complete crap. Just a bunch of sleazy love songs." he says in an irritated tone.

Maggie feels like she's been punched in the face. She has been sitting all evening, enjoying the music, the humour and the memories, and then he...he... shit! How can he feel that way about such a wonderful, touching film? Her heart wells up with sorrow. This is probably the final straw. Proof that they don't belong together. It doesn't work, they are simply too different.

"Well, then," she says, "you'll have to find someone who isn't so fond of love songs!"

Maggie turns around and walks angrily down the street away from him, her heels clicking. Her stomach is a tight ball of disappointment.

How do you respond when your partner, friend or relative has a completely different opinion from yours? Do you say, "That's interesting, tell me more?" Or do you tend to respond more like Maggie and Johnny did?

The truth is, behaving like Maggie and Johnny is very common.

We often get the idea that it's difficult to live together if we are different; that "birds of a feather flock together" and that there is a *right* way and a *wrong* way to think, feel and be. Instead we ought to be curious about the other person. Examine, discover, sniff, taste, ask… *visit*. We simply need to "move apart" in order to be together. We need to celebrate the fact that You are a different person than I am, and that we sometimes hold different truths. This sounds both natural and easy. But is it?

Sometimes we work hard at making our partner think like we do. Then, when he or she finally does, we find that our partner is not such an interesting person any longer. Sometimes we also get the idea that if we understand the other, we also have to agree with him or her. Not so.

Everyone knows that each individual is unique. Why, then, is it so difficult to accept differences? We can have different genders, experiences, values, DNA, opinions, tastes in furniture, food, films, and so on. But we need to learn to listen to others with great respect, be curious about the differences, differentiate (move apart), and dare to "step into" the other person's reality *without fear of losing our own identity*. We need simply to connect, step into the other's world, and in that process allow ourselves to be touched by the other person. With attunement, resonance and curiosity, we embark on an adventure – toward the other

– and at the same time stay connected to ourselves. When we do that, we are a You and an I in safe connection.

Far Away and Near

Commonly, partners either communicate with too much distance or too few boundaries. Sometimes, when a couple tries to bring up a difficult subject, they are so differentiated that there is no contact at all; each is so separate that they can't enter each other's world. Other couples are so emotionally joined that everything is mashed together; there is no healthy sense of self. Either way, nobody is crossing the bridge to the other.

Daniel Goleman says: "The fact that we can trigger any emotion at all in someone else-or they in us- testifies to the power mechanism by which one person's feelings spread to another. Such contagions are the central transaction in the emotional economy, the give-and-take of feeling that accompanies every human encounter we have, no matter what the ostensible business at hand may be." [35]

Yes, emotions contaminate through mirror neurons and resonance circuits, and that goes for both positive and negative emotions. So we must be vigilant.

On our natural ladder of development – from infant to adult – we learn how we *can* and *may* bond with people close to us. All the time we get signals from our surrounding telling us whether it's safe to attach, be close, dependent, needy, similar, and connected, and also whether it's safe to leave, separate, differentiate, express our individuality, and think differently – and then get back and bond again. Our brains encode and read off the signals. Signals that we as babies ourselves experience, but also what we see our parents and other people close to us experience – between them. Everything lives in the space.

---

35 Daniel Goleman, *Social Intelligence; The New Science of Human Relationships,* page 16

A person that learns that it's safe to be close *and* to be separate knows his or her own boundaries and identity. This person has a strong "I" that doesn't easily get mixed up with others. This individual knows that he or she can visit a "You" with a loving contact and presence and still remain himself or herself. The natural and healthy development is that we attach as children, let go (differentiate), attach again, and let go again and again. I call this process "hello and goodbye."

Hello! Goodbye.
One Hello… and one goodbye
Hello……………………..goodbye
Hello………………………….goodbye
Hello……………………………..goodbye
Hello………………………………….goodbye
Hello……………………………………….goodbye.

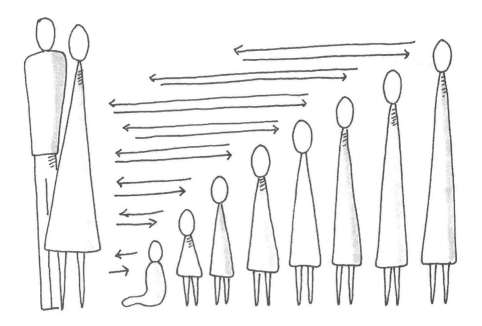

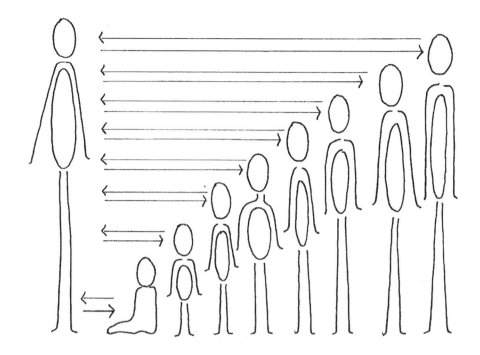

Our natural impulse as infants (from birth to 18 months) is to attach and bond. We move between needing, not needing so much, and then needing again. Step by step, piece by piece, we move towards the world around us – and then quickly return to the safe harbour again. The safer we feel, the further we go, knowing that whenever we need security and regulation, we can get it.

As babies, we *attach* and then we differentiate by turning our gaze away, and then back to the safety of Mom's or Dad's face (or that of another primary caregiver). We learn to crawl, begin to *explore*, and then scurry back to safety. We learn to walk, and run, and then... back to safety.

When we are about three, we begin to test our *identity* (who am I?) by taking on different roles: Superman, princess, monster, policeman, banana. We dare to say *no* when Mom or Dad says *yes*. We try to find out if we can be different, and then... back to safety.

We test our *competence* and build with blocks, draw, climb, run, jump, try various things, and then... back to safety. We start to feel *concern for others*, start school and bond with one or more friends, and then.... back to safety.

We become teenagers and say *no*, because we are once again *exploring and testing our identity*, and then... back to safety. We move – physically, emotionally, and mentally – further and further away, and then... back to safety.

For every such experience, we store memories (both implicit and explicit) of how the experience worked and how we felt. We remember whether we were *both* allowed to physically move away and experience the world *and* allowed to have our own opinion and be an individual... and at the same time know that someone will be there when we return.

The basic question throughout the bonding process is the same over the years: "Are you there when I need you?" All of the answers we get and the experiences we make are stored. Neurons get fired, make their tracks and draw the map of our ego.

This process goes on throughout life and with everyone who is close to us. We link together, move away and differentiate, and then come back again. Ideally, by the time we are adults we have gained so much safety from this ongoing process that we know who we are, what we think, where we begin and where we end. A natural result of this repeated experience of safety is that we can calm our nervous system ourselves when we get worried or frightened. We can emotionally regulate ourselves and others.

The natural steps of development described above are clearly connected to the development of the brain. It's natural that small children get worried and anxious when Mom or Dad disappears. These feelings are universal. Naturally, there are differences depending on the nature of the bonding, but also depending on such factors as religion, gender, class--that is, how both parents and society look at the different steps on the ladder of development. The important thing here is not that we become worried and anxious–that's normal – but that we can learn to *calm ourselves down* and feel balanced again.

If we follow the natural steps of development, we will learn to separate from our parents or guardians bit by bit and become more independent. If we always have a safe harbour to return to we will go out into the world with confidence and curiosity. We know our value. We have a body and soul in harmony and balance. As grownups, we can regulate ourselves and others.

The Dance of Defiance

One way to move away from our parents is to say *no* when they say *yes*. Or to say yes when they say no. Or to say pizza when they say casserole.

As we go through the process of separation, we tend to test limits and find out whether we can be different from the ones we love and need. This natural process is especially evident in teenagers. Unfortunately, we refer to this natural period in a child's development as "teenage defiance." It is, of course, a difficult time for parents, teachers and others who are close to the teenager, but there is more reason to worry if it *doesn't* occur.

From adults, teenagers may hear:

"You're so cheeky! How can you say that?"

"No, that's just *wrong!*"

"In this house (or school or family), we believe…"

"Now you're really being stupid; that's not how it works in the world."

"I'm so upset that you feel that way! Now I won't be able to sleep all night!"

"I know *exactly* what you need, and it's not…"

In daily life, adults express in countless ways that they can't really accept differences. If we, as teenagers, think or feel differently than our parents, teachers, or grandparents, then those adults become angry, sad, or disappointed. And in our brain-map, it is inscribed a truth that *it's not okay* to separate physically, mentally, emotionally, spiritually, or intellectually, and at the same time stay in contact. Many of us react by putting on an Armani suit of docile obedience or flagrant disobedience, which is problematic either way because they control our actions. The suit limits our free choice.

In saying this, I definitely don't mean that we should let our children do as they please. But we do need to understand the importance of respecting differences, and the importance of listening to teenagers and separating their signals from ours. And when we have to say "no," it's very much a question *how* we say it. It's a question of acknowledging the differences in the child, even as we guide them in the direction we think is best. When we have to say "no," we can do so in a soft, clear and understanding way.

I know that it can be difficult to be a parent when children are testing all limits. I know that I have a tendency to get stuck in tiresome discussions with my teenagers! Right now, I'm practising (with a capital P) to have a little sense of humour and distance and realize that their favourite phrases right now are "you can't tell me what to do" and "I don't care." It's not easy to remain calm and firm. But I'm trying.

Finding the Balance

When children and teens experience safe bonding and differentiation, they are preparing themselves to become part of a healthy couple. When partners feel safely attached to each other, they can express different opinions, even in emotionally difficult discussions, and maintain a soft, respectful contact. They can be apart and together at the same time, because each partner feels secure and whole.

When we feel unsafe, on the other hand, we have great difficulties tolerating differences. When someone feels differently than we do about something, we have a tendency to feel threatened. And when we feel threatened, we take everything much more personally, and in a flash we jump into our Armani suites.

Many of us have never learned to "go away and come back" safely. Not necessarily because we had "bad" parents, but because of some lack of safety in our lives--in our families, in our culture, in our society, between different religions, between different countries—yes, it's everywhere! Some of us also have experienced external danger that makes it impossible to leave safely: war, poverty, illness, abuse, and difficult losses are such factors.

As a couple's therapist, I can see that it is very difficult for a lot of people to leave or be left. But I also see that many are afraid to get "too close," shying away from intimacy and possible dependence on another. Both responses can be problematic.

Our ability to differentiate and yet be connected – that is, *integrated* – deeply affects our sex lives. When we have difficulties differentiating, we often lose our sense of excitement and passion. We become like twins, where the one knows what the other one feels before he or she does. By contrast, when we are *too* differentiated, the gap between us is so great that a truly intimate sex life is impossible. We are not in contact.

Many choose to live in physical closeness – but not be close at all – by being attracted to relationships in which *being unsafe* is the fuel for the sex life. In some cases, we may feel we must desperately keep the fires burning and maintain a highly erotic sex life – otherwise he or she may leave us! This is usually fear, not intimacy.

The Myth of the One Truth

When we have difficulties differentiating and at the same time staying connected and integrated, we have difficulties accepting differences. We have problems accepting a no when we are convinced it should be yes. We easily get the idea that there is *one* truth. This "truth" – everything that we have experienced on our way up the ladder of development – is connected in our brain like a map that we automatically orient to in our relationships. Our experience is repeated directly or indirectly in our everyday life, especially when we get into arguments about sensitive subjects. As we learned in an earlier chapter, this is when we get into power struggles with our partner. We find ourselves saying things like:

"I can never tell you how I really feel – because then you just argue with me."

"You keep trying to control me."

"I don't need your help; I can do it myself."

"You always have to be right!"

"You never help me when I need it.

"You don't see me!"

"You think you know more about how I feel than I do."

"Just listen! You never hear what I say!"

"Everything is about you!"

"Talking to you is like talking to a wall."

"Damn it, realize that *I'm* not *you!*"

"_____" (Fill in whatever is missing.)

Who's Feeling--You or Me?

If we are either too "mixed up" with another *or* distance ourselves too much, it can be difficult to maintain a dialogue as two distinct individuals--individuals who take each other in emotionally while thinking and feeling differently. Below are a few examples of what I mean by being "mixed up" together.

A 13-year-old to his math teacher:

"It's no fun in class. Everyone yells and I get nothing done."

"Well, pull yourself together! Grow up and deal with it."

Lovers:

"We never have sex anymore…"

"O yeah, why do you say that? It's not like it's my fault!"

"I didn't say it was your fault, I just said that we don't have sex anymore, and I wonder why…"

The one party responds emotionally to what the other one says, so that the reaction has nothing to do with what was actually said, but rather how we react to what the other one says. We don't listen, since we perceive what we hear as critique of us, and then it becomes all about us--what we think and feel about what the other one says. The one person's feelings simply become the other person's feeling. Are you with me? Here are a few more examples:

A teenager to her mother:

"I found a pair of jeans, they are so cool, with these rips on the legs and…"

"You will never be allowed to pay money for jeans that are torn from the start. I'm not made out of money!"

Anyone:

"It doesn't feel like you are listening."

"Look who's talking, you never listen, either!"

We are hijacked by our own emotions, and thus we can't listen to the other person. We must understand this phenomenon first, and then learn how to find the difference the other person's signals and our own. On top of this, we must find effective ways to calm our nervous system so that we can build a little bridge and cross over to the other person's world.

The Quiet Magic of Listening

When we visit the other person's world, we need to do so with great presence. We need to listen and with great respect really hear what the other person says, no matter what we *think or feel* about what is said. In this moment, what we think or feel is not important. It can be very important later, *but not now*. Now, you are visiting another person's reality.

If we dare to lean back and listen with presence and curiosity, the miraculous thing occurs is that we begin to be genuinely interested in what the other person has to say. "Tell me more!" we respond. *We want to keep on listening.*

Now you may think: If we're not supposed to take what the other one says personally, how can we truly listen to each other? Well, we can listen without concluding that the other is "right." Maybe there isn't any right or wrong. Maybe the world becomes what we see – depending on who is looking.

Imagine that someone yells at you: "You are completely worthless!" Are you worthless, then? No, of course not. Now, imagine that the same person yells: "You don't listen to me!" Does this mean that you don't listen? Not necessarily, but one thing is certain--the other person doesn't *feel* heard. If we take what they say personally and perceive it as critique, then we throw on the Armani suit and begin to defend ourselves! But if, instead, we learn to calm our nervous system and just listen, it will help us *in the moment* to separate what is yours from what is mine. And, interestingly enough, it will also help us to separate what feels from what is.

With effort and practice, we can begin to understand (with the aid of our prefrontal cortex) that You and I are not the same. Granted, this is sometimes very difficult, especially when someone is looking at us with angry, sad, disappointed, displeased or hostile eyes. But if we can learn to take in what is said with curiosity, we can sometimes really see our part in what is said without becoming "the bad guy."

And here is the really interesting part: When we can calm our own nervous system and truly listen, we help to calm down the other person's nervous system as well. As a result, this person becomes less inclined to project malice (or whatever it is), and instead begins to show respect and love, with both words and body language. We create a snowball of respectful and loving actions. In short, we regulate each other.

I'm not saying that this process is easy. It's not. But I have seen this transformation occur in so many clients that I know it's *possible* for us to create this avalanche of love. Now, let's find out how to make it happen.

*The purpose of relation is the
relation itself – touching the You.
For as soon as we touch a You
We are touched by eternal life*

MARTIN BUBER

1 0

Crossing the Bridge

Tell Me More!

So, we need to be curious about another person--curious and present without getting emotionally "mixed up" with that other person. We simply need to go apart – so that we can be together.

Because our nervous system is incredibly sensitive to other people's nervous systems, we're capable of feeling as if we're walking in someone else's shoes. A resonance is then created between our experience and the experience of the other. In the same moment that your face shows an emotion, mirror neurons make it possible for the other person to experience the same emotion. Whenever human beings make contact face-to-face or skin-to-skin, our brains and mind are connected.

Okay, now that we know that we constantly infect each other with our emotional states and that this interplay lives in the space between us, what do we do about it?

For starters, we can humbly ask others: this feeling that I have now, does it correspond to what *you* feel? We can check whether the emotion is ours alone or whether it also exists in the other person. For while we are capable of feeling what other people feel, we also know that it's easy to mix ourselves up in others and project our own emotions onto the other person. I think that this is vital for everyone to understand, and especially those who are in a profession where we hold other people's emotions in our hands (therapists, doctors, priests, psychologists, teachers, social workers, and so on).

With curious eyes and hearts, let's learn to recognize our signals and natural responses and see what works and what doesn't. Conflicts that we repeat over and over again tell us something important about ourselves. If we let them, our conflicts can be our guides.

In the Jaws of the Dog

Daniel Siegel often relates the following parable: "We can compare our trauma and strong negative experiences with a dog bite. What happens automatically when we are bitten in the hand by a dog? Well, we pull our hand away, as quickly as we can! What happens to the wound? The hand is torn and we probably get a fairly large wound."

So, what can we do instead?

"Well, we can, if we have presence enough, face the dog bite by forcing our hand a bit further into the mouth of the dog. What happens then? The dog will let go. The result is that we get a wound, but not as large as if we quickly pull away our hand, which is the natural reaction when we experience physical pain." [36]If we apply this metaphor on the small and large traumas that get stuck in our consciousness, then we can *softly* and with curiosity meet what we get stuck in, and even quietly cheer it – not because of what happened, but for the possibility of meeting the difficulty in another way this time, so that we can understand and

---

36 Daniel J. Siegel, Allan Schore, Michael Stone, Bessel Van der Kolk, Marion Solomon, Francine Shapiro and John Lang, Cd, *Understanding and Treating Trauma*

heal it. Then we can consciously choose to let go of the event and learn a new way of responding to similar events in the future.

There are many ways to "meet the dog bite." In close relationships, we can help each other to find the inner craters that each of us repeatedly fall into, examine them and understand why we keep falling down there. Then we can learn to calm down our nervous system so that we can choose how we act. We can learn how to climb up out of the abyss and then to fill in the hole, so that we never fall into it again.

Become Your own Brain Surgeon

Daniel Goleman says: "Our social interactions even play a role in reshaping our brain, through "neuroplasticity", which means that repeated experiences sculpt the shape, size, and number of neurons and their synaptic connections. By repeatedly driving our brain into a given register, our key relationships can gradually mold certain neural circuits." [37]

This is brain surgery, then?

In a way, yes. The key thing to understand here is that in order to form new, healthier neural circuits, we must look squarely at our traumas. We must confront our dog bites in order to get the liberating "aha" reaction. This process allows us to experience the link between then and now. When we do that, we can choose to let go of the pain of the dog bite to welcome something new. But if we repeatedly choose to step down and thrash around in the painful crater, we continue to feel how much pain this dog bite gave us. In the process, we only strengthen the negative neural circuits.

In my work, I teach contingent communication through the dialogue - *crossing the bridge*. Bonnie Badenoch says:" The very heart of secure attachment is *contingent communication*. This involves receiving people´s signals (nonverbal more than verbal) and responding in a way that lets them "feel felt". Much of this nonverbal conversation

37 Daniel Goleman, *Social Intelligence; The New Science of Human Relationships*, page 11

takes place below the level of conscious awareness, implicit process to implicit process, in the right hemisphere. Resonance circuits including mirror neurons, are the heart of this process" [38]

This carefully designed, powerful ritual helps both couples and singles to invite another person on a guided tour of their mind and brain. Sometimes this journey goes back in time, while other times it remains in the present; either way, it can lead to new tracks in the brain. As new nerve paths are established, we begin to see new possibilities and make new choices. The dialogue can engender a feeling of being deeply heard, understood, empathized with, and respected.

Crossing the bridge offers an opportunity to create new neural pathways and inner healing with the aid of mindful attention, attunement, limbic resonance and empathy. In his book, *Mindsight*, Daniel Siegel says that this process allows us to "SNAG" the brain, that is, Stimulate Neuronal Activation and Growth. Wherever neural firing occurs, existing neurons can make new or enhanced synaptic connections through the process called *synaptogenesis*. New neurons can be stimulated to develop as well, via a process called *neurogenesis*. [39] With this information in mind, let's return to Lisa and Michael.

---

38 Bonnie Badenoch, *Being a Brain-Wise Therapist; A Practical Guide to Interpersonal Neurobiology,* Page 57

39 Daniel J. Siegel, *Mindsight; The New Science of Personal Transformation,* page 110

Michael and Lisa

All We Need is Contact

"Put your chairs closer, as close as you can come," the therapist says to Michael and Lisa. "But mind your heads so you don't bump them together. We don't want any brain damage here, do we?"

As she says this, the therapist gives the couple a warm smile. As Michael and Lisa comply with the request, Lisa thinks: What if some people actually bumped their heads together by mistake when they got their courage to step up in front of all the other couples? Lisa envisions this slapstick scene and giggles nervously, which gives rise to subdued laughter from the others in the room. Maybe they imagine the same scene. The laughter is liberating and releases some of the tension in the room. Many in the group of fifteen couples seem just as nervous as Michael and Lisa.

"The rest of you can also come closer," the therapist directed.

Most of them pull their blue conference chairs as close to the couple as they can, while others sit on the floor nearby. Michael and Lisa sit with their knees close together, their feet firmly on the floor. Outside, rain is pouring and some candles flicker on a table in the corner. There is the sound of chairs scraping and people clearing their throats. Then, silence.

It's Saturday, the second day of the weekend workshop for couples. The evening before, there had been introductions. Some couples admitted that they were in an emergency situation; one couple was in the process of divorcing. Others were still in love. One couple got the seminar as a wedding gift, another one as an anniversary present from their adult children. Yet another one was sent by an employer. Whatever their situation, nearly all of them wanted to learn to communicate better.

So far, Saturday has been filled with lectures, with even the husband of the therapist participating actively as a lecturer. Against his will, Michael has become interested. This didn't seem to be the mushy bathing in emotions that he'd feared. You could hardly call it group therapy, either. Instead, he'd been hearing interesting lectures about brain research and new theories about how the brain and mind can be affected and altered. Actually, he found himself very stimulated by the new theories. The therapist seemed knowledgeable and sensible, too--surely, she would help him pick up the pieces of Lisa, he'd thought.

But now he's feeling anxious. He'd lowered his guard and suddenly, he's here in the midst of everybody's attention and is supposed to talk about his emotions. How the hell did this happen? How could he have been so tricked?

Lisa, meanwhile, feels a cramp in her stomach. Help, what have I done? she wonders. Why did I have to be so damn quick to rise and volunteer them as a demonstration couple? Mike had protested--Mike, who didn't want to be here at all! But, as usual, she'd coaxed, pressed, pulled and pushed, and he'd probably given in just to get her to stop nagging.

She lets out a trembling sigh; her breathing is so out of sync that she feels she might faint. The room spins.

Michael wipes his forehead once again and looks out over the couples seated so close to them. Thirty pairs of eyes watch them. All of his pain and flaws are about to go on display. A public execution. The only reason he'd agreed to demonstrate a dialogue was so he wouldn't be seen as a pathetic coward. Well, he can't escape now; he must go through with this. He can barely breathe.

Though Michael is terrified, he realizes that a small, small part of him is also curious. But this doesn't stop his knees from shaking. In desperation, he tries to catch the therapist's gaze, to find courage there. She meets his eyes with great enthusiasm.

"Hello, you courageous couple," she says, smiling.

Lisa manages to smile back, but Michael looks down at the floor. The therapist continues:

"I have asked the other couples to sit close to us because, you know, when one couple really makes *contact*, or 'crosses the bridge' as I usually put it, most of us tend to recognize ourselves in the dialogue. We are so incredibly much alike, we humans. But tell us if you think they're too close, because then they'll move back a bit. Is it okay?"

Lisa nods. Again, Michael seeks the eyes of therapist and whispers, "It's okay…I'm almost used to it now."

The therapist looks at the middle-aged couple in front of her: the slim, energetic, slightly squirrel-like woman with dark curly hair and big brown eyes; and the man, angular and muscular, with a furrowed face and greying hair. She knows that they have lived almost half of their lives together and that now they're locked in a kind of war. Probably they have hurt each other a lot. Probably, they both feel very unsafe.

The therapist is seated in the middle facing Lisa and Michael, so close that her chair forms the stem of a T. Once the dialogue begins, she will move back to make room for them as a couple. She's really just there to facilitate and "hold" the process. She will help them put words to the emotions that flow between them, their body language, and everything else that they place in the important space between them--the interval.

One member of the couple will make an emotional journey – cross the bridge – to the other one and visit that partner with curiosity, love and mindful presence, like an explorer in a foreign country. The task of the receiver is to dare open the door and welcome the visitor inside.

Once the journey has started the process often continues by itself, but the therapist is always there for support. From long experience, she knows how hard it can be to walk unarmed over the bridge and leave the ego and defences behind. She also knows how difficult it can be to open up and receive the threatening visitor that you may have been at war with for a long time.

She looks out at the group and says:

"Now, I want to ask you to make it really safe for this courageous couple. One way to make it safe in here is for everyone to go to something that I call our 'safe place.' It's a place where you experience wellbeing. This can be a place that you remember, for instance by the sea, in the forest, at home, or in the car. Or it can be a place that you invent here and now – you can just make it up, it doesn't matter. What is important is that it is a place where you can feel safety and wellbeing – a *comfortable* place."

Many participants get a distant gaze as they look for this place in their memory. Others close their eyes. She goes on:

"Once, a man said to me, 'a safe place for me is when I sit in the centre of the city eating an ice cream cone. The sun is shining, it's hot and the ice cream melts and drips a bit, and I see myself licking frantically at the ice cream. That's comfortable!'"

Subdued laughter can be heard in the room. She continues:

"Close your eyes and see if you can find that place. If you don't find any, it's okay. Just move around in your imagination and see what happens."

The room goes silent. Eyes close and heads bend in concentration, as brains and minds search for memories of safety. Lisa and Michael also close their eyes. Their breath is strained.

The therapist takes a slow, deep breath, in order to inspire the brave couple in front of her to follow her own relaxed breathing. Then, after a few minutes:

"When you are ready, meet your partners gaze."

Michael's eyes quickly move towards Lisa's. The therapist asks them both to carefully observe their body language, and she asks them to close up their bodies as much as they can. Both of them slouch and fold their arms. Michael crosses his legs.

"I must cross my legs to feel closed," he explains, surprising both Lisa and himself. The nervousness seeps out as laughter. It feels good.

"How does it feel?" asks the therapist.

"Horrible," says Lisa. "Do I look like this when I'm closed?"

"Closed and cold," her husband sighs.

"Okay, good," says the therapist. "Now, open up your body language as much as you can. Have both feet steady on the floor. Relax. Open your chest, bring out your curious gaze and look at each other with the softest eyes. Relax your arms and hands."

After a moment, she says, "See how your hands almost touch each other?"

Both look down. Michael reflexively pulls back his hand.

"Do let your hands touch," the therapist says gently. "We often do that automatically when we feel safety and closeness. So hold each other and give each other some of the oxytocin hormone that helps create contact between you. Sit like you are romantically in love.

"On the other hand," she continues," maybe that's not a good idea, because in that stage, you sit on and in each other!" The therapist now has a twinkle in her eyes.

The group laughs.

"Okay, instead, sit like best friends do. Like two friends who feel safe together and are about to experience something new and exciting together. You are going on a journey. We have no problems to solve, just an adventure to live. Hold each other if it feels natural."

Cautiously, Lisa and Michael stretch out their hands until they are touching.

"How does it feel now?"

"Wonderful," says Lisa.

"A bit more open. Friendly... and a bit too pressing," says Michael.

The therapist leans in. "Ok, now I want you to look... just *look* at each other," she says softly but urgently. "Look and see whatever is."

They stare at each other a bit stiffly, with embarrassed smiles.

"For how long have you been together?"

"Twenty one years and seven months," Lisa says.

"A long time," Michael says and turns his eyes to the therapist. With a nod, she directs him to look at his wife again, and she encourages them to keep looking, just keep gazing into each other's eyes while she speaks to them.

"Everything that you are going to do now is just between the two of you... and all the other couples in this safe room, of course!" Many in the group smile.

"Look at each other... *Wow!* You have a lot of memories together, and your brains and minds have photographed many, many of these images. Images of wonderful moments and also some difficult events, I believe. Is that right?

Lisa nods and suddenly, tears flood her eyes. It's so painful, so unbearably painful to think about what has happened.

"Yes, you carry a lot with you."

Michael turns his eyes away and hangs his head. He can't handle Lisa's despair and his own bad conscience. His jaw begins to twitch.

"Gently, stay with your eyes," says the therapist. "Stay with soft, warm eyes and let everything that you have shared and share right now, be there, in the space between you two. It is okay." Her voice is soft. "See if you can show love, respect, and humility with your eyes... respect and humility for everything that you have done and shared through the years, all that concerns only the two of you. Respect and humility for both yourself and the other, because you are so brave that you sit here right now, open to understand a bit more."

Lisa's tears keep running down her cheeks; she can't help it. She feels great warmth when she looks at her husband.

"You are brave enough to look at difficulties and visit each other in a new way," the therapist continues. "That says quite a lot about both of you, that you have enough awareness to choose, and want something *new* – no matter whether you have a future together or not."

As Lisa blinks away the tears, Michael's gaze wanders for a short moment. Then they resume looking at each other. Slowly, their bodies soften and open to each other. It's as though they have laid down their weapons. Maybe for the first time in a very long time, the therapist thinks.

She says: Soon I will teach you the dialogue, "crossing the bridge." But before we start the exercise, I want to say one very important thing. You see, I believe that we all need to recognize and focus on what actually *works* between us, and let that energy carry that which is painful. Everybody needs to be seen and appreciated. We all depend on contact, even if we work hard to avoid it sometimes."

Michael thinks of all the contact he has denied Lisa in the last few years, and especially the last six months. A lump of guilt grows in his chest. At the same time, he thinks about all the criticism he has had to take. If Lisa hadn't been so accusing, he wouldn't have had to hide.

"Stay in mindful contact," he hears the therapist softly encourage them. He focuses again on his wife's beautiful brown eyes. It's easier than he thought to sink into her gaze.

"Just look at each other and see if you can express some of all the things you appreciate in your partner, just with your eyes. Put everything else away just now, everything that hinders, is painful and destroys. Put it away for a while, and just open yourself to the things you like in your partner – right now, in this moment."

Each of them begins to smile, slowly and tentatively. The smiles grow warmer. The entire group can see that this couple carries with them a lot of fine memories, even if they've been buried deeply for a long time.

"Perfect! Now take some imaginary photographs of your partner's eyes just now, when they are warm an appreciating. Click! You can save them and keep them in your memory together with all the others."

As Lisa gazes into her husband's unusually warm eyes, she etches the images into the photo album of her memory. It feels so good! At the same time, a knife cuts through her chest as she thinks about how many times she has complained and criticised, heaping accusations and demands on Mike and making him feel insufficient. But on the other hand, if he had not been so extreme in turning off and hiding out she'd have no reason to complain. If they only could start over again...

The therapist interrupts her thoughts. "Now, in a clear voice, I want you to express appreciation for one thing in your partner, the one that feels strongest right now," she says. "But keep it totally positive! It's so easy to blend in a bit a criticism, and then it's a hard compliment to take. It is as if we think, *now that he's finally listening,* I better take the opportunity to say what I don't like, as well!"

"So you cannot say, "I appreciate that you finally did the dishes, because you never do..."

Subdued laughter in the group.

"Do you recognize yourself?"

Both Lisa and Michael nod. He thinks about all the times that he felt Lisa was criticising him. She thinks about all the times he seemed completely disconnected, his eyes full of judgment.

"Okay, are you ready? One thing that I appreciate about you right now is ..." says the therapist, like a prompter in a theatre.

Lisa looks at Michael, silently asking. Shall you or I begin? An angry little voice inside her says that after all the pain Michael has caused her, *he* should be the one to start!

Seeming to read her thoughts, Michael clears his throat and says:

"Lisa, I appreciate your energy and your enormous power and will to get on in life."

Lisa raises her eyebrows, presses her lips together and lets the air seep out in a weak "oh." Then she opens her mouth to comment on what Mikael said.

The therapist puts a hand softly on Lisa's arm.

"Wait a second, Lisa," she says. "Look at Mike and allow yourself to really take in what he says. Look at his face! Listen to his soft voice and *see* what it actually means to him that you have such energy and power."

When Lisa stops long enough to really read his expression and look back at him with a warm gaze, something happens inside Michael. He suddenly realizes how long it's been since they've really cared to see each other, to try to feel *with* each other. Very touched, he repeats in a whisper:

"Yes... I really appreciate that power."

Lisa smiles, her brown eyes glistening behind the tears. Suddenly. Michael sees her face as he remembered it--and loved it.

"Now, Lisa, you are going to take in this information in a new and special way. You will *mirror* what Michael says, in order to stay in his world – not just copy his words, but rather 'tone in' to his world, find his frequency, like when you tune a radio! It may feel strange to repeat everything that he says, but I want you to trust me, okay?"

Lisa isn't sure she understands. "I just say what he said?"

"Yes," she says. "But as you do that, also stay in his gaze and openly receive whatever he has to say. Do you remember what he said?"

Lisa nods eagerly and whispers. "So ... one thing that you appreciate with me is my energy and power to move on."

"Did I get you?" prompts the therapist, still looking at Lisa.

"Did I get you?" Lisa repeats, looking into Mike's eyes.

"Yes, you did." Michael's face gleams with satisfaction.

The therapist leans toward him and smiles.

"So *tell* her what is best for you about that energy!"

Michael ponders a moment. "The best thing is that your energy is like an engine that moves me forward, helping me to evolve. Your energy is so alive!"

Lisa listens with eyes big and shiny, like saucers. Then she mirrors:

"So my energy is alive and makes you move forward so that you evolve. But... can't I comment on this?"

"Good question," says the therapist. "No, you can't. Because what happens if you comment right now? Where would you then be on the bridge--with Michael or with yourself?"

"With me, of course," she acknowledges. "But I'm going to say something positive!" Lisa is almost jumping on her chair with eagerness.

"You want to say something positive, I can see that. But you see, it's not really a question of what you want to say. It's a question of staying in his world and just being *with* him. Bit by bit, I think that this will make sense to you, but right now it may feel a bit confusing. Is that right?"

"Well… yes, it is," Lisa admits. "But right now I should just mirror and follow him, then."

Michael peers with his green eyes and sighs with relief. The therapist turns to him and asks:

"How does it feel when you experience this living energy in Lisa that pulls you forward? Say *one* emotion, or one word."

"Prerequisite for life," says Michael, sighing again.

Lisa raises her eyebrows and mirrors in a surprised voice:

"It feels like a prerequisite for life…?"

The therapist steps in. "Michael, this feeling of a 'prerequisite for life' where in your body is it located?" she asks.

"In my *body*?" Michael frowns.

"Yes, where in your body would you say that a 'prerequisite for life' is situated?"

He ponders this for a while, and then he says hesitantly, "In my stomach…"

"In your stomach. Can you show us with your hand? It's important to include the body, because all our memories live there."

Michael slowly moves his hand towards his stomach and whispers: "The feeling of 'prerequisite for life' is in my stomach."

Lisa automatically moves her hand to her stomach as she mirrors:

"The prerequisite for life is in your stomach." Did I get you?"

"Yes, you got me."

Time moves very slowly.

"You are doing this mini-dialogue perfectly," the therapist says gently. "It feels a bit strange to start with, but you are doing it very well. It is also beautiful to see how you, Lisa, mirrored Michael's body movements. It is so important, because of what I said before about mirror neurons and resonance circuits. Now you are helping Michael to 'feel felt,' and to highlight a positive feeling associated with prerequisite for life.

"Okay, Lisa, now it's your turn. Say what you appreciate most about Michael right now."

Lisa quickly says: "I appreciate that you are here, and that you came along on this weekend workshop even though you didn't really want to."

Michael flushes with embarrassment. Taking a deep breath, he mirrors: "So you appreciate that I'm here, although I didn't want to go to this workshop. Is that so?"

"Yes, it makes me feel that you care, that I--we and our family--mean something to you. That we are important."

"So… when I come along for such a weekend, it feels like you and the family means something to me. That you are important."

"And check with her: Did I get you?" the therapist prompts.

"Did I get you, Lisa?"

Lisa nods energetically and continues with glistening eyes:

"Yes, it feels like I exist then!"

Now the therapist asks Michael to stop and just look. Look and look and really take in Lisa and the warmth and joy she expresses with her body and words.

"Look, Michael--this is the way this woman looks and sounds when you come with her and show her interest. When she feels that she exists."

Michael halts and looks at Lisa with apparent curiosity and sympathy, seeming to really take her in. Lisa begins to weep.

"Just look at her tears, just visit Lisa's world and see the wave of sorrow that bubbles within her," the therapist says. "Wait until the wave has calmed down."

Michael looks at Lisa's tears, takes them in, and keeps looking at her. His chest tightens, and for the first time in a very long while he feels the impulse to stretch out his hand and stroke her cheek. To his surprise, he feels touched by her pain.

When the flow of tears ebbs, the therapist says, "Lisa, tell Michael how it feels when you experience the feeling of existing – existing for him. Say it in one word."

"Warmth," whispers Lisa.

"So, where in your body do you feel warmth?"

Lisa slowly puts her hand on her heart.

"So ... it feels... warm," says Michael slowly. He is having difficulty keeping his voice steady. His hand moves to his own heart.

Everything in the room stops. It is as if all the time in world could fit into this moment. Lisa and Michael continue to gaze into each other's eyes, and Lisa feels as though the entire group is breathing at a common calm pace, like the sea.

The therapist quietly moves her chair back and whispers to them:

"Just take each other in. Take in whatever is in the space between you right now. Take your time."

It is quite a long but pleasant time.

"Soon one of you will take an exciting trip again," the therapist says. "One of you will get the chance to cross the bridge to the other's world. Which one of you usually talks, want to sort things out, maybe comes running after the other?"

"Well, that's me, of course," Lisa says.

"Good. It might be wise to try something new today, since I'm here for support," the therapist says.

Michael sighs with relief. Maybe he can avoid the disaster of having her criticising him in public.

"Is that okay with you, Michael?"

"Of course, I don't know what I'm going to talk about... but sure, it's okay."

"Is it okay for you, Lisa? That you visit Michael to see who he is today at 3:05 pm?"

Lisa nods enthusiastically.

The therapist prepares Michael. She tells him how important it is to put away--as well as he can--his fears and previous experiences and "truths" about what will happen when he tries to communicate with Lisa. Here and now, Lisa will get the opportunity to understand more about how he works, and how his brain is really wired. In order for her to be able to see and understand him, he must open the door and let her in.

"Lisa can build a thousand bridges, but if you don't open the door, nothing will happen," she says. "Today, both of you are supposed to learn something new. You are going to see how the 'tracks' in Michael's brain and mind have been created through years of experience. You will get an insight into how the neural pathways actually live their own lives and can mess things up between you as a couple. Because, as we already know, 'neurons that fire together wire together and survive together!'"

Michael doesn't understand everything that the therapist is saying, but he has confidence in her competence and for the first time in a long while, he feels a flicker of hope. He knows how it is to fail during a conversation with Lisa. She usually nags, yells sometimes, criticises – and then she gets sad and starts to cry. When she does all of this, he feels terrible. He can't bear to listen, so he does what he has to--turns her off or leaves the room.

Now, he muses, it will be interesting to see if Lisa can listen to him. But how great are the chances of that, really? Despair wells up inside of him again.

"Okay, how do I do this?" he asks with a sigh.

"You sigh, Michael," says the therapist. "Now, let's see if you can become a little curious about what your sigh stands for – and at the same time, choose to put it away for now. Just open up as much as you can, so that Lisa has a chance to step in and visit. I'm here to support you both. Take your time and go to your safe place, and when you are ready and as open as you can be–in this moment--tell your wife that you are ready to let her in."

Now, the therapist turns to Lisa. "While Michael is preparing himself, see if you can let go of everything that has to do with yourself. Instead, go to *your* safe place and muster all of your curiosity, love, presence and interest in getting to know your husband. A man that you have thousands of pictures of inside your brain. Many of them are good to have with you. But you also have images that are disturbing and get in the way of seeing something new. There is also the risk that you feel that you *know* how he is and always will be. Is that correct?"

"Yes," Lisa nodded. "I know that since he usually…"

The therapist interrupts her softly. "Lisa. I hear that you know, but I want to teach you that it is up to you to decide to be *curious*. To be curious about your husband. Curious about understanding how it is to be him. Enthusiastic about stepping into his head! Curious about how it feels to be one of those who shaves his face."

Now Lisa begins to laugh. "Well, that I don't need to do that, not yet. at least."

The entire group laughs with her.

"Okay, perfect, now you understand," the therapist says. "It's about realizing that you are not him and he is not you. You shall only visit him, find his frequency, tune in and see who he is today. Exciting, isn't it?"

"Yes, now I'm beginning to feel curious!" Lisa says and playfully rubs her hands.

"Very good, keep that feeling. This can be very difficult, to actually leave the focus on yourself and what happens in you, and just be curious about someone else. When you fall in love its quite easy, but then…"

Lisa looks intently at Michael with wide brown eyes. She really does want to listen.

"Now Lisa, when you feel enthusiasm and curiosity, you are automatically in the part of your brain called the prefrontal cortex. That's the area we must have access to when we visit, to be able to understand someone else's view of the world."

Michael is quite amused. He suddenly feels calm. Lisa's positive energy and loving eyes are contagious – as usual.

"Tell your wife when you are ready to let her in to your world, where you have your own DNA, your own taste, your own pace…"

"Okay… welcome to my land," Michael whispers.

"Thank you," Lisa says. "I'm on my way over the bridge to you...,"
She closes her eyes. A few moments later, she says,

"Now I'm here."

To Michael's big surprise, his eyes fill with tears. He is deeply touched by the feeling that Lisa is with him now, in his world. It has been ages since he felt that Lisa was actually interested in *him*, who he really is, what he thinks and feels. She has only been so disappointed, dissatisfied, angry, and sad. As tears helplessly run down his cheeks, he understands how much he missed this contact.

"Welcome in," he says in a voice full of hope.

All actual life is encounter

MARTIN BUBER, I AND THOU, 1923

11

Welcome to My Brain – Here You Can Reach my Heart

On the Grey-Pink Surface of the Moon

We will return to Michael and Lisa, but first we'll revisit our amazing mind and brain.

In order to more easily visit each other and take in each other's reality, we need clear structures to help us. We need structures that allow the brain to relax and signal that it is safe although it may *feel* unsafe sometimes. It also helps us see that we are distinct individuals and that our truths can be completely different. That's why we only *visit* when we listen to someone else.

When we calm down our nervous system with this structure, we don't end up in a defensive situation, in the bottom of our own crater where we can't see anything except its walls. Down there, we move around each other like fighters in the ring and defend ourselves as best we can.

Some of us aim external energy towards our partner. For others, the energy is turned inwards and we try to move away from the partner and turn off. If it is too difficult to be together, we may seek happiness elsewhere with someone who can make us feel alive again for the moment. Many of us are drawn into the rush of falling in love, only to find ourselves back in battle gear, once the "love drugs" wear off.

If you can easily see images, imagine a grey-pink mass of brain tissue up in your head. Now, imagine that the grey looks like the surface of the moon. There is flat land but also deep craters. Some paths are barely visible, but if you look closely, perhaps you can see a row of lonely footsteps. Some of the paths have been used so often that they are again like deep craters or ravines that you might slip down into. Maybe they have become at safe place to hide; a place that you may not like, but that you recognize. Maybe you've tried to become more comfortable there by installing cosy lights and expensive carpets.

Now, imagine a colourful ladder leaned against the wall of the crater. It's wide and steady. Using the ladder, you can climb to the top and into your adult, conscious, friendly life, any time you want or need to. What luck! Once you are up there, you have an overview. Now you can easily visit yourself or someone else, or you can invite a visitor to look in and see how you are wired. You and your partner can safely explore the grey mass, in the process discovering how everything – your life experiences as well as other people's minds and brains – formed your brain. No matter how difficult your earlier life looks, you can invite your partner into this conscious space to recreate a safe attachment, a deep contact and integration between two persons. Daniel Stern describes this experience as "a special kind of mental contact – namely, an intersubjective contact. This involves the mutual interpenetration of minds that permits us to say, *"I know that you know that I know"* or *"I feel that you feel that I feel"*. There is a reading of the contents of the other's mind" [40]

In order to experience a real shift within, another person must often be present. We need "limbic resonance," which arises from the emotional part of the brain. If we don't experience this resonance, we can understand a lot of things rationally and theoretically, but nothing new happens. We can't seem to change our behaviour. The dialogue of "crossing the bridge" can help us to achieve limbic resonance and therefore, real change.

Mirroring

The structure of the dialogue begins with "mirroring." In this context, to "mirror" means to follow the other person and be tuned in to the language, expressions, body movements and tempo of this person. It means to be mindful--to just listen and receive, and then mirror back every word your partner says, along with any shifts in body language. We do this very slowly and with great curiosity and presence. When we mirror, we help ourselves to differentiate and see that I am not You and You are not Me.

You may think that it sounds a bit parrot-like to repeat every word your partner says. And it can be – if we mirror without emotion and empathic presence. But if we mirror with an open heart, it can be a powerful experience for both the speaker and the listener.

If you choose to try this, I suggest that you focus *all of your attention* on the other person. That means following with great curiosity not

---

40 Daniel Stern, *The Present Moment; In Psychotherapy and Everyday Life,* page 75

only the words, but also the details of the face, expression, eyes, voice, posture and gestures. When you mirror what you hear, be sure that you do so accurately, so that the speaker feels truly heard. After you mirror the speaker's words, ask: "Did I get you?"

Another powerful aspect of mirroring is that it helps you to differentiate – and thus experience what it is like to be someone else. You can do this by keeping all of your focus on the other person, in spite of the fact that difficult feelings are gnawing at you, too. When your attention is focused on the other person, you may start to feel in your own body what you think your partner feels in his or her body. You begin to access your empathy.

A prerequisite for really understanding another person's internal world is that you share feelings. As you now know, our mirror neurons and resonance circuits make empathy possible--the ability to feel pain when someone else feels pain. The more attentive we are, the better we will understand and feel another person's inner condition. [41] What I call attunement is a kind of attention that goes deeper than occasional empathy; it's a presence that doesn't yield or fade. We listen fully, with every fibre. We do everything we can to understand this other person, instead of arguing from our own perspective. To achieve this attunement, we need to listen to more than words. We need to mirror the words, of course, but mirroring is merely the structure that allows us to follow and be in harmony with the other person's body language, gaze, tone of voice and everything else that belongs to the right half of the brain. We accept and rest in what IS right now, in the present moment.

As we do this, we "take in" both explicit memories (factual and autobiographical), but also implicit memories (those that are seen in our emotions, senses, perception and body impulses). If we don't understand how important this is, the dialogue may simply be a way to talk, talk and talk some more, which may lead to *no contact at all*, in spite of

---

41 Marco Iacoboni, *Mirroring people; The Science of Empathy and How we Connect with Others*, page 119, 123, 126, and Daniel Goleman, *Social Intelligence; The New Science of Human Relationships*, page 57

our effort and good intentions. Mirroring then becomes a way to mimic the other or simply repeat the words without any feeling.

But when we become really attuned to each other, magical things happen. Often we reach each other's heart.

The ability to perceive what goes on in another person is one of our most valuable human abilities. Scientists usually call it "the theory of mind," and it refers to our ability to see into the mind of others, experience their emotions and intuit their thinking. Daniel Siegel and others use the expression "to feel felt," which means that I feel that you feel that I feel! Without this capacity for empathy, our relations are hollow. We would relate to others as if they were objects without emotions and thoughts.

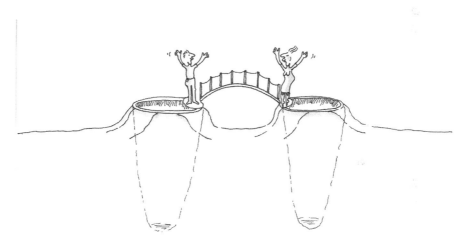

Validation

Everything makes sense once we *understand* it. When we dare to listen long enough with presence and curiosity, another person's story and behaviour become understandable. We can suddenly feel how it is to be the other person, and understand why our fellow humans behave as they do. We can also more easily understand ourselves and why we feel and behave the way we do. We become understandable to ourselves.

I heard a story about a man who was on a tram with four rowdy kids. There were a lot of people on the tram and it was hot. The man sat motionless, staring dejected through the window. His four kids screamed, yelled and ran around. The passengers around them muttered in irritation: "How can he let his kids make such a noise in a public place?" "Unbelievable." "No upbringing." "A good spanking wouldn't hurt"…

The noise grew louder and louder, but the father didn't seem to hear. Finally one woman couldn't take it anymore. She rose out of her seat and stepped up to the father. "Now you have to take care of you kids!" she snapped. "They are making a heck of a lot of noise and we want some peace and quiet!"

The man looked up with an empty and despairing gaze. "Oh, I'm sorry," he whispered faintly. "My wife just died and I am on my way.. home and I don't know what to do… the kids they…" The words died on his lips. Tears welled in his eyes. In a fraction of a second, the woman's emotions changed.

"Oh no, poor you," she gasped. The other passengers sitting close by overheard the exchange, and began to gaze compassionately at the father. A young man moved from his place and sat beside the four- year-old who had just lost his mother.

"Hi there," said the young man. "Do you know how fast this tram can go?"

Something had happened on that tram. The pervasive sense of irritation was gone and the air was filled with warmth, concern, and empathy. So quickly our emotions can change when we suddenly understand the behaviour of another person. When we understand the story behind the actions, compassion flowers.

We all have a background, a history within us that we need to tell, both for others to understand us and so that we can understand ourselves. We also need to tell our stories because the story *itself* helps to integrate different parts of the brain. We can create a kind of meditative flow in the moment, together with another person. We can heal both the other and ourselves.

Forty thousand years ago, man told his story in cave paintings. To tell a story is a natural and significant way to let the brain review things that have happened, make them understandable and thus create an internal balance. Then we can put a heart around ourselves and start to look with empathy at our defences and how they have come between us and our close ones. We can choose to put away fear, hostility and anger, and instead be curious, clear, present and aware.

Even if our stories are made up of words and the left half of the brain, the right half must also be active in order for the story to be comprehensible. The deep understanding comes when both halves of the brain are involved. Otherwise it's just words--words without any connection with the heart and the body. This also explains why it is healing to write down your emotions. To a certain degree, this is because our story can help us make sense to ourselves. But writing is also healing because the process integrates the left and the right domain of the brain.

I got the chance to experience how my wonderful mother--after four heart attacks and a heart transplant with numerous complications and crises--healed and revised her experience by writing. This resulted in *Waiting For Someone to Die* (available only in Swedish), a book that many people experience as powerful and moving. She made her horrible experiences understandable to herself. The emotional, writing helped her come back to life and joy. [42]

Maybe you have written down your story, or some part of it, and thereby helped yourself to heal and integrate? Whether you're writing gets published or stays in your journal, the process is healing. Everybody has a story that needs to be heard – by others but also by ourselves.

---

42 Carin Ritzen-Sick, Swedish book; *I väntan på att någon ska dö*, Brombergs,2005

Empathy

Now that we have heard what our partner has said and understood his or her story, empathy follows naturally. Consider the man on the tram; as soon as the other passengers realized his grief, despair and desperation, their compassion was aroused. They could feel what he felt in themselves. So even though his behaviour did not change (he did not quiet his children) everything in the space between people on that tram had changed – in the moment of understanding.

Let's return to wisdom of the philosopher Martin Buber. When we are not in contact but just throw the words or defences between us, he calls that encounter "when an I meets a That." What signifies the "I-That" interaction, according to Buber, is that one person lacks sensitivity to the other person's subjective reality and doesn't feel any empathy for that person. Buber created the "I-That" expression for an entire spectrum of relations that ranges from unengaged to exploitative. In this kind of relationship, the other part is more of an object than a person. Daniel Goleman says: "That egocentric mode contrasts with "communion", a state of high mutual empathy where your feelings do more than matter to me-they change me. While we are in communion, we stay in synch, meshed in mutual feedback loop. But during moments of agency, we disconnect." [43] This is very important, since we can spend many hours (even years) in an I-That-interaction that doesn't lead to contact and empathy. It's not until we let go of the focus on ourselves and are in *limbic resonance* that we can step into another person's reality.

You have surely experienced the view of your pain or joy reflected in someone else's eyes mind and body; and probably you have experienced someone else's pain or joy in your mind and body. When we are right there, *in contact* – as most often when we are romantically in love – then it feels right. What is it that feels right in this communication? Well:

The *first* ingredient is total attention, especially with the eyes.

---

43 Daniel Goleman, *Social Intelligence; The new science of human relationships*, page 106

The *second* ingredient is tone of voice and facial expression. The nonverbal messages can be more important than the words we use.

The third ingredient is coordination, tempo and timing in the interaction – and our body language.

Having worked with more than six hundred couples, I'm convinced that these three elements are the most important in an effective dialogue. They are a prerequisite for achieving contact and intimacy. When couples have a dialogue that is filled with words but lacks eye contact, there is often very little limbic resonance. We are not touched in the same way. Matching posture is an example of an important element for deep contact. It doesn't work if the listener is sitting with folded arms, busy with his or her own defence. An open body language and a loving, strong gaze open a link to resonance and understanding. Then we can identify with each other, deeply connect, and unconsciously respond to our partner with the same sympathy as we give ourselves.

Compared to the I-That interaction, the I-You interaction that Martin Buber wrote about is a *ramifying relationship.* In it, we experience the other person as separate from all else, unique and more important. These deep encounters are the moments we remember best in our close relationships--indeed, in our lives. As Buber wrote: "All true life is encounters."

If you want to learn more about empathy, I recommend the book *The Social Neuroscience of Empathy* by Jean Decety and William Ickes.

Talk is Not Enough

The world looks a bit different depending on whether you "see" life more from the right or the left domain of the brain. Again, it's especially important to understand this when we are in dialogue with someone else.

Let's simplify and look at the left and the right domain like this: *The left part of the brain* has characteristics that start with an L, including:

Linear – mathematic, structured, calculating

Logic – analytic; cause and effect, "Why?"

Linguistic – spoken and written

Literal – concrete, sequential (one thing at the time)

The right part of the brain represents the holistic. It interprets images, symbols, facial expressions and sees what IS in the present moment – it doesn't analyse! Other right-brain abilities we may not be aware of are intuition, creativity, sensitivity, sense of locale, sense of shape, musicality, and the autobiographical memory. The right side represents a non-verbal language where body, voice and gestures carry the meaning. Communicating with facial expressions, eyes, tone of voice, posture, gestures and emotional "timing" are performed by the right side of the big brain.

Dividing the brain halves and their abilities isn't quite that simple, of course. They depend on each other, interact, and ideally area integrated. Still, we can say that the two parts have different functions and "see" the world quite differently. The description is naturally simplified so that we can more easily understand our behaviour. I bring this up mainly to show that when we meet in a dialogue, we need to give both the left and the right side scope to let integration and new knowledge arise between us.

The right half is of the brain very important in our roles as parents, partners and friends. It is necessary for our ability to be attuned, "fade in" (fade into another person's world.) and feel. Unfortunately, our culture often favours and praises the left half of the brain at the cost of the right one. We can find plenty of examples of this in school and at work. We very seldom learn to ponder what happens inside of us.

The differences between the brain halves are especially important to understand for parents. A small child sends out signals from the right brain with eye contact, facial expressions and tone of voice, a nonverbal communication. In order for us adults to understand these signals, our right bran must be active. As the child develops and get more access to the left brain, the parents need to help the child develop a language and thus integrate body, word and emotions. The child will not automatically learn to regulate his or her feelings, know who he/she is, make contact with other people and show empathic ability – if there isn't a mirror image of these abilities. [44]

Almost every day in my line of work, I see that a lot of people think that communication is all about talking – sorting out problems, negotiating and understand each other with words and more words. A lot of people call this "communication." Unfortunately, I see far too many couples get stuck in talking things to pieces.

In the West, we often get stuck in the left domain of the brain and forget to focus on the right. But there are also many of us who live mostly from the right domain, where we also can get stuck. For a right-brain person, "communication" can become a constant flow of tears, pain, sadness, hopelessness and implicit memories, and there is nowhere for the left, logical (and somewhat happier) half to fit in.

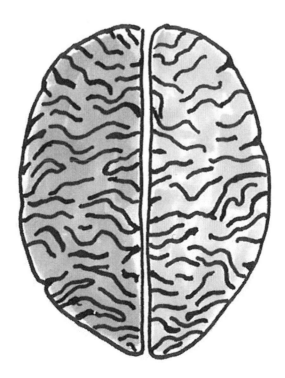

---

44 Daniel J. Siegel and Mary Hartzell, *Parenting from the inside out*, DVD.

When we as partners try to solve a problem – whether it is in the kitchen or with a therapist of some kind – the integration between the brain-halves has significant importance.

In their book, *How To Improve Your Marriage Without Talking About It,* Pat Love and Steven Stosny describes how important it is to understand that words *can* make things much worse. Generally speaking, you can say that a woman who experience problems calms down by talking about the problem. She then produces the attachment hormone oxytocin. A man, on the other hand, usually produces cortisol, a stress hormone that help the body prepare for danger. This is often because the man experiences some obscure responsibility to "solve" the problem in question, and thus he can feel criticised. The result can be that he turns off and the woman feels abandoned. It's important to understand that the phrase "Darling, we need to talk about this" can mean completely different things for different individuals.

I don't mean to generalize and say that men are like this and women are like that; we are all unique individuals. It only means that we can notice with curiosity how *different* things affect us. Some men produce oxytocin and feel close and loved when they talk and share feelings. Some women pull back and find talk about problems to be difficult and stressful. But in a relationship it is usually one partner who wants to feel contact by talking, understanding and reconciling. The other usually wants to establish contact another way, for instance through hugging or sex. Maybe each has something important to offer to the other. Sometimes we get the mistaken impression that we need the same thing and that there is a RIGHT way and a WRONG way.

So, how much does talking help you and your partner? Does it take you where you want to go? When you talk, do you then talk with the left domain of the brain and let the words bounce between you as if in a game of tennis and you have to win or at least get as many set points as possible? Is it just words without any deeper meeting? Or do you get stuck in strong, raw emotions that no words can help to calm down?

There is a wonderful saying: *Name it to tame it – but never explain it*. When we name it, we activate the left domain, but if we explain it, we get stuck. To me, this was very important, a real *aha* experience, both as therapist, partner and parent. For a long time, my brain was "leaning left" and I wanted to talk all the time--talk and analyze and talk and find logical solutions. I talked my relationship with my husband, friends, and children practically to pieces. But I can also thank my left brain for taking me on a treasure hunt to find a better way.

With the importance of left and right brain abilities in mind, let's now return to the workshop, where Lisa is just about to cross the bridge to Michael's brain.

Michael and Lisa

Lisa Steps Onto the Bridge

"Welcome in," says Michael, his voice filled with hope.

"Thank you," Lisa says. She leans forward curiously, and her hands rest softly in her lap. They sit very close, which makes eye contact easier.

"So, now as I sit looking into your eyes and you are here with me, Lisa, I feel…", prompts the therapist.

Michael says quietly: "Now that you are here with me, Lisa, I feel… warmth. I'm glad that you want to come to me… and…" His voice wobbles and his left hand is in a tight fist. "I don't quite know why my tears came," he said with a shivering voice.

Lisa looks at him with open surprise, touched by his tears. Michael almost never cries – he simply isn't one who cries. In recent years she has just seen a closed man, and when she now sees his tears she gets a bit edgy. At the same time, it lights a bowl of hope in her.

"So when you are with me, you feel warmth?" she says, expectation rising in her chest. "Please tell me more."

It's totally silent in the room. Fifteen couples and a therapist breathlessly follow their words and mirroring. Lisa's and Michael's eyes rest in each other.

The therapist whispers to Michael:

"What I *think* my tears are all about is…"

"What I think my tears are about is that I seldom feel heard," Michael says. He clears his throat and continues with emphasis: "During all the years that we have been married, I have almost never felt that you are strong enough to be able to listen to me."

Lisa sighs aloud and snaps like a reptile: "No, and that's not so strange! You never say any…"

The therapist stops her with a hand on her arm and says:

"Lisa, I can see that you feel hurt and that you directly reacted to what Michael said. Where are you, then? In his world or yours?"

"In my world," Lisa snaps angrily with tear-filled eyes. The therapist turns to her and says with a soft but firm voice: "I understand that you react when you are in your world. There is a lot of pain between you two that hurts. Do you feel that things are working between you and Michael?"

"No, you can't say that. He wants to leave me!" Lisa spits the words out as if they were poisonous.

"So he wants to leave you. If I got you, you are here because you want to experience something new. Is that true?"

"Yes… if it's possible," Lisa sighs.

"Yes, I'm convinced that it is possible. But it is important to realize that in order for something new to happen, you must be prepared to do something new--both of you. It can be difficult, most likely it is, but it can actually lead to understanding each other in a totally new way. That was why you dragged your husband here, wasn't it?"

Lisa nods. Michael looks at his hands.

"Lisa, I want you to once again build a little bridge in your imagination." The therapist makes an arc between them with her hand. "I want you to pull yourself together, regulate and calm yourself so that you can leave Lisa-land and cross the bridge to Michael's country again. This means that for now, you have to put your own pain, fear, sorrow, anger or whatever it is that you feel, aside.

"Then you will slowly but steadily cross the bridge again. If it feels better, you can row or swim or pole jump – if it is comfortable, find a playful way to get back over to him and his heart again. You are an explorer! Maybe you can see how you wade around in red rubber boots in Michael's grey mass and witness a natural phenomenon for the first time – namely, how his unique neurons fire away. Use your imagination!"

The corners of Lisa's mouth twitch.

"Maybe you can with a sense of humour say: 'Whoops, I went back to my own land. I'll soon be back to you again.'"

Lisa gave the therapist a fiery but humorous look, wobbled her head and said playfully in a theatrical voice:

"Whoops, whoops! Mike, I stepped back into my land… but wait a minute and I'll be back on your side of the bridge again."

Michael looks up and meets Lisa's eyes. They have contact again. While they gaze at each other, the therapist says to them and indirectly to the entire group:

"It's not so strange that we fall back to ourselves sometimes; it happens all the time. The thing is that we need to cheek where we are when we communicate. Are we with the other one or are we with ourselves? Where are we on the bridge? It's good to have some distance from yourself and say: 'Darn! Whoops! Sorry, I seem to be back with myself now.' Your partner will feel that anyway. In a fraction of a second, we know if we have a receiver or not. But it becomes very *safe* when we dare to say what you just said, Lisa: 'Whoops, I stepped into my land, but I'll soon get back to you.'"

The therapist pauses to let this sink in. Lisa looks at her with big, shiny eyes. A second ago she felt offended, reproved, like a small child, but now she really starts to understand. *Safe*. That is how she wants it. Safe is the keyword here, she thinks, as the therapist says:

"It becomes safe, because then Michael can really know when you are with him, 'tuned in' to his frequency, and when you get stuck in yourself and your own reactions. Most of us know only too well how it feels to communicate when there is no receiver."

"Well, yes! But it would never have worked If you didn't help me," Lisa says, now in a much happier voice. The therapist nods.

"Just as you say, it's difficult to keep such a dialogue without a therapist present, at least to start with. Some can do it, others can't. If it's hard to get over the bridge, we can always say, 'Sorry, this isn't working, we have to take a pause, calm down and then I'll try to cross the bridge again.' If it feels impossible, you can work with the aid of a therapist. And now you have me here. You are doing great. Welcome back Lisa." She smiles.

Lisa nods pensively. She feels much calmer now. Sure, she was back in her land for a while, but now she wants to go back to Mike's land.

"Lisa, look at Michael, see what happens to him--right now–when you have all this courage to be a grown up and to take responsibility for where you are on the bridge. Look!"

Lisa looks at her husband. Her chest fills with curiosity and warmth again.

The therapist continues; "Okay... when you are ready, tell Mike: 'Now I'm back with you.'"

Lisa breathes deeply from her stomach, looks steadily at her husband and says in a firm voice.

"Now I'm back with you again."

"Welcome back," Michael whispers.

"Do you remember where we were, Lisa?" asks the therapist.

"Hmm... it was something about how he can't talk to me."

"Tell him."

"So... what you said was that you can't talk to me," Lisa says to Michael.

"Did I get you?" prompts the therapist.

"Did I get you, Mike?"

"Oh, yes. You got me all right!" A moment ago, Michael felt in high spirits by being listened to, but Lisa's outburst made him pull back into his shell again. He nods suspiciously. "You react so violently, like just now," he says with a deep sigh.

"Breathe... take in what he says... and mirror," says the therapist.

Lisa's eyebrows are lifted high and she leans eagerly forward.

"Okay, you think that I react violently, like just now."

"Yes."

"Tell me more," the therapist softly prompts.

"Tell me more!" Lisa notices that this time, she really means it. She really wants to know how this man that she has lived with for so many years' works.

"Well... every time I try to say something important about how I feel, there is real hullabaloo. It always ends with you crying and me being the big asshole," he mutters.

"Breathe, Lisa, breathe and stay with him. You are doing fine."

"So when you want to talk about something you feel is important, I cry. Have I understood this right?"

"Say 'did I get you?' or 'did I hear you?' – so that we don't get stuck in 'right or wrong,'" whispers the therapist.

"Did I hear you?"

"Yes, you heard me," Michael says, nodding. "I'm glad that we are here... and have help, because then you might listen."

"You are glad that we are here and have help, because then I might listen?" She is quiet for a short while then she says: "I'm here now Mike. I'm listening. Tell me more."

Michael's gaze leaves Lisa for a couple of seconds and moves around the room as he searches for words.

"You... always gets so sad, and it always feels like I have hurt you. And that feels like shit."

The therapist quietly move her hand to her chest, and with that gesture she shows that Lisa need to find a place close to her heart; a place where she can place the words that her husband just uttered.

"Listen to what he says, Lisa. Don't defend yourself, don't analyse, just take in his body language, all of him, his words, his voice. Put them close to your heart where it is warm, and see if you can be open, open and *curious* as to how this happened. Look at his face... look at his mouth, his chin, look at him with love, Lisa."

She looks and looks, sees her husband's chin with the dark stubble, the cheek that twitches a bit, the eyelids that blink nervously... and the eyes filled with tears. Both his hands are clutched in tight fists like a cramp.

Filled up with tenderness, she starts to mirror:

"During all the years that we have been married, you seldom felt that I listened to you. Did I get you?"

"Yes. I didn't know if you were strong enough to listen," whispers Michael.

"So you haven't known if I was strong enough to listen to you and what you feel. Did I hear you right? Eh, I mean: did I hear you?"

"Good, you're doing fine Lisa. Because there is no right or wrong here," whispers the therapist.

"Have I heard *you, you, you*?" asks Lisa and looks attentively at her husband.

Now Michael nods vigorously.

"Yes, you got me."

"Tell me more!" Lisa surprises herself because her invitation comes automatically and in a strong voice. She really wants to know more. She doesn't feel afraid now.

"Like I said, it feels like you don't have strength enough to listen to me. Every time I have tried, it ends with you crying... and then it's better for me to be silent."

Michael throws a quick glance at the therapist to make sure she really is there to take care of Lisa if she should snap again, get angry or cry. She gives him a calm look back and says to Lisa in a clear voice:

"If it feels alright for you, Lisa, you can tell Michael that you can handle anything now. That you are here for him, with him."

Lisa nods and moves a bit closer to her husband.

"I'm here for you Mike. I'm strong, and can listen to *you*. Tell me more!"

Inside Michael's chest grows an unfamiliar, warm feeling, a perception he almost forgot, it was so long since he experienced it. The words get stuck in his throat. He looks at his wife's warm, compassionate eyes, feels her strong will and suddenly thinks: I really like this woman very much. It's silent and it feels warm and safe between them, in spite of all the misery the have been carrying. He is amazed.

The therapist leads Michael on: "The worst thing for me when you are sad and angry is…"

"The worst thing for me then… is that… I get… so *angry!*" Michael's words come out jerkily. "I feel… a horrible anger that I don't understand… and… I feel such an enormous guilt…" He can't continue, but presses his jaw together; he turns his head to the side and looks down into the floor. As the tears sting his eyelids once again, he is so ashamed.

"It is okay," says the therapist in a very soft voice. "Stay with the feeling. And Lisa, look at your husband with loving eyes. Look at his face, his tight jaw, the anger, the shame… and everything that is within him, look with respect at that which *is now.*"

Lisa watches Michael's red face that works so frenetically to stay in control. Much to her surprise, she has moved still closer to him. Usually she backs off when he looks this angry.

"Tell me more, it's okay," she says.

"Tell Lisa what lies behind your anger," encourages the therapist. "Notice what your body wants to tell you."

Lisa can see that Michael is absent; he looks at her but his eyes are glassy.

"The worst thing for me when you are sad and weak is that I can't help you. It feels like you *break into pieces* because of me… that I'm mainly in the way, and that your misfortune is my fault… I feel insignificant, worthless, wrong and helpless, completely helpless!" The words nearly explode out of his mouth.

"You are in the way and feel…", Lisa starts to mirror.

"Yes! It's like you are going to break and everything I do is wrong. I'm simply not sufficient!" His voice is coarse with desperation and suppressed despair.

"Look at your husband… keep your heart open and really take in what he says, the therapist urges Lisa. "Look at his body language and all the pain that you see there, hands, face… take in the gravity in what he says,"

Michael starts to cry. He sobs piteously, hiccupping like a small child.

Time stands still.

Lisa hasn't seen her husband cry since their first child was born, and then it was tears of joy and emotion. It's frightening, but yet in some strange way it's moving to see him lose his armour completely. She breathes deeply, stretches forward carefully and touches the back of his hand with her thumb.

Michael's tears and snot flow; his chest pulls together and he stutters out small helpless, whining sounds. Can he really handle this? He cries so hard that Lisa looks anxiously at the therapist for support. She looks completely calm.

"Michael… when possible, stay in eye contact with Lisa for a while, then you won't have to be so lonely in your sadness."

Michael raises his eyes, meets Lisa's, and they share this moment of deep sadness in a truly painful and humble meeting.

"Just look at him Lisa, just follow him in the wave of sadness, and just wait there a little while."

After a while, the tears ebb out in small sobs and in time Michael can breathe normally again. Lisa's loving gaze has calmed down and regulated his nervous system, and there is a respectful silence between them. Her thumb still caresses his hand, and it feels good. A calm that he hasn't felt for a long time spreads through his body.

The therapist whispers to Lisa: "Ask him what he would wish from you if he could do magic."

Lisa smiles in the midst of the almost sacred moment.

"Okay. If you could do magic, Mike, what would you want from me?"

"I would want you to always be happy!" he exclaims with great energy before he gets a chance to think, and then he laughs at his own eagerness.

The couples around them laugh quietly, too. The sadness in the room has shifted to joy in a flash.

"So you would want me to always be happy," Lisa says, giggling.

"YES! If I could do magic I would make you always happy."

"Lisa, hurry to take some imaginary photographs of him," smiles the therapist. "He is so happy, because he can do magic. Take ten pictures, take thirty-six, take a hundred! Freeze this moment so that you can remember how *well* he would feel if you were happy." The therapist continues turned to Michael:

"Tell Lisa: if you were happy all the time, then I would feel..."

"If you were happy all the time, then I would be able to relax and enjoy life!" comes bubbling from Michael. He feels relieved, light, as if he lost tons of ballast from the top of his head.

"If you... no, if *I* was happy all the time, then you would be able to relax and enjoy life," Lisa mirrors.

"Yes, exactly," Michael replies instantly, brimming with newfound lightness and smiles.

The therapist also smiles, but then she asks: "Where does this sadness come from, Michael? When did you really need joy around you? When did you experience that made you feel that you couldn't say what was inside you?"

Michael stares at the therapist. With wide-open eyes and a startled voice, he says: "Oh! I felt that way since my sister died as a child." The tears well up again, but this time Michael receives them without shame; strangely enough, he feels calm about his own grief, although it hurts terribly. "When my sister died, my happy mother died, too."

You could hear a pin drop in the room. Everyone holds their breath, some with pain shining in their eyes, others with tears running freely down their cheeks. Michael and Lisa look into each other's eyes and share this deep insight that just landed in the space between them.

"Now Lisa, can you create a nice little room close to your heart for Michael's story? It is a place where you can keep the memory of the little kid in him who tragically lost both his sister and his happy mother. It will be a place filled of empathy that helps you understand your husband better."

Lisa nods, her eyes filled with tears. She looks at him with a gaze filled with tenderness. The therapist continues:

"Put all that you have heard him say in that safe, warm place close to your heart and keep it there. Now we are going to make a journey in time and step into an album from that time when Michael was a small boy. She turns to Michael. "Is it alright that Lisa goes for a visit in your story? So that she more easily can understand what you experienced as a small boy?"

Michael nods. In his mind, he is already there.

"Would it feel better if we symbolically brought your mother here for a short while? Would you like Lisa to *act* as her, and then you as a small boy can talk directly to your mother? Or would you rather talk about her?"

"Eeh… I think I'd rather talk about her," Michael says, perplexed.

"Okay, you want to talk about her. Let's now step into the album and visit the time when… how old were you when this grief befell you, Michael?"

Michael looks motionless into Lisa's eyes and says in a hollow voice: I was eight when Carina died."

"You were eight when your sister died," mirrors the therapist.

Michael bursts into tears.

"Look at him and just take him in… you are just visiting Michael, his tears, his story." She prompts Lisa: "Ask him what was best about having his mother for a mother."

"What was best for you about having your mother as a mother?"

"That she was so loving to everyone," he whispers barely audibly.

"She was so loving to everyone," Lisa repeats. "Tell me more!"

She sees that Michael's cheeks are wet with tears and that his beloved face is sagging with emotion.

"Yes, she was happy before Carina died... there are such wonderful pictures of her when she is happy..."

Lisa mirrors and then the slow and tentative communication between them continues with great presence. At times, the therapist asks Lisa to lower the tempo and just look at her husband. To listen to the words but also register everything else: tone of voice, sounds, gestures, posture. Michael cries again.

"When Carina died I was the one who was supposed to comfort Mom," he sobs, "I was supposed to be all that Carina had been ... too. My brother was already a teenager and on his way out... he is barely at home... dad neither...I'm supposed to take care of everything... but me, I'm not allowed to exist!" he sobs, not realizing that he has changed to the present tense. In his emotions he is now Michael, eight years old. The tears well up with such force that he can't say another word. There are only salty tears and pent-up grief.

Lisa only sits there, receives his gazes and follows him in his grief. She follows him in that which *is*, in this moment. She can feel the pain, inside of her, a kind of cutting pain in her chest. She doesn't know if Michael had been crying for a minute or an eternity, but suddenly she exclaims spontaneously:

"Poor, poor Michael!"

The therapist asks Michael to breathe deeply down in his stomach and look at Lisa, feel her presence, look her in the eyes so that he won't be alone in his pain. She encourages him to let the wave of sadness roll through his body without stopping it.

The room is quiet. Some of the other participants cry soundlessly and hold each other's hands, hard.

Slowly the tears subsides, and calmness spreads over the boy Michael's face; a boy who slowly moves back into a grown man. He looks up at his wife's loving eyes with a gaze that is newborn.

"Is there anything more?" the therapist prompts Lisa, who is so moved that she has forgotten to mirror.

"Is there anything more?" she whispers.

Michael shakes his head. "No, there isn't anything more now."

Lisa looks at him with a tenderness that aches in her chest. Time stands still in the room.

The voice of the therapist breaks the silence.

"Before we leave this event, ask Michael what he did as a child to deal with his own grief, and the fact that his mother vanished into her grief."

Lisa nods and asks.

"The grief I kind of turned off," Michael says, sighing and shivering. "I never cried and we never talked about what happened at home. It was too difficult, too heavy to talk about. After the accident, Mother became a zombie… she sat there staring out the window, filled up with tranquilizers. Nobody talked. I was all… alone."

Lisa listens with her mouth agape. This is entirely new information. Michael always talked about his childhood as so safe and good, almost *perfect*.

"So what did you do then, when you couldn't talk about what happened?" asks Lisa.

"I played soccer… turned to my friends…"

Once again, the therapist asks Lisa to slow down, look, register all that she sees and put it close to her heart. "And don't forget to mirror. You don't have to mirror everything, but do repeat the essence of what he says."

"I am so touched," Lisa said softly. "I never heard of this before…. So, you never talked about this at home. You turned off your grief. Your mom became a zombie… and you went out to play soccer and…eh… went to friends. Did I get you?"

"Yes. I studied a lot too, got good in school and managed on my own."

"You studied a lot."

"Yes, I did. I studied, played soccer… well, I don't know… I just managed on my own! I didn't need anyone," says Michael.

"You didn't need anyone. But where was your father in all this?" Lisa asks, eagerly leaning forward.

"He just worked and travelled as usual, came home and visited sometimes, sat in front of the news and hushed… I guess it felt terrible to him to be home, so he kept away… I think… I hardly remember him from that period."

"So your dad worked a lot…"

"Yes, Dad never showed very much feelings, he put the lid on." He looks at Lisa with a fiery gaze. "Just like me."

"Where did you take your longing for your mother and father when they couldn't be there for you?" the therapist prompts Lisa.

Lisa poses the question to her husband.

"I managed on my own, worked in school and… sometimes I spent time with my grandfather. Him… I loved him." Michael's voice cracks and the tears run down his stubbled cheeks. "What would I have done… without… my grandfather?" he sobs.

Lisa watches Michael's heavy brows wrinkle up in pain, and how he rubs his wrists with his big hands to calm himself as he talks.

"You loved your grandfather," Lisa says. Grief bubbles up in her and the tears run down her cheeks, too.

"Lisa… do you think that you can check now if your tears are empathy for Michael or if you have slipped into your own world, perhaps a grief of your own?"

"It's both… because my grandfather…"

The therapist says softly: "Lisa I can see that your grandfather has affected you, too. But right now I want you to stay in Michael's land, with his grandfather. You know, sometimes we have a tendency to mix ourselves up with the other. But it is important to avoid that now, especially considering what Michael has just told us – that he couldn't be in his grief because everything was about his mother's and his father's grief. Put a heart around yourself and choose to stay with him.

Lisa nods. She understands.

"Let your emotions for you grandfather remain within you, but stay with Michael for a while. Prepare to return to him again… see the bridge ahead of you!"

"Yes… I'm okay now," Lisa says.

"Good. Now, tell Michael: Whoops, I must have slipped away to my grandfather and me. Wait a minute and I'll be back to you again."

Lisa looks Michael in the eyes again at the same time as she repeats the words in a very soft tone of voice. Michael's smile is pale when he replies: "Thank you, Lisa, for wanting to be with me."

"So," the therapist says, "before we leave this album and this event, check if there is anything else Michael wants to say about his grandfather or his childhood."

"Is there more?" Lisa asks.

"No, nothing more," Michael says after a while.

"Good. You are both doing so well. And now Lisa, can you try to guess how it was to be Michael when he was eight and his sister died? Tell him."

"Mike… I can only imagine that it must have been terrible… frightening… lonely. Is that right?"

Michael nods, and the therapist says: "Use your own words Michael. Lisa can only guess."

"Well… I felt lonely, powerless… and empty."

"So you felt lonely, powerless and empty," Lisa mirrors quickly and naturally, as if mirroring always had been her way to communicate. "I can really understand that."

The therapist asks Lisa to keep everything she heard about the boy Michael close to her heart, and continues:

"Good work Lisa! You did this so well, mirroring and following your husband. Now, dear, you will have a chance to sum up, validate and offer some empathy. Simple isn't it?"

"Help!" Lisa says. "What does all that mean?"

Michael beams in his chair. He is very happy to have his empathic wife visiting him and is looking forward to the rest. His chest feels unusually well right now.

"Well, Lisa, this is how we do it: first, you are going to sum up everything you have heard Michael say about the present, that which was important to bring up."

"Nothing about his childhood?"

"No not now, not yet – you are only going to recapitulate the essence of everything you heard Michael say about the present."

"Help, I've almost forgotten that," Lisa whispers.

"That's alright; Michael and I will help you. And you, Michael, are just going to lean back and receive what she sums up. Okay?"

He nods and leans back in his chair. Love and confidence flow through his body and he enjoys the feeling. Lisa leans forward and begins:

"Well… you wanted to talk about how I can't listen. I'm not strong enough to hear you and you are afraid that there will be a lot of tears if you say what you feel… you are afraid that I'm not strong enough… did I get you?"

"That's perfect. You have really heard everything." His eyes glisten. "And the most important thing is that you are happy!" he quickly adds.

"Good that you praise her, because she worked really hard here!" says the therapist. "You could always use a bit of humour and say 'Good Lisa, you got ninety-eight per cent! What I want to add, and which is the most important two per cent is that I want you to be happy… because that is the most important!' Because if you say so, then you help Lisa by praising her, but you also help yourself to receive the other ninety-eight per cent that she actually heard. Okay?"

Michael nods pensively.

"I guess that you have quite a few tracks in your mind and brain, maybe even a highway, that says 'no one is going to listen to me'… so when it happens, like now, it's not so easy to recognize or receive. Does that fit you?"

"Yes, unfortunately it does."

"Okay, let go on," the therapist says, nodding.

"Lisa... you have understood everything very well, to ninety-five per cent. What I want you to add is the fact that I want you to be *happy*."

Lisa smiles proudly. "So I have understood almost everything, but you want to add that you want me to be happy."

"And now, Lisa," says the therapist, "you are going to tell us a little story about your husband's history."

"Oh."

"Start like this, like in a fairy tale," says the therapist, "'Once upon a time there was a little boy. When he was eight...' and so on. I want you to do this so that we show Michael that we were only *visiting* today. The eight-year-old doesn't actually exist today; he only exists in his memories. By telling a fairy tale, we help ourselves to separate what was then from what is now. Then we can put the fairy tale about the eight-year-old *here*." She points to the floor beside Michael's chair.

"Okay. Once upon a time there was a little boy who lost his younger sister in a car accident when he was eight years old. His mother and father disappeared into a kind of... haze of grief so that the boy almost felt like an orphan. The little boy learnt to manage on his own, turned off all emotions, went to friends, and sometimes he lived with his grandfather...Nobody talked about feelings in his home," Lisa sums up with all her heart, and Michael looks at his wife with eyes filled of tenderness, respect, pain and love. He is impressed how much she remembers, more than he does.

"Did I remember most of your story?" Lisa asks.

"Yes, one hundred percent," he says proudly. Now that he has some distance to the story about the boy, and can see the compassion in Lisa's eyes, Michael feels very touched by what the little kid in him was forced to go through.

"One hundred percent," Lisa whispers with tears in her eyes.

"Good work, again," the therapist says. "Now let's go on to the next step--validation. It means that you will help Michael make sense of what he learnt as a child, and show him how *brilliantly* he responded to his sister's death and his parents' pain, because it was a way to survive. This is how it might sound: 'It really makes sense to me that you learned to shut off your feelings as a child, because nobody talked about them. And it also makes sense that you got scared of feelings because you felt your parents' pain....'"

Lisa thinks about this for a moment. "It really make sense to me that you shut off, Michael, because it must have been horrible that there was no one there for you when your sister died. Did I get you?"

"Yes, no one could handle the grief and the horrible."

"So, no one could handle the grief and the horrible," mirrors Lisa. The therapist nods at her to continue. "I can also understand that you wanted to be good and that it mattered to you to manage on your own when they weren't there for you. Is that correct?"

"Yes, that's so true. I became an achiever." Michael has tears in his eyes again.

"You became an achiever."

"You are doing this so beautifully, Lisa. You just follow him and tune in to his world. Ask if there is anything else he needs to get validated."

"Is there anything that I didn't understand, Michael?" says Lisa.

"No, it feels like you really have understood," says Michael, and Lisa shines like the sun.

"Now, Lisa, we shall move to one of the most important parts in the dialogue. You shall validate and see the 'red thread,' namely how *you* fit in this drama."

The therapist sounds very enthusiastic, as if she were a game show host on TV. Lisa wrinkles her eyebrows. "Oh… I see it clearly. I'm terribly critical and unfortunately, I fit in just too well," Lisa sighs.

"It isn't 'unfortunately' at all – it's *fantastic* that you can see it, because now there is a chance to do something new. Tell him!"

"I fit into the drama because I'm often sad, disappointed and critical. Is that so?"

In spite of the long and intensive dialogue, Lisa and Michael still maintain intense eye contact and mindful presence.

"Yes," says Michael, "You are often sad and disappointed. It feels like it doesn't matter what I do because it's wrong anyway." He makes a hollow sigh.

"So, it feels like it doesn't matter what you do. You know, I can really understand that, since I unfortunately often see what is wrong. But I think that you are also very…"

"Stay, *stay* with him, Lisa!" The therapist interrupts quickly. Lisa takes a few deep breaths and continues. "Well, Mike, I can see that I fit in to your world because I have been sad, disappointed and negative for a long, long time. Did I get you?"

"Yes, you got me. When you are sad, I feel like it doesn't matter what I do because you will find something wrong with me, anyway."

"So it doesn't help, because I will find something wrong. Well, that makes sense because we get trapped here. I do complain and I can see that you give up."

"Perfect, Lisa. Now ask Michael what he would need from you."

"What would you need from me?" Lisa asks eagerly.

"That you listen like you do right now."

"That I listen like I do now. That is what you want…"

"Yes and that you sometimes smile when you see me…"

"Put his needs by your heart, and just let it lie there. Now ask him what he would need and wish from himself."

"What do you need and wish from yourself?"

Michael is silent for a long time. Then he looks at Lisa, looks out the window, up at the ceiling and then intensely at Lisa again. Lisa can see that he takes this question very seriously, and that makes her happy and relieved.

"Well… maybe I should try to express myself, talk a little more with you, Lisa… tell you how I feel about things?"

Lisa mirrors with the speed of lightning: "So you're thinking that you should talk a bit more to me about how you feel? Did I get you, Michael?"

"Yes, you did."

"Look at Mike, he is now thinking of doing something that he really needed to do as a child," says the therapist. "To express himself, to depend on someone, to get regulated and to be able to need. Can you see that, Lisa?"

"Yes," Lisa smiles, feeling softness bloom in her chest and heart.

The therapist then asks Michael to take a picture of Lisa, really seeing her energy and how her face changes when he says that he wants to talk to her. He smiles, picks up an imaginary camera and says:

"Click, click!"

The therapist prompts Michael: "So... if I practice talking a bit more to you Lisa, expressing myself, I think I would feel..."

"Hmm... if I would practice talking a bit more with you Lisa I would probably feel... aah... a bit frightened perhaps... but mostly I would feel contact, that we share something. Community... and that I'm not so closed."

Lisa mirrors.

"Let this moment be etched to your memories and senses," says the therapist. "Community and contact are of course things that Michael should have been able to feel many times as a child. If we could change the story, we would see to it that his younger sister lived, or that his parents had been able to regulate and talk about difficult feelings, and that he would have been allowed his grief... right?"

Concurring hums were heard from the entire group.

"Lisa, how would you react if Mike came home and talked to you a bit more?"

"Well, then I would open my arms and listen. I wouldn't feel so lonely"

"Can you mirror that, Michael?"

"If I talked to you more, you would open your arms and listen... and you would not feel so lonely. Did I get you?"

"Yes, one thousand percent," Lisa says with a pleased smile.

The therapist prompts Michael again: "So if you opened your arms and listened…"

"If you opened your arms and listened, I would feel that I was important, and that I meant something to you. If you listened instead of at once telling me what is wrong…"

Lisa takes his hand and caresses it.

"So if I listened instead of complaining, then you would feel that you mean something to me… is that so?"

"Yes," whispers Michael.

The therapist once again asks them to freeze the magic moment and take a mental picture of each other, take each other in completely.

"Everything you now share is in the space between you two," she says. A moment of silence follows.

Then she turns to Michael and says:

"Remember that you can practice to open up, not just to Lisa, but to yourself. For such a long time you have learnt to close things in, so it's understandable that you do it again. But when you notice that you do it, you can put a heart around yourself and try to look at that part of you with compassion. Then you can practice at your own pace to dare to open up."

The therapist now turns to Lisa. "So, when you sometimes see that he is turned off, don't be so afraid! This way of shutting down has really protected your husband many times before. Find a way to differentiate, him from you, and see that his reactions say more about him than about you. Then get a little curious about your own implicit memories. Why his shutting down becomes so terrible for you. That way, you can calm down your nervous system and regulate yourself. Give it time. We humans don't change our behaviour in fifteen minutes."

"I will try."

"Michael, I can imagine that when we first sat down here in these 'hot seats' you felt…"

Lisa hears the prompt and smiles.

"Mike, I can imagine that when we first sat down here you felt terror, embarrassment and… yes, anxiety," says Lisa.

"Yes, I felt damn anxious about how this would end."

"So you felt damn anxious about how this would end," mirrors Lisa.

"Yes, definitely!"

The therapist whispers to Lisa: "And I can imagine that you now feel…"

"I can imagine that you now feel relieved, surprised and perhaps a bit shocked," Lisa says a bit tentatively. "Is that right?"

"Yes, shocked actually… and relieved… and completely exhausted."

"You feel shocked, relieved and completely exhausted. I can really understand that," says Lisa.

"Completely finished, and interestingly enough, happy. Happy!" The words come without any thought.

"You feel finished and…happy," says Lisa, the words sticking slightly in her throat.

"So, each of you… say like this: 'one thing that I really have appreciated with you in this moment is…'" Michael immediately catches on and says in a strong voice:

"One thing that I really appreciated about you Lisa, is that you came back after flipping out earlier, and that you really have listened to me."

"So… one thing that you appreciated is that I came back after getting angry before, and you felt that I really listened," says Lisa.

"Yes, thank you, Lisa!"

"You're welcome," she says with a soft smile. "And one thing that I have appreciated about you, Mike, is that you have opened up and let me into your world. Thank you. It has been very rewarding."

"You appreciate that I opened up and let you in, because it was very rewarding. Thank you, too." His eyes shine with gratitude.

"And now," says the therapist, "I will ask you, brave couple, to put words to what you have created in the space between you. For instance: 'I experience love, respect…'"

"Warmth, respect, love, tears, need for happiness, contact," Lisa, says.

"Freedom," adds Michael, smiling happily.

After a moment, the therapist asks them to softly turn their gaze outwards to face the group of couples that is sitting around them and has followed them on their journey.

"Oh, I almost forgot about them!" says Lisa and glances at the clock. "Oh, my god! It's been an hour and a half! I thought it was maybe 30 minutes."

"Me too," says Michael, feeling the warmth spread slowly from his stomach and out to all of his limbs. He feels...carbonated. Light and happy. He can't actually remember the last time he felt this light and... well, *alive.*

The therapist asks them to seek eye contact with everyone in the room. Slowly, they turn outwards and around in the room and meet the others with shy but yet proud gazes. One by one, Michael and Lisa meet the gaze of all of the participants. They can see that many of them are deeply touched. There are many lingering meetings of smiling mouths and loving eyes filled with tears. Once more, time stands still.

The therapist now turns to the participants. "To finish up, you will all get the chance to put words to what you've experienced that Lisa and Michael have put in the space between them, and which now rests in this room."

In the room, a feeling of deep, almost sacred respect prevails. The other people in the workshop have witnessed a true encounter between partners that have been in struggle for so long. Lisa and Michael sit calmly as they listen to the other participants describe what now rests in the space between them all.

"Presence."

"Hope."

"Sorrow."

"A small sister."

"Life."

"Vulnerability and playfulness."

"Pain, love."

"Something new!"

"Differences, respect, will."

"A life story."

"Power!"

"Gratefulness."

"Compassion."

"Courage!"

The therapist adds:

"Mirror neurons."

Catching on, Michael adds enthusiastically:

"… and new neural pathways!"

Lisa nods, laughing, as they catch each other's hands.

You must be the change you want to see in the world

MAHATMA GANDHI
INDIAN POLITICAL AND SPIRITUAL LEADER (1869-1948)

1 2

When an "I" Meets a "You"

The Miracle of Presence

This dialogue is fantastic each time I experience it – no matter who visits whom, what they carry along, whether they continue their journey together or decide to go separate ways. It's miraculous because it often leads to a feeling of being heard, respected and understood--for some couples, an experience they haven't shared for years. The dialogue leads to loving relationships.

We all need to slow down the pace, focus all our attention on the one who speaks and adopt a kind of mindful awareness – we call it *trance* or *flow* – where we are really present and meet the presence with both the past and the future embedded *in that moment.* It doesn't mean that we have to go back in time during every dialogue, but rather that we understand in the moment of NOW that everything already is there.

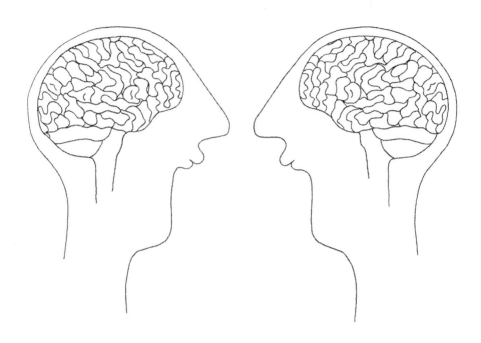

I repeat: When someone hears our signal, when we feel heard and get a response that meets our need, *harmony and safety are created.* We get regulated. When we get a response that has more to do with the other person's emotions, there is very easily chaos, confusion, anger, rigidity and hopelessness. The feeling corresponds very much to what happens in the first bonding in life, that between the child and the parent or guardian (remember Chapter 6 on attachment).

Notice what happened in the contact between Michael and Lisa when she fell down into her "crater." When she reacted defensively and angrily, he quickly retreated again into his familiar turtle shell. The therapist's presence helped them to restore contact. With a little practice, many couple can learn how to reconnect themselves.

Kidnapped

When we fall down among our own painful memories, we lose the ability to listen. We take everything we hear all too personally, everything is about us – we think. Put simply, we become kidnapped by our amygdala and thus lost in our own reactions. The only signals that we hear at that time are the signals from the brain's survival center. We lose our ability to calm down, regulate and tune into the other person. Sadly enough, we also lose contact with ourselves and our core--our *essence*.

But when we can differentiate and "just" visit, we can stay in the other person's world and there experience contact. We can listen curiously without becoming defensive or "falling apart." In my view, empathy is crucial for communication to work.

The Experience of Attunement

Relationship is about attunement, that is, tuning in to each other's subjective experiences. When we get a positive response to our signals, we experience that we are valuable and our story gets a context: "I make sense!" And when we know that we are valuable, we treat others as important and valuable. We know that we are only visiting, and that the other person is different from us. We show respect for both I and You, regardless whether the communication is between intimate partners, teacher and student, doctor and patient, therapist and client, parent and child, friend and friend, or whomever we're in contact with. When we are differentiated and still linked together, we can be truly present with the other and not occupied with ourselves. With a little practice and guidance, we can learn to see the differences.

Even though the most important period for bonding is during the first years of life, we can create the experience of safe attachment all through our lives. In Bonnie Badenoch's book, *The Brain-Savvy Therapist's Workbook – A Companion to Being a Brain-Wise Therapist,* she says: "Research tells us that attuned relationship is the single most important variable in the healing endeavour, and that non-judgmental acceptance is the most efficacious component of attunement." [45]

Let's look a bit more at the role of the therapist. It is important that the therapist be emphatic, present and completely "tuned in." He or she must take care to avoid getting stuck in condemning or thinking about right or wrong, and instead just *hold* the process; *hold* whatever comes up during the therapy with warmth, warmth and more warmth. The therapist must see every individual in his or her office as a You.

Daniel Goleman has this to say about therapeutic empathy:

"The crucial role in therapy of finely attuned empathy are those moments, when the therapist feels "on target" with the patient, accurately sensing what feelings are roiling through the patient. Unfortunately, part of what the analyst feels come from his own emotional baggage, a projection of his own inner reality onto that of the patient. Projection ignores the other person´s inner reality; when we are projecting, we assume the other feels and thinks as we do. [46] When we see an act and a supposed intent in another person, it is sometimes hard to know what happens to whom. That is because our mirror neurons and resonance circuits read off actions and intentions in others, and when this occurs; similar nerve cells light up in our brain, too. So, it is important to ask questions like "Did I get you? Is this true for you, or does this say more about me? Are you feeling what I am feeling?" Of course, it is also important that the therapist understand his or her own neuronal map of implicit memories and how this can sometimes interfere with the process taking place in "the space" between therapist and client.

Goleman further writes: "Neuroscience now tells us something akin to the poetic idea that eyes are windows on the soul: the eyes offer glimpses into a person´s most private feelings. More specifically, the eyes contain nerve projections that lead directly to a key brain structure for empathy and matching emotions, the orbitofrontal (or OFC) area of

---

45 Bonnie Badenoch, *The Brain-Savvy Therapist's Workbook – A Companion to Being a Brain-Wise Therapist,* preface
46 Daniel Goleman. *Social Intelligence; The New Science of Human Relationships,* page 115

the prefrontal cortex. Looking eyes loops us." [47] Imagine an emotional moment when two people in love look deeply into each other's eyes and feel an endless affinity, love and desire. Neurologically, we can playfully reduce this process to the fact that they have linked their orbifrontal areas together. It doesn't sound quite as romantic as "I drowned in her eyes" – but a bit simplified, that is exactly what happens!

When a dialogue really works, the harmony in the brain of both parties is reflected. We regulate each other.

47 Daniel Goleman, *Social Intelligence; The New Science of Human Relationships,* page 63

Paths to Integration

Of course, there are other ways to create integration of the different parts of the brain. If you know that you carry difficult trauma, EMDR therapy (see Chapter 5) can for instance be an effective way to treat and solve them. I have had a good experience with EMDR treatment. And it's not only a trauma tool; EMDR is also very effective in treating helping people become free of reoccurring negative feelings of all sorts.

There are other ways to help the brain begin to integrate, including dancing, aerobics, writing, and, above all, practicing mindfulness. When we practice mindful presence – or, for instance meditation, yoga, qi gong or tai chi – we help important parts of the brain to develop. In time, these practices make it easier for us to calm a galloping nervous system and thus choose healthier behaviour. We don't have to put on our Armani suits and react out of habit. We can more easily enjoy and take responsibility for the present. We can regulate ourselves.

For instance, meditation helps us differentiate from our own thoughts and emotions; to "move apart" within ourselves. It really means that we *are* not our thoughts and emotions, but that, bit by bit, we learn to live in the *space* between the thoughts. Then we can see that thoughts and emotions are only activities of our mind.

When we feel or think, we sometimes identify with these emotions and thoughts too easily. We *become* our emotions and thoughts, and then respond to what we think occurs instead of what actually occurs. We respond on impulse and call this impulse our Ego.

Meditation changes the structure of the brain, thereby slowing down these automatic, reactive processes. As Daniel Siegel says in *The Mindful Therapist,* "From a different set of reasoning and data, we do know that mindfulness meditation does promote our nine middle pre-frontal functions:

1. Body regulation: Balance of the sympathetic (accelerator) and parasympathetic (braces) branches of the autonomic nervous system.

2. Attuned communication: Enables us to tune into others state and link minds.

3. Emotional balance: Permits the lower limbic regions to become aroused enough so life has meaning, but not too aroused that we become flooded.

4. Response flexibility: The opposite of a "knee-jerk" (or "being kidnapped") reaction, this capacity enables us to pause before acting and inhibit impulses giving us enough time to reflect on our various options for response.

5. Empathy: Considering the mental perspective of another person.

6. Insight: Self-knowing awareness, the gateway to our autobio-graphical narratives and self- understanding.

7. Fear extinction: GABA (an inhibitory neurotransmitter) fibers project down to the amygdale and enable fearful responses to be calmed.

8. Intuition: Being aware of the input of our body, especially infor-mation from the neural networks surrounding the intestines (a "gut feel-

ing") and heart ("heartfelt feelings") enables us to open to the wisdom of our non-conceptual selves.

9. Morality: The capacity to think of the larger good and to act on these pro-social ideas, even when alone; appears to depend on an intact middle prefrontal region.

And so we can say that helping ourselves to practice mindfulness can be considered a form of "brain fitness," in that it stimulates the growth and presumably maintains the functioning of our integrative prefrontal circuits." [48]

Creating Safety: A Brief Review

Let's now briefly recap how we can learn to create the experience of safe attachment in our adult relationships. We must:

1) hear the signal from another person;

2) make sense of that signal;

3) respond to that signal.

In other words, we need to:

1) **Mirror**: As the other person speaks, just follow and be attuned to him or her. Say in response: "I hear you say..... Did I get you?"

2) **Validate:** We see the logic in the other's statements, and reflect back that understanding. "Hearing you say and feel this really make sense because....." or "You really make sense, because....."

3) **Empathize**: We guess what the other person might feel by feeling in our own body what we think the other person feels in his/her body. Then we check out whether we've guessed correctly. "I can imagine that you must feel angry and helpless. Is that so?"

Let's return now to Lisa and Michael. How are they progressing in their efforts to create mutual safety?

---

48 Daniel J. Siegel, *The Mindful Therapist; A clinican's Guie to Mindsighy and neural Integration*, page 180

-Tell me more, darling. (The translation from Swedish to English by Eva Berlander)

Lisa and Michael

Two Trees

The sun shone over the park's natural grass plains. Above them galloped a yellow dog almost exactly the same color as the withered grass. She was chasing a Frisbee and every time she went after it, she barked happily. When she came back and gave the plastic disc to John, she ran eagerly beside him, tongue hanging out, waiting for the next throw – the next mission. After all, she was a retriever!

"No, it's my turn now!" shouted Jimmy.

"What about me, I haven't had a single throw." Anna said sulkily. Much to everyone's surprise, Jimmy collected the Frisbee and generously handed it to his younger sister.

It was a clear, sunny day at the end of March. Lisa and Michael walked hand in hand some ten yards behind the kids and the dog. Everyone in the family was dressed warmly since there was a chill in the air, but they also noticed that the days were longer and spring was not so far away with the first small flowers.

Lisa was enjoying herself completely. She had suggested that all the family take a walk in the park together and round it off with a small feast of coffee and cakes in the city – and everyone said yes! It was the first time in years that the entire family had taken a Sunday walk together. That the kids had been willing to let go of computers and friends and go with them felt like a great victory.

Maybe it did have something to do with the pleasurable atmosphere that had prevailed in the home lately. During the two months that had passed since the couple's workshop, things were more open and relaxed at home. There was more laughter. Michael and Lisa had hugged several times in front of the children (who looked at them and elbowed each other), and Michael had really been home more. The reason for this was their current topic of conversation.

"Alice Jacobsen is the perfect office manager!" Michael's eyes shone. "She's incredibly competent and her CV is really something. Only terrific reviews from everyone! And she's been married fifteen years--a merit in itself!" He squeezed Lisa's hand, winked and continued:

"Honestly, she seems to be a generally stable person, and very nice. The other guy we interviewed, Stefan Newman, also seemed good, but in some ways he felt more like a career guy-- and maybe a bit of a brat."

"Sounds like you made a good decision," Lisa said. "I think it's nice that you chose a woman."

"Yes, women can manage, and ladies try," Michael said in a high, squeaky voice and gripped Lisa's waist so tightly that she screamed and hit him with her mittened hand. In response, he ran away and hid behind a big fir with an enormous trunk a bit away. Lisa looked up at the tip of the tree, which had vanished in the air.

Lisa ran over to the tree and sneaked around the trunk, but when she got there, Michael was gone. She ran all the way around it, but he wasn't there. She ran the other way – not this time either! He had vanished. The kids had disappeared behind a small hill. In a second, her old horrible feeling of abandonment seized her.

"Mike?" she shouted in a pitiful voice. She looked around her. Did he just leave her here in the middle of the park? He couldn't...? Then she heard a rustling behind her, and suddenly she was lifted off the ground. She howled in mingled shock and joy.

"You scared me," she gasped.

"Just kidding," he said, laughing, and let her down. He took her mitten in his big glove. "Let's go after the kids." They went back down into the field, where they found their teenagers romping around with the dog.

Michael watched the kids with satisfaction. He felt good. The decision to hire an office manager to relieve the pressure on him had been wise. The company could afford it, and now he could be more creative and slow down a bit. He was able to be home a bit more, and spend more time with Lisa and the kids--and with himself.

Things definitely felt better now. They had continued working on the jigsaw puzzle of their marriage with the therapist, and started to understand more how their past experiences affected their relationship now. And, primarily, they had provided themselves with the tools to actually listen to each other.

It had been nice to be with Lisa again. A number of times, their increased intimacy had led to sex--sex that felt different than it did before. Maybe not the burning passion that he'd felt with Cecilia, but... more intimate. It felt safer, and strangely enough exciting, as if they'd discovered each other anew. In some ways it was more genuine. Cecilia had faded from his life, and the passion he'd felt for her was ebbing, like the bubbles going flat in a glass of champagne. Sometimes the bubbles stirred, but it was more and more seldom. He felt a certain confidence. Maybe he would be able to continue with Lisa?

They did have two intensive days booked ahead with the therapist: one in May and the other in October. Knowing this gave Michael a sense of security, since he didn't know if their newfound feeling of love would remain or if they would fall back into their old, boring tracks.

Michael had decided that he wanted to give Lisa and himself a year to find their way back to each other. He had come to realize that this therapy actually wasn't about saving a marriage, but rather a kind of individual genealogical research; each of them was learning to see the connection between their past and the way they experienced life with their partner now. And especially, they were learning to communicate. He found the tools useful at work too; in his conversations with his colleagues, he'd had become a much better listener.

Even more important, he had come to understand that the feeling of being *dead* that he'd been carrying with him for so long really didn't have anything to do with Lisa. He had learnt to run away from himself and his emotions much earlier, and the consequence had been a devastating loneliness.

Much to his surprise, he'd realized that he also needed love and contact – as much as Lisa did, but in a somewhat different way. If he could experience that with Lisa, it would be best. If, in the future, he could sit on a sunny veranda with her beside him and their grandchildren on his lap, that would be quite wonderful! And if they couldn't make it work – well, they would still have learnt a lot on the way. He also knew that if they had to separate after the year, after all, the experience would be completely different than if he had just walked out.

One important thing he'd realized was that he needed--and wanted--to spend more time with Lisa. As the therapist put it, they needed to be *source of joy* to each other instead of just yelling problems or walking away. Surprisingly enough, he had come to realize that it was fun to be with his wife! She elicited emotions in him that he hadn't felt for her in years. Reluctantly, he'd also come to realize that he and Cecilia would also have gotten stuck sooner or later, once the first stage of love passed and everyday life took over. He and Lisa had the kids, the dog, the house, the garden, their friends, and the memories they shared. Maybe it was his small fortune that Cecilia didn't want to take her chances with him; it made his decision to stay and fight for his relationship with Lisa easier. The way things were now, with this wonderful feeling of getting contact and appreciation, he found that he no longer wanted to leave.

Michael himself had suggested a holiday trip to England just for him and Lisa at the end of July. Jimmy and Anna were going on trips of their own and John wanted to stay home. They would drive through Cornwall to Land's End, up through Wales to Scotland, staying in small, romantic hotels and bed-and-breakfasts. Lisa would be able to visit English gardens and the Eden Project--the largest indoor rainforest in the world--that she'd been talking about for years; he would come with her and get involved. He actually felt a wish to make her happy. He wanted to look at some architecture himself: he wanted to be inspired by Welsh stone houses with thatched roofs for his next big environment-adjusted project – a big ecological housing area. And he wanted to challenge himself by driving on the left side of the road and turn the wrong way in lots of roundabouts!

But what actually made Michael happier was something completely different. When he first suggested the trip to England, Lisa said:

"Of course, darling, I'll be glad to! But first, I want to go away on my own for a week or so. Perhaps with Petra... But if she can't go, I'll go on my own. I want to go to go some place in June. It won't be expensive! If that's alright?"

"Of course it's alright!" Michael had exclaimed, at once perplexed and happy. Lisa had never wanted to do travel on her own before; she seemed to be worried to leave the family, as if she thought that everything would stop functioning without her. Or, as if she couldn't manage without *them*. This seemed like a step on her way to becoming more independent, and he welcomed it.

They emerged from the trees and into the sun, which felt warm on their cold noses.

"It's getting time for that coffee. Shall we go back?" asked Michael.

"Okay."

"Hey, kids!" Michael shouted at the top of his voice. "Time to go back!"

The youngsters waved and approached them in a playful zigzag over the lawn. They seemed to be busy stuffing grass in each other's collars. Hollers and protests echoed over the field. Lisa and Michael stood still, listening to the kids' voices and the wind singing in the trees. Suddenly, Lisa said:

"Mike. Do you see the two trees over there?" She pointed and peered. Michael shaded his eyes with the hand and looked.

"You mean the two straight ones beside each other?"

"Yes, the one with bare stems and their crowns sort of twined together."

"Yes, what about them?"

"That's how I would like to see us, Mike. Like two straight trees standing together but beside each other... almost like the pillars in an old Greek temple."

She paused.

"Because... those trees don't need each other to grow and stand strong, but the crowns still touch. They brush against each other in contact. Nice isn't it?" she said, catching his gaze. "It feels like I always have been a small... well, clinging vine needing to grow protected by you, or climb on your stem. I don't want to be that anymore. I want to have the contact, but I don't want to be over dependent. I want to be like that tree. Do you understand what I mean?"

Michael looked up at the crowns of the two trees and thought that it was a quite beautiful picture.

"Mmm, I think so," he said.

Their three teenage kids now were with them and Jimmy said:

"What the heck are you looking at?"

"Trees," Lisa and Michael said at the same time, laughing.

"Trees?" Anna said. "Well, cool. Is it feast-time now?"

Back into the Crater

"You don't seem to have understood anything the therapist says! You *never* listen, damn it!"

Lisa tore open the door to her husband's hiding place, and her screams echoed through the entire house. Michael stood by the bedroom window with his back to Lisa and eyes toward the pale grey landscape. His jaws were locked in a cramp and a knot of hopelessness ached in his stomach. He knew that he ought to act differently, but his body had decided: he had to get away from there! Now that she was on the warpath, nothing could stop Lisa.

They had crashed – again. He apparently didn't listen well enough when she'd said something about work and Jimmy's birthday. First, she'd been disappointed and then angry; within minutes, the conflict had been turned up full force. He'd actually *tried* to counteract his impulse to flee by making a partial retreat to another room, but it didn't help – Lisa had followed. Now she stood there yelling and he just had to get away! He couldn't take her shrill complaints.

So he did the same thing that he had done so many times before. With decisive steps he pushed past Lisa in the doorway, ran down the stairs, yanked on his shoes and jacket, tore open the door and slammed it shut with such force that the entire house vibrated.

Lisa stood alone in the bedroom, dazed by the bang. After a few minutes, she walked tentatively to the kitchen and stood in front of the sink, staring. There were the yucky, dirty plates after the casserole they'd for Sunday lunch. But it was the smell of her enormous failure that hurt her nostrils, made her cheeks damp and pushed thousands of hopeless thoughts into motion.

"Well, *leave then*! Go! Run away as usual and *don't come back*!! She yelled until her voice was hoarse. The screaming turned into angry tears, and then more screaming:

"I hate, hate, *hate* when he just leaves! Shit, he will never change."

Somewhere beneath all that anger, she was grateful that the kids weren't home. They would have been so disappointed. Slowly, the anger transformed into misery, and she sank dejected onto a chair.

"Why, why, *why* is it like this again?" she sobbed out loud.

She had been so certain that they had come further in their development and that such a shitty row was a past stage. That those fights were gone for good.

With the back of her right hand, she wiped the tears from her eyes and took a deep breath. The tears slowed down a bit. The words of the therapist started to move around in her head. They repeated again and again:

HURRAY! What luck. Interesting. Conflicts are such an opportunity. HURRAY! What luck. Interesting. Conflicts are such an opportunity. HURRAY...

But the words tasted bitter. So incredibly stupid. How could she ever experience this painful cat-and-mouse game as a possibility and shout "hurray?" It was like some kind of hopeless tango where they were one step away from each other all the time and never in contact. Lately, she had begun building up new confidence and hope, but it had been cruelly turned into nothing. Nothing would ever be different with Mike. In this moment, she just wanted to die.

But with a sense of remembering another woman in another life, she thought about how it had been at the workshop; the sympathetic eyes of the other participants, the safe atmosphere among them, the warmth in the room. So easy it had seemed then!

Then, as she was thinking about the workshop, she noticed that she had stopped crying and was breathing almost normally again. She remembered the drawings on the big pad: *reptile brain, amygdala...*

She noticed that she was feeling less panicky now. How strange. In some way, she must have managed to calm down her amygdala, made it less noisy. Instead, an unfamiliar feeling of decisiveness grew in her. With quick steps she went to the mantelpiece, where two plastic figures were positioned.

"Go and get yourself a couple of small reptile toys," the therapist had said to the participants when they finished the workshop. "To remind you that it is your reptile brains that governs you when you get into a conflict." Then, when she had chosen the little green crocodile in a local gift shop, she had smiled tenderly and thought that this little reptile would never run her again. Ha ha. Next to the crocodile was the turtle she'd bought for Michael. She looked at the two ugly little plastic figures. Lisa and Michael, two adults, in the middle of their lives with children who were nearly grown.

In the midst of her despair, Lisa couldn't help seeing the humour in how silly they behaved when the reptiles ran them once again, creating misery. It was actually quite comical. Tragi-comic. They behaved like small children whose feelings had been hurt. Or lizards in Armani suits. She surprised herself by laughing. No, she wouldn't go on like this!

Trying Something New

Suddenly, Lisa craved a cup of coffee and went back out into the kitchen. While the coffeemaker gurgled, she decided to calm her nervous system even more by lighting two candles on the kitchen table. She lit them almost devotionally--one for her and all of the lonely, deserted feelings that so easily took over her body and mind. A bit reluctantly, she lit the other candle for Michael, for that damn turtle in him.

"Well, here we are again," she said out loud. Imagine that Mike had once again triggered all those old feelings of being invisible and insignificant. This time it felt even worse since in the weeks after the workshop, both of them had felt as though they'd fallen in love again. It made the disappointment and shock even greater.

Lisa thought about their latest session with the therapist. Several times, she had repeated:

"If you like the result you get, keep doing what you do. But if you don't like it, try something new!"

But how could she try something new, now? Wasn't it too late?

Lisa sat by the kitchen table with her eyes locked on the flame of the candle, as though she were hypnotized. She slurped the hot coffee, slowly and thoughtfully. It made her warm. Then she rose and slowly went to the phone on the table in the hallway. Her heart nearly stopped beating and she could almost feel the crocodile lying in wait for her in her stomach. Her index finger hung in the air.

No.

She wasn't going to call Michael now. She would do something completely different, something new. With decisive steps she strode into the living room to the fireplace, took wood from the basket, built a good pile and lit it. It sparkled and smelled nicely of resin. As the fire got started, she stood there for a while and looked into the dancing yellow flames, feeling warmth and calm spread through her body.

After a while, she closed the damper a little and walked over to the bookcase. There were so many books that she wanted to read there--but who had the energy? Lisa loved to read; when she was younger, she read all the time. In recent years, she'd done much less, unable to find the time and peace for reading between dishes, cleaning, work and the kids. But it was time to change that now.

Her eyes moved along the books until they rested on one, a novel by an author she particularly liked. She brought it with her to the couch in front of the fire and took out the woollen blanket – she would indeed be cosy. The kids would be gone until the evening, so she had the entire Saturday afternoon to herself.

What could make this wonderful time alone with her book complete? More coffee? But… a glass of red wine by the fireplace would be lovely. No. She couldn't just sit and enjoy a glass of wine all alone… that was… that was horrible, it was… alcoholism! Or? Why couldn't she have a glass of wine if she wanted to? She wasn't her father! Damn it, she would drink a glass in one of those big rounded glasses that made the wine smell so heavenly. Then she would sip her wine and read for hours.

And when Mike came back, she would say:

"I'm sorry that I yelled and was so accusing, I know how tears and screaming affect you, how tough they are on you. I'm really sorry for that, Mike. *Forgive me.*"

Yes, that's what she would do.

With a straight back, new courage and new pride, she went into the kitchen to open a bottle of wine.

*

Michael's steps, which had been so angry a minute ago, suddenly felt heavy as he continued up the hill. How fit was he, really? He had been exercising a bit less lately, but…

Huffing, he reached the top. The sea spread out in front of him while the cold wind pulled at his hair and reddened his ears. It was very cold. He ought to take the car and go to the office and be useful, since he couldn't be at home. It was hopeless to walk back into Lisa's minefield. Or… was he to blame for this, too?

If you like the result you get, keep doing what you do. But if you don't like it, do something else!

That's how the therapist had put it. Well, well, that was easy to say, but to walk unarmed into enemy line of fire--you don't do that voluntarily.

He felt the turned-off cell phone in his pocket. It was an hour since he'd rushed away from the house. Lisa was probably bombarding him with calls and text messages right now. Maybe he should….He hesitated. Then he picked up his cell phone and turned it on. He clutched it at an arm's length in front of him while waiting for the aggressive signals that announced a hundred missed calls and messages.

Nothing happened. Nothing at all. No messages. No calls.

Contradictory feelings grabbed Michael, bouncing him between relief, worry, anger and surprise. He stood staring at the empty display, trying to understand what it meant. Suddenly, he felt how tense his shoulders were, and slowly, he let them sink down again. He let out a long sigh.

Then he began the long, bumpy climb down towards the parked car.

I walk down the street
There is a deep hole in the sidewalk
I fall in
I am lost. I am hopeless
It isn't my fault
It takes forever to find a way out

I walk down the street
There is a deep hole in the sidewalk
I fall in again
I can't believe I am in the same place
But it isn't my fault
It still takes a long time to get out

I walk down the same street
There is a deep hole in the sidewalk
I see it, it's a habit
My eyes are open
I know where I am
It is my fault
I get out immediately

I walk down the same street
There is a deep hole in the sidewalk
I walk around it

I walk down another street….

SOGYAL RINPOCHE,
FROM **THE TIBETAN BOOK OF
LIVING AND DYING**

1 3

Repair, Repair and Repair Again

Mending Our Fences

Maybe the most important condition for safe attachment and intimacy is the ability to repair, repair and repair again. The most devastating thing for a relationship is not that problems occur. *Shit happens, and that's normal*! The most devastating thing is when we break contact and don't reconnect. This is especially important between parents and children.

Small children can't see the difference between themselves and their parents. Children depend on us adults and need to be able to rely on us to behave like adults--calmly and responsibly. That doesn't mean that we can't ever be angry, nagging or upset. On the contrary, we are human beings with flaws and failings, and we must be allowed them. But, as adults, after losing it and *falling down into a crater,* we can take the elevator up to the prefrontal cortex and choose how we want to behave. We can take responsibility for our behaviour, correct, apologise, and reconnect.

When our implicit memories play tricks on us and we don't understand them, they are very easily triggered by our close ones. And when that happens, we almost always blame others.

If I, for instance, yell "DON'T YELL" to my children (which I've done many times), I can't expect them not to yell back. Children do as we do. Most of us know this – and yet we easily "get started." Afterwards, we are often hit by feelings of guilt and shame. If, instead, we can get curious about our reaction, calm down our nervous system and then repair the contact, then we teach our children to calm down their nervous system themselves and take responsibility for their actions.

But I repeat: this does *not* mean that we can't get angry. To sometimes get angry is completely natural and even important. Stefan Einhorn says in his book, *The Art of Being Kind*: "When we live in close proximity to each other, as in a family unit, it is unavoidable that we should sometimes act out our anger and frustration. Studies of couple's relationships have shown that in principle there are three ways in which couples behave in conflicts. They either avoid confrontations entirely, have a listening and responsive attitude, or act out their anger in quarrels. It turns out that the third group is not necessary the worst type of relationship. On the contrary, these relationships may be very loving, in between quarrels. Studies of our closest relatives, the apes, have shown that conflicts within a group can be followed by tender scenes of reconciliation". [49]

---

49 Stefan Einhorn, *The Art of being kind*, location 721 (kindle version) Swedish version; *Konsten att vara snäll*, page 89.

Apologising

Bit by bit, we can choose how we want to be with our near and dear ones. When we act badly, which we do all of us from time to time, we apologise. We take responsibility for ourselves. That doesn't mean that we can't establish limits for another's behaviour toward us. Nor does it mean that we take responsibility for what the other person says or does. Let's just let go of potential guilt and be adults who take responsibility for ourselves.

We need to learn how to read our own signals, appreciate ourselves and "put a heart around" our "terrible" reactions, see the need behind the frustration – and choose a new behaviour. We are beautiful, valuable human beings, and when we mess things up we apologise for our behaviour. In other cases this behaviour can lead to something we don't want.

To Heal Together--or On Our Own

Let's get back to the story about Lisa and Michael.

When Michael told his wife that he had met another woman and had decided to leave their marriage, she almost went to pieces. In spite of the fact that his newfound love would not leave her husband Michael felt that he must leave a marriage that felt dead. Lisa, who has experienced abandonment many times in her life, was not only sad and disconsolated but initially lost her will to live. Then, she found the couples workshop.

That Lisa became distraught when Michael wanted to leave her was natural. To grieve and suffer is a part of the mourning process. On the other hand, the feeling that we "don't want to live" a long time after the shock has subsided is *usually* mixed with something else. It may be that things happening in the present are mixed with things that happened earlier and haven't been made explicit yet. A new "trauma," in this case enormous loss, has been mixed with earlier events in our implicit memory. For Lisa--as for most of us--it is a mixture of many things, including the feelings from her childhood of not being seen and being abandoned together with the fear of separation planted by her mother.

Fortunately, Lisa and Michael chose to get help. Lisa started to understand more about her old "dog bites" and why she tended to live through her husband, She began to understand why she felt so abandoned and was always longing for more--more reassurance, more attention, more love. In time, she realized that the fear of divorce and abandonment was a mixture of her own "old" feelings of being abandoned, which in turn had a lot to do with her parents' feelings and reactions. It was a revelation to Lisa that some of her fear had more to do with her mother's "old" fear than with her own.

In the "laboratory" of couples therapy and in the space between her and Michael, Lisa started to see how she was "wired," and how that has shaped her way of looking on life. She put her personal jigsaw puzzle together and found various ways to calm herself down, especially when she was worried. Lisa noticed that meditation and writing in her journal helped her to calm down. She even learned to look at her husband's (and her own) reactions with soft eyes and empathy. The calmer she became, the more independent she became, while still staying in contact. She simply started to take responsibility for herself and her own needs.

Michael could also see that time and time again, he contributed to Lisa's feeling of being outside and invisible. He also made his own exploration and began to understand why he so easily "turns off," flees and leaves the relationship in various ways. Now, Lisa can also see this.

The adventure that these two have embarked upon isn't primarily about saving their marriage. It's about meeting each other for real and, during that process, create integration between distinct and isolated parts of the brain and mind. Bit by bit, they *heal* themselves and each other. In doing so, they create the *possibility* of living in love.

Becoming Whole

Many clients of mine have stayed in therapy long after their partner left them to start a new life with a lover. The one who is left feels shattered. There, at the bottom of their feeling of abandonment, they have sought and received help, started their exploration and slowly came to realize how the past and present are connected. Then they have been able to integrate their experiences into a whole in their brain, finish their mourning, heal and move on.

The feelings of abandonment and grief that usually accompany a relationship break-up are natural and should be expressed fully. If the person in question doesn't carry within them any serious "dog bites" and deep craters, the grief can fairly quickly leave body and soul. But if you do have gnawing, implicit memories, the separation will probably give rise to panic, despair, resignation and a sense of powerlessness. Many people who set to work on their "dog bites" when they fell down into the abyss after a divorce say that the crisis became a priceless starting point for personal development. A number of my "abandoned" clients have learnt to regulate themselves, consciously open up to new love and have found a new partner who chooses to be truly with them.

Others, like Michael and Lisa, use the crisis to try to heal and re-create a good life together. I don't believe that either one of these ways is better than the other. It is just as important to say "hello" fully, fully, fully as it is to say "goodbye" fully, fully, fully. The important thing is to dare to commit ourselves to one or the other. So many of us hang in between, trying to both say hello and goodbye at the same time. We both want to be together and don´t want to be together. Usually, such "hanging" gets in the way of intimacy.

Through our development, we can very slowly let go of what we thought was "I" and instead create the "I" that we want to be.

It's important to remember, though, that we shall not wander around endlessly down in the crater, but only make short visits in order to understand our context. Then we shall choose a new route – one that goes where we want to go. The simple truth about the past is this: it's over and gone. Everything that happened more than a second ago is gone. It's old news. But, of course, this is only the case *if we don't live through our implicit memories.* If we do, we will relive the same emotions, the same problems and the same pain over and over again.

Bike Ride to Hell

Of course, I have endured many of the same relationship "disconnects" as everyone else. As I mentioned earlier, the important thing is not to try to avoid them, but to do your best to repair them. Here is a story from my own life

It is a Sunday afternoon in summer. Sven and I are going to take the motorcycle to an outdoor café, where some fifty bikers are going to meet for coffee. The sun is shining and we both enjoy the feeling of freedom, the beauty of nature, the smell of fresh-cut hay and the company of each other. The bikes drive in a row and the sound of the engines is one that only a bunch of Harley Davidson's can make; it's music to my ears.

My colleague Elsa, and her husband, Peter, are also at this outing. When we arrive at the café, we sit down with them and enjoy some coffee and cake. Then Sven stands up to greet some old friends who have just arrived.

Suddenly, something happens within me. I can see that Sven is like a fish in water and I start to feel more and more "outside." Earlier, on the way to the café, we had a fine time together. But now, I feel like he is completely absorbed with his old bike-riding friends. As I watch him laugh and talk with the other guys in leather, I feel completely forgotten.

A conviction awakens and grows strong within me: Sven doesn't care about me! I sneak up beside him, hoping to be able to work my way into the conversation, but they are all so busy with some common story from the past that no one seems to notice me.

Slowly but surely, I feel increasingly invisible, lonely and actually a bit *humiliated* by my husband. My anger rises. I turn around and walk away with quick, furious steps to a small grove where I can be alone. Now I'm boiling with rage. I want to go home at once. If I weren't depending on Sven and his bike to get away, I would have left.

From my perch on the hill, I turn around and look down at the group of leather-clad, happy people talking and drinking coffee. My husband is still in the same place where I left him, still laughing and obviously feeling good. Hasn't he even noticed that I left? Now I'm very close to marching out onto the road and hitching back home.

From my vantage point, I can also see Elsa and Peter talking cheerfully. I see Elsa glance at me, wondering. I feel like it's been hours since Sven bothered to see where his wife has gone. But now he does. He comes toward me in the grove.

"What are you doing up there? Are you calling someone?"

"No, I just wanted to be left alone," I reply sharply (and untruthfully).

Sven shakes his head. From his gaze and body language I realize that he feels very criticized, pressured and angry. And I feel outside, lonely, invisible and angry. He takes long strides – away from me.

A few minutes later, the bikes start up again, now for a nice trip back home in the sunshine. Angrily, I jump up on the back of the bike. The journey home is silent and dull. No comforting smells reach my nose, I hear no birdsong, and notice no music from the engines. Sven and I are completely out of sync. The evening is just as tense.

The next day I go to work early. During the drive, I think about the Sunday outing and our boring power struggle. I have two voices inside my head. One clearly and loudly says:

"Damn Sven, who is so nonchalant toward me! He could have been a bit nice and friendly – I'm the one who felt expelled! He doesn't care about me, and now I don't care about him."

The other voice whispers:" What if I was the one who invited this negative dance? What if I only *got the impression* that I was left out? What if it wasn't as bad as it felt inside? What if we are both dancing this dull dance?"

Elsa is already there when I arrive. I decide to ask her what she feels about Sven and his apparent arrogance. Since I help couples with similar things every day, there is a small doubt: *maybe, maybe, maybe* I don't see it quite clearly after all.

"Sven was nonchalant yesterday, wasn't he? Or am I blind again?"

Much to my surprise (and my great annoyance), Elsa says that she didn't perceive Sven as nonchalant or arrogant. Rather, she thought that I had been closed, strange and nonchalant.

"What happened, Eva?" she asks in a soft voice.

I sit down and tell her the entire story about what took place in my head. Elsa smiles and says: "Then you make sense!"

My annoyance was gone; instead I'm curious. "What did you see when you looked at Sven?"

"That he was having a good time, that he liked talking to his friends and that he was happy."

Now I understand that I have fallen down into a crater…just as I have so many times before! This one is called the "I'm invisible and not important" crater. Automatically, I put on my Armani suit and did what I so wisely learnt early in life--to walk away with my body full of anger and hopelessness. A suit that made me a martyr and filled with self-pity. My amygdala sounded the big alarm, twisted Sven's facial expression and read "busy with others," which to my brain means danger: *I don't exist any more; I'm invisible, forgotten, and all alone.*

Do you remember the example of a person who lifts his arm to wave? For a confident person, this probably means a greeting or some other positive thing. For a person who has been beaten, the arm can mean, "Now I will get beaten again." Unfortunately, the amygdala shouts its warning whether or not actual danger exists.

When I realized, with the aid of Elsa, what really happened and how my neurons connected, I feel great warmth for the little girl inside of me. I realize that I must see Sven for a moment--now.

Sven is in his office when I knock on his door.

"Yes!" he shouts.

Tentatively, I open the door. "Hi… do you have a moment?"

Sven glances up and looks both surprised and guarded. "Okay," he replies hesitantly. I step in and close the door.

"I'm the one who started our struggle yesterday. I'm sorry, Sven."

He sits quietly for a while, looks out the window and presses his lips together hard. Then he looks at me and says: "Thank you."

His voice is calm but his eyes aren't warm, not yet. And I understand that he hasn't been able to process what I have said.

"With the aid of Elsa I have realized … that I ruined a large part of your day yesterday. You must have felt angry and maybe abandoned and criticised when I just left. Is that right?"

"Yeah, that's right… but mainly I was confused. I didn't understand anything. We were having a good time and suddenly you were gone and when I found you, you were angry as hell." Sven pulls his hand through his hair and leans forward.

"Yes I know. Sorry. I fell down into a crater."

"Okay, what happened?"

"Oh, this is a bit shameful and vulnerable… I got the impression that you like your bike-riding friends much better than me… and I just wanted to go and leave you." Suddenly the tears come flowing and my chest is in a cramp. "Ugh, I recognize this feeling," I sob. The five-year-old within has come out and tears are running down my cheeks.

"I have always, always felt invisible and deserted, even though I was the cute little princess on parade. Mother was busy with her emotions and Daddy was drunk!"

Now I'm crying full force. Sven rises from his chair, come around and sits on the desk close to me; he puts his hand on mine.

"Tell me more," he whispers.

The words rush out of me. My body is filled with feelings of loneliness and shame, but this time I have my husband's presence, his breath, voice and warm hand. He listens and listens and finally he says:

"It wasn't so easy for you then, Eva."

"No," I reply in a whisper. And at the same moment, feelings of guilt rush in. "It feels embarrassing and difficult to say this about my mother, since I know she loved me so much. I know she didn't mean any harm."

At once I hear my therapist voice inside: *Eva, memories are not truth, just memories. Let go of the guilty feelings. It's okay! Remain in that feeling for a moment, so that you can live and understand it.* While I continue to sob, my built-in therapist continues: *To feel guilt is natural, but you don't have to carry it with you. She did what she could and it is okay.*

Sven interrupts my inner voice: "My dear wife, you are the most important person to me." Sven's words wake me up from my self-analysis, and I look shyly at him with red, swollen eyes. He continues: "You and the boys are the most important persons to me. You *can* need me. I can even understand that you felt a bit outside, since these friends are such an important part of my life. But I don't want you to feel that my bike-riding friends are *against you,* only that they are *for me."* He pauses and strokes my hand. Now I can look him in the eyes. They are warm.

"Does it feel better now?" he asks.

I nod silently. Yes, it feels much better, now that I'm back in my adult body as a forty-four year old (this happened a few years ago), a full-fledged grownup who really isn't afraid to be outside the group. My back straightens and I raise my head so that I can feel my spine creaking as the tendons stretch. I squeeze Sven's hand and say:

"You know, Sven, I am beginning to understand this. I will really make an effort to see what is what, and learn how to take care of myself when I get started like this. Will you help me a bit?"

"Sure, what can I do?"

"Next time we go away with your bike-riding friends, maybe you can wink at me; flirt a little, so that I know you are still in contact with me. And above all, if I get scared or look cold, don't take it personally, now that you know."

Sven laughs and says: "I'll be more than happy to do that. But remind me the next time, so that I don't forget it. I understand that this is important for you."

"I will also try to find some positive trigger so that I can regulate and calm myself when I start to feel invisible," I whisper.

"That sounds like a brilliant idea."

"Thank you for listening."

"Thank you for telling me all of this."

We hugged for a long time in his office. Then I went out to the car and drove back to work.

When I step into my office, Elsa looks questioningly at me. I smile and say:

"Thanks!"

She nods kindly.

With a straight back and a big ball of warmth in my stomach, I greet the first couple of the day at the clinic.

Again and Again, We Tumble Down

Later, Sven told me that he naturally had fallen into his own quite frequently-visited crater--that is, the feeling of being criticized and trapped. Interestingly enough, he quickly jumped into his own Armani suit and turned off towards me (and maybe opened up more than usual towards his other – safer – friends). His response made him realize that he enhanced my feeling of being outside and invisible.

In the dance of the power struggle, the two of us play out our implicit and explicit memories in the space between us. But we can learn to notice when we plunge, build a colourful ladder and learn to climb up out of the crater. One way to get up the ladder is to find positive triggers. By a "trigger," I mean a behaviour, word, gesture, thought, smell, or sound – anything that triggers a certain reaction or feeling. The feeling can be positive or negative. Personally, I found a small pebble that I often carried in my pocket to remind me that I'm not outside or insignificant. When I didn't have the pebble with me, I just had to think about it, and the thought helped me get my ladder in place.

So, once again, let us look at conflicts as exciting opportunities. They put the searchlight on our unconscious memories and give us the chance to learn new things! With the aid of our imagination, let us see all of our little Croatian, Indian, English, Nigerian and Swedish men and women run around in our head, digging tracks and deep craters. Let us see how our brain works when, out of habit, we run around in these tracks and how strangely *right* it feels to be there, in spite of the fact that the track doesn't lead us where we want to go.

We can stop building an immune defence system for experiences that the amygdala sounds the alarm for. When I talk about the "immune defence system," I like to use a simple metaphor:

One of my sons is allergic to, among other things, cats. To enable him to visit friends who have cats, a little "cat" is planted inside him every six weeks. In an allergy office, he gets tiny doses injected into his bloodstream, which increases his tolerance to cats. Because this has been going on for a number of years, his body is now used to cats. With time, the body learns to protect itself. It's the same way with our brain.

If we return to the example of the fire alarm in the hotel, we can see that I gained a new experience: when the fire alarm goes off, it does not necessarily mean disaster. My brain has "fired and wired" neurons that have given my mind a new experience.

And when Sven is angry, negative, closed or under stress, I do not have to conclude that it is a disaster, even though it feels that way. Nor do I have to get it into my head that I don't exist, don't have any right to needs, and must arrange and take care of everything. Through experiences like the false fire alarm, I have "scanned in" new truths that tell me I'm safe and fine. This means that I can have experiences similar to ones that were previously very painful, but now with a strengthened neural "immune defence" and the calm of an adult. My son can let a cat pass by him without suffering shortness of breath. This does not mean that he should have his lap filled with cats--or that I should start working as a firefighter. If we have a strong "allergy," we must of course be careful; but we can learn how to build up a tolerance so that we are less affected than before. Of course, there are some things that we should *not* try to get immune to, such as physical or emotional abuse.

Mindfulness

There are many ways to help the middle part of our prefrontal cortex to become more active and in charge, so that our reptilian brain doesn't so easily kidnap us. It's indeed too late to change things that happened in the past, but it's never too late to repair, take responsibility for what is NOW and create new memories for the future.

Daniel Siegel describes how our prefrontal cortex is altered when we are mindful. The more often we use that part of the brain, the more neuron-connections are created there. So, remember: *use it or lose it!* [50]

As you remember, the prefrontal cortex is the part of the brain that is in contact with all three main parts of the brain: the cortex, the limbic area and the brain stem. When our prefrontal cortex grows, it helps us to get access to the nine abilities that lead to integration, harmony and balance; regulating the body, attuning to others, regulating and balancing emotions, being flexible in our responses, soothing fear, creating empathy, creating insight, creating moral awareness and intuition.

Researchers have seen that the seven first also arises in safe attachment. Many people claim that we can get access to these abilities when we practice meditation and mindful presence, or *mindfulness*. Mindfulness is defined as paying attention, in the present moment, on purpose, without making any judgment.

The "Crossing the Bridge" dialogue that I use is one way to be mindful in the present moment, first within yourself and then together with someone else.

Another way to practice being present is a short, simple exercise that you can do yourself and requires only 20 minutes of your time and

---

50 Daniel Siegel, *The Mindful Brain*, page 42 and *The Neurobiology of We,* cd.

a chair. (No yoga mats, sitar music or crossed legs are needed, though of course they can be used.)

Sit down in a comfortable chair and place your feet flat on the floor. Once you find a comfortable position, put your hands on your lap. Close your eyes and *experience* your breathing, without trying to control it. Just observe your breathing, in and out, calmly and quietly. Don't try to change anything. When your attention floats away toward a thought, a sound or something that you can feel in your body, just calmly return your attention to your breathing.

Carry out this practice for 20 minutes, both morning and evening. After a while, you will notice positive things happening in your mind, brain and your relationships. You may notice that you become more flexible, adaptive, coherent, energized and stable. [51]

If you want to learn more about *mindfulness*, there are a number of books, DVDs and CDs on the topic. Jon Kabat-Zinn's book, *Wherever You Go, There You Are* is one that I recommend. You can also listen to a wonderful piece called "Wheel of Awareness" at Dr. Daniel Siegel's home page: www.drdansiegel.com

---

51 Daniel Siegel, *The Mindful Brain, page 78,164,199,207-8,226,288*

Are you the result of your past?
Or a cause of the future?

Lᴀʀs-Eʀɪᴄ Uɴᴇsᴛåʜʟ

1 4

You Can Make it Happen

Envisioning Your Life

In this book I have discussed how the brain, memory and interpersonal communication work, and how they can help us to achieve--or hinder-- our life goals. Do you know what direction you want to take in your important relationships and your life in general?

Think of it this way: at some point, all of us have found ourselves in the wrong place without actually knowing how we ended up there. When I'm really tired, I can sometimes sit in my car and drive to work like a robot although it's not there I'm going. Autopilot rules! That's how it is in much of life: we have a tendency to do what we've always done. So, in order to do something new, we must program ourselves anew. It is very important to get a clear image of our goals, so as not to get lost on the way. If we don't have a clear goal, there is nothing to motivate us to act, and we may even feel that life has little meaning.

A sense of purpose primarily gives us a feeling of being in control of a life that we choose ourselves. It strengthens our self-esteem and gives everyday life a structure. We learn to organize our days wisely. A vision helps us keep our motivation alive. That goes for sports, private enterprise and our personal lives – including our loving relationships. Therefore, we need to consciously choose images that we want to run our internal autopilot. If old "truths" have burrowed into our brains, creating deep neuron tracks, they will sometimes guide us towards something we don't want. Think about the pile of sand and the bucket of water! Let's instead dig new channels in the sand and consciously create our *future memories*.

Mental Training

When you think of a loving relationship, what do you see in front of you? How do you want to feel and behave with your partner? What does love look like, for you? Can you easily paint pictures of what you want, or do you tend to get stopped by everything that's in the way? Do you get stuck in what you *don't* want instead of what you *do* want and need?

It's easy to get mired in obstacles and problems, especially so in our culture, which tends to focus on disaster, conflict, threat and danger (especially in the media). But as I mentioned earlier, *everything we focus on grows.* That means that if we only see obstacles, obstacles are what we will meet.

In order for a company to be successful, it must create a vision, goals and a business plan. The same goes for us as individuals. We need to have a clear idea about where we are *right now* and to define *where we are headed.* There is a gap between the place we are and the place we want to be in the future. If we want to reach that new place, we must get the map out, take out the course and with enthusiasm start the trip with our nose pointed in the right direction! To do otherwise would be like playing soccer without a goal; we would just kick the ball around without having any idea where to go. What are the chances, do you think, that we would kick the ball through the goalposts?

I have helped myself install new, goal-oriented images through a process of "mental training." Mental training means, simply, to train our brain and mind. The way we do that is to create a "room" in our minds. During a relaxation session, I could create a safe mental room inside of me where the target images could steer my autopilot. The founder of mental training, Lars-Erik Unerståhl, says:

"A main task for the basic mental training is to create a mental room. This room gets to define the alternate awareness or state of mind where a large part of the mental exercise is placed. With advanced EEC-technique it has been possible to show that the brain uses another "operating system" in the mental room. Among other things, the differences in activity between the front and the back of the brain disappear. The differences also disappear between the left and the right half of the brain. There is thus an integration and synchronisation of the activity in the brain." [52]

When we create a mental room during deep relaxation, it is easier for the brain to accept the new images as possible "truths." You could say that the brain ignores the old map and *passes by* what we have experienced earlier.

If the mental training is to be successful, establishing the mental room is of great importance. For me, it was crucial since I didn't have any experience of having a "safe place" to go to. I remember the first time I listened to a relaxation tape in which Lars-Eric Uneståhl said: "Go into yourself... into your mental room...." I was very surprised, but also relieved as I started to realize that I did have a safe place inside myself! A place where I could decide how I wanted to feel, live and be. Until then, my craters had been filled to overflowing with powerlessness and fear. In my separate mental room, I slowly built up new tracks of safety, power, relaxation, joy and possibilities. I could choose and have an influence on my mind and life!

We are most open to self-influencing when we are in our mental room because in that space, thoughts and ideas can slip by our critical, logical thinking processes. Under *deep relaxation,* the mental obstacles we normally put up are out of order and the new information we send to ourselves is accepted. In this alternate state, we are open to new ideas and goals. We can see what we want to see, feel what we want to feel, and behave as we like.

Our nervous system has great difficulty distinguishing between a real event and an imaginary situation perceived in a lively and detailed way. The negative side of this (as you probably know) is that time and

---

52 Lars-Eric Uneståhl, Swedish book: *Integrerad Mental Träning,* page 17 Translated by Eva Berlander (web site in English: www.siu.nu)

time again, we are triggered and *get the idea* that terrible things are happening. But the positive side is that we can also create new, energizing "truths" that are just as strong. When we have decided what self-image we want and have created goals for the future, we can begin to integrate these images into our mental room. Gradually, these images begin to take over the steering function in our brain, like an autopilot.

Our autopilot runs us all the time. As I mentioned earlier, it often steers us towards what we don't want instead of towards what we want. A simple example: I'm going to fetch something but suddenly realize that I'm standing with the door to the refrigerator open and wondering what I'm doing there. Or, I think I'm putting away the butter but later I find it among the coffee cups. And I drive to work when I've meant to go to the store. These things easily happen when we're tired and unfocused.

When you create new pictures in your mental room, you can actually steer yourself towards a chosen outcome *in spite of the fact that you live in the midst of the process* and are completely focused on what is happening now. So, instead of creating a self-image that is based on the past, you choose new "memories" from the future.

Mental training is achieved by practicing systematic, long-term exercises at a slow pace. After acquiring basic knowledge of the process, you then practice, practice, and practice until you become competent. Gradually, new images will be integrated in such a natural way that they'll automatically alter your behaviour. Often, people around you are the first to notice the changes in you.

Here is a simple target picture: Think about a time when you were really pleased with yourself. For the moment, put all your self-critical ideas away. Close your eyes and take a moment to remember and imagine this time when you felt wonderful about yourself.

Now, how did that feel in your body? How did you move; what did you voice sound like? How did you look? What do you think others saw when they looked at you? What was it that made you feel so pleased?

Freeze this image. Remember, we're not including negative thoughts here. Write down all of your positive images, thoughts and feelings.

If you want to, you can bring this feeling with you into an imagined relationship. See yourself and your partner in the relationship. How do you look, how do you move, and what does your voice sound like? How do you feel in your body? Once again, put obstacles and impossibilities aside and see your goal. Look at yourself and see how you are *just the one you want to be.*

If you'd like to learn to install such images in your mental room, there are numerous relaxation CDs and tapes to help you. You find more information in English at: www.mtsweden.com

The Power of Positive Triggers

In our mental room, we can replace negative triggers with positive ones. Everyone knows that elite athletes often use positive triggers, that is, some symbolic act or gesture that helps them to enter a state of mind where everything goes as they've programmed. They fly over the bar, cross the finishing line first, make lots of goals, and so on.

When I first began to meditate, I found it trying when the house was filled with sounds. But with time, I have managed to shift my brain in such a way that when I hear the sound of voices, they become a positive trigger that help me relax and go deeper into my meditation. Such reprogramming is not done in a jiffy, but everything that we practice sooner or later is learnt. So the more often I choose to focus on sounds in a positive way, the easier it is for me to find my calm.

The most common way to approach change is by force of will and teeth-gritted effort--which often doesn't work. To succeed, we need to create new, positive triggers so that we can gradually make our chosen images and behaviour automatic. Using this process, we bypass the force of will that can easily lock us into the problem rather than free us from it.

For me, another positive trigger is a small sticker--a little red dot--that I often use in my workshops as well as at home. The dots symbolise things that we like about ourselves and each other. So, when I see the dots in various places (in the car, on the mirror, on the fridge), my thoughts and emotions automatically go to appreciation of myself and others. They go straight to the small picture of appreciation that I placed earlier in my mental album.

The Happiness Factor

If you can imagine a rewarding life in the future, you'll start becoming happier today. Since you now see yourself as a person who is capable of making the change you want, you automatically become more satisfied in the present. You realise that your state of mind isn't dependent on your partner, money, boss, weight, wrinkles or coincidence. You experience that you actually have power in your own life.

Research about what makes us "happy" confirms that in our society, we often get the impression that true happiness equals material well-being, fame, a beautiful partner, perfect health, and so on. But this is not so. We must be able to tell the difference between true and false success so that we don't vainly chase after the wrong things. Many studies show that strong, loving relationships are the key to satisfaction, not things or money. Often, we don't realize what is important in life until it's too late--we get ill, or a loved one dies. Let's not wait that long.

Still, I think we should "put a heart around" our chase for material happiness, since it is a way that we automatically try to calm our nervous system. It's natural, especially in a society that so openly encourages us to consume. Of course, we try the things that are offered! We want to feel calm and alive, and it often feels good--at least in the short term--to buy something new, make a good investment, trade in our car, have plastic surgery or switch our partner. We may do some things fanatically or excessively often: work, eat, drink, exercise, redecorate, clean, sleep, have sex, smoke, shop, go to therapy, argue, divorce, remarry, and so on. We do it because it feels better, we feel more alive – for the moment. Some people get addicted to adrenaline rushes by often exposing themselves to risks, such as mountain climbing, dangerous driving, making risky investments, committing crimes or having sex with strangers. These activities can become a kind of drug.

Unfortunately these behaviours rarely lead us where we really want to go. To try to calm the nervous system when it's out of balance is a natural reaction. But when we do things excessively, it often means that we are trying to avoid "the dog bite" by dulling its pain. We are simply kidding ourselves. The feeling of happiness is often short-lived, since happiness is not about food, money (well, maybe a little), drugs, luxury or sex. Naturally, I don't mean that it's wrong to climb mountains, enjoy sex or eat a delicious dessert. It's just that genuine happiness resides in relationships, *in the space between us* and in the limbic resonance.

Let's now continue the story of Lisa and Michael. When we left them last, they had just contacted the pain behind their own addictive behaviours. What's in store for them?

Lisa and Michael: Going Inward, Reaching Out

With help, Michael was able to recognize his "allergy" to emotions (especially sadness and hopelessness) and his strategy to close down all contact and softer emotions through anger. What would have happened if he had not understood that? What would have happened if he had not realized that he actually was *screaming* for contact, to be heard?

When his parents closed off their feelings and couldn't deal with their own grief, the loss became locked in Michael as a trauma. It was a trauma that he learnt to deal with by closing off his softer emotions, just like his parents had done. His amygdala now had an important mission: to make sure he never ended up in that kind of pain again! Michael was totally unaware that this had happened.

When Lisa cried or was demanding, dissatisfied and sad for a long time, Michael automatically closed off his feelings for her. He symbolically felt abandoned – again – and as powerless before Lisa's tears as he had before his mother's. To turn off was a very intelligent strategy for avoiding the old pain. He tried to further diminish the isolation and imbalance in his nervous system by, among other things, hard work, hard exercise and excessive achievement. Now, finally, he'd begun to see the bigger picture.

If Michael had not started to understand his jigsaw puzzle of neuronal networks, what would have happened? Maybe he would have divorced Lisa, thought that love was "over" and continued to blame himself. He certainly would have tried to find experiences that made him feel alive again. He may have continued to fall in love, over and over again. Or perhaps he would have married Cecilia or someone else, felt excellent and become reconciled with his past in some other way. Perhaps he would have chosen to live alone.

But my guess is that, sooner or later, Michael's implicit memories would have caught up with him, triggering depression, burnout, illness or another kind of crisis.

Meanwhile, what would have happened to Lisa if she had not understood the connection between now and then--that she so often felt abandoned and exploited because of her early experiences? What would have happened if she'd continued to believe that only *someone else* could fill the emptiness she was carrying? If Lisa and Michael had divorced, she would probably have found a new partner in a panic to feel that she existed, someone who could help her feel alive. But in time, that wouldn't have filled the gap either – since no one but she could accomplish that.

What did happen was that Michael and Lisa started to put together their jigsaw puzzle, understand the connections between present and past, and help each other to honour and nurture the space between them. With tentative steps, they chose to try something new. Michael's falling in love with Cecilia had been very real and very tangible. But now, he understood that falling in love wasn't the same thing as genuine loving and that in time, he would likely end up in a similar power struggle with Cecilia.

At the same time, Lisa was learning some important things about herself. She was learning to let go of the powerlessness that she sometimes felt over not being seen or loved. She could calm and regulate her jumpy nervous system herself and didn't have to get stuck in a tangle of emotions. Instead, she could cross the bridge to Michael (and herself) and lay out the puzzle. Give and receive.

Michael could practice to dare to be close, and dare to need Lisa and cross the bridge to her (and to himself). Give and receive. Both choose to face their "dog bites," reconcile with their past and put in new pictures for the future that they have chosen themselves. If they continue along this path, they will eventually behave this way without even thinking. They will have treaded new paths--paths the size of highways.

Walking A Fine Line

Important caution: We are supposed to only dip our toes into our craters. If, when we get this far, we continue to descend and then swim around in our old pain, dwell on it and analyse it, we either create new negative tracks or strengthen the old ones. And they can lead us seriously astray. We must choose not to step down too far or too long, and instead let go of our pain as soon as we understand the connection between our present and our past.

This is important because many who are, or have been, in therapy run the risk of building a kind of identity from the negative experiences. It can sound something like this: "I am terrified of being abandoned because I was abandoned as a child" or "I drink because I was beaten by my father" or "I turn off all emotions because I had to do that as a child." Then you mix the present with things that happened a long time ago – and stay stuck in the past. Remember: *everything we focus on grows*. Instead, we can understand and acknowledge what happened to us as children, feel that pain again for a short while, and then--importantly--move on to a different and better present.

How Do We Calm Ourselves?

I now want to invite you to try to look at what you use to calm your own nervous system--but which doesn't lead you where you want to go. One way is to ask yourself: "Which way is my energy directed? What do I think I need to feel good?"

Now, this is a bit tricky. After all, it can be good to find conscious ways to calm ourselves down. It can be very good to exercise, read, bathe, light a candle, clean, meditate, sing, play the violin, get more sleep or whatever else we do – just to give ourselves a gift and treat ourselves as valuable. Many things that we do *feel* like they are leading us where we want to go. Some do, but others don't. How do we know which is which?

Well, once again we can observe where we get stuck in life. Where are our lights directed? Maybe on continued rows with our partner or our kids, conflicts at work or with friends, aggression, bad health, unsound use of alcohol or food, or excessive pill-taking. Yet, we may not recognize those activities as unhealthy. If we are stuck in abuse, we are also often in such strong denial that we are deaf and blind to our own havoc.

But the people around us do hear and do see. Do you dare to ask your close ones: *What do you think that I'm doing that's bad for me?* Do you dare to listen to the reply and with objective ears and eyes discover whether it's true? If, for instance, we have an alcohol or other substance abuse problem, we need to receive help with great love for ourselves. Recovering from addiction is rarely something we can do all by ourselves.

When our unhealthy behaviours knock hard and long and we still don't listen, they usually finally show up as some kind of crisis--a crisis that gives us the opportunity to face what is hiding implicitly in our mind. Often, these crises show up around "big birthdays," such as when we turn forty, fifty or sixty. They might show up as a sharp increase in dissatisfaction in one's marriage, losing interest in one's job, or a stress-related illness such as high blood pressure or chronic stomach problems.

What luck!

What I previously and unconsciously did to calm my own nervous system was to talk. That's right: Talk about emotions, preferably about problems, analyse emotions and so on for all eternity. Talk, talk, chatter, chatter. Talking was my drug. No wonder I became a therapist!

In the beginning, it calmed me down. Purely hormonally, many people (especially women) feel calmer when they talk, so to a certain extent it fit in physically. But in my case, I talked and analysed so much that I permanently moved down into the crater and decorated it. Sven, on the other hand, let himself be engulfed in his work, or took the car or his bike and drove away... far away.

When we engage in escapist or addictive behaviours, what we are really screaming for is limbic resonance. We scream so that someone – sometimes ourselves – will really hear our signals. Will hear them and receive them with empathy. Sonja Lyubomirsky, professor of psychology at UCLA, writes: "In order to become happier, we must learn to imitate the habits of very happy people. Happy people are exceptionally good at their friendships, family and intimate relationships." [53]

How Do We Do It?

The psychologist John Gottman films married couples and then observes systematically how they speak and behave towards each other. In his research, Gottman has filmed hundreds of couples in everyday situations. From these observations, he claims that he can predict, with 90 percent certainty, which couples that will stick together and which will divorce.

---

53 Sonja Lyubomirsky, *The How of Happiness,* page 139

Can you guess how many loving actions those in intimate and safe relationships perform every day? It's more than 100! They stroke their partner's back, give hugs, offer tea, say "hi" in a loving voice, make eye contact when they talk, listen attentively, behave playfully, call each other often, join hands in everyday situations …and the list goes on.

According to Gottman, for every negative thing we do in our marriage, we need to do five positive ones to balance it! Couples in very good relationships do this automatically. They appreciate each other and choose to do what works.

The interesting thing is that all couples have the same kind of problems, more or less. The difference between harmonious couples and the ones who get struck in power struggles is how they *deal* with those problems. Often, we get the idea that we have to sort out and solve every problem before we can be kind, respectful and loving to each other. This goes for all close relationships, not only our romantic relationships. When we dress up in our Armani suits (that is, stay hidden behind our defences), focusing on the negative is a natural response. But when we live from the knowledge that we are valuable, we don't need to do that. We can shed the suit and act from a place of generosity because compassion and kindness are integration made visible.

Holding Both: Connection and Individuality

What is the secret of a successful marriage, according to John Gottman? Well, we need to listen to each other, make time for each other, stay in contact, appreciate each other and show our gratitude in a variety of ways. According to Gottman, we then bring out the best in each other and help each other to become whole.

We also need to value and respect the other, acknowledge our differences and appreciate what we see – that is, to *differentiate*. The ability to deal effectively with conflicts is also of great importance. If we learn to hear each other, be tolerant and even curious about our differences, and communicate our message and needs with respect for each other, our conflicts can lead to true intimacy.

Of course, all of this is easier said than done. No book can do this for us. But a book can help us create a vision of the kind of relationship we want. It can inspire us to take our relationships, ourselves and our lives seriously--and then to act in ways that help us to meet our goals.

A small exercise in appreciation:

Take three minutes a day to show appreciation and gratitude for something someone else has done. You can express appreciation toward your partner, a child, a friend, yourself – or why not all of the above? You could say something like: "I really appreciated the e-mail I got from you today, because that made me realize that you think of me" or "I love when you look at me this way, because that makes me feel seen" or "I really appreciated that you got me up this morning, because I really needed to get to work on time."

These small acts of gratitude can make a big difference in your relationship and create many new positive tracks in the mind.

"Thank you for…. Thank you……" (Translation from Swedish to English by Eva Berlander)

*Our deepest fear is not that we are inadequate.
Our deepest fear is that we are powerful beyond measure.
It is our light, not our darkness that most frightens us.
We ask ourselves, who am I to be brilliant, gorgeous, talented, fabulous?
Actually, who are you not to be?
You are a child of God. Your playing small does not serve the world.
There is nothing enlightened about shrinking so that other people won't feel insecure around you.
We are all meant to shine, as children do.
We were born to make manifest the glory of God that is within us.
It's not just in some of us; it's in everyone.
And as we let our own light shine, we unconsciously give other people permission to do the same. As we are liberated from our own fear, our presence automatically liberates others.*

MARIANNE WILLIAMSON (AND NELSON MANDELA)

1 5

Living Instead of Surviving

Valuing the Self

How many of us wake up in the morning, look in the mirror in the bathroom and happily exclaim: "Good morning, wonderful person!" No, most of us have learnt not to boast or emphasize ourselves, and instead to be modest and even to criticize ourselves. Early on, we learned that "self-praise is no recommendation."

Or is it? I still remember the day that I opened a white envelope from the hospital, my stomach gnawing with anxiety. The letter said that my latest mammography examination had shown changes in my right breast. I was told to call immediately for further tests.

In an instant, I saw a horror-vision of my maimed body--radiation therapy, chemotherapy, baldness and death. With sweating hands, I called Sven at work. In my world, I was certain that I did have breast cancer.

Three days later, I lay exhausted with anxiety on the examination bed. My usually calm husband sat stiff with fear in the waiting room, holding all fingers crossed for me to be well. He had promised to rush in, whether permitted or not, if the result was negative and he heard me scream in despair.

I cannot express the relief I felt when the nurse came in and told me that they hadn't found any unnatural alterations. My breasts and I were completely healthy.

Oh what a fantastic experience! I felt like I'd gotten my life back. I'd entered the hospital with my back bent and body half-paralyzed, breathing in gasps high up in the throat like a frightened dog. Now I almost danced out the door, my back straight, my breath calm, my body bubbling with life. I could feel joy of life, enthusiasm, gratitude and humility. I thought about everyone else who that day was told that his or her body carried a life-threatening disease.

That evening, I really felt like I loved life! But, you can't love life without loving yourself--can you? After I'd brushed my teeth, I looked in the mirror, smiled widely and said aloud, "Good night, wonderful you!"

I often give a lecture that I call "Living Instead of Surviving – in Relationships." By that I don't simply mean that we should be glad to be alive. I mean that we look at ourselves and the world in a completely different way when we are grateful and happy that we are alive. We see our entire existence through a lens of appreciation and gratitude, and then we can look underneath the Armani suits to our inner being, the core in both ourselves and others. When we see the best and treat ourselves and others as valuable, we can *live* rather than just defending ourselves and surviving. And isn't it sad that many of us fail to be really alive until death throws a shadow over us?

Why Be Kind?

There is a Tibetan saying: "When you smile at life, half your smile is for your face and half for someone else's." Isn't that beautiful?

One way to be true to your inner being is to put kindness, friendliness and concern in the space between yourself and others. Stefan Einhorn says that "A person that is kind is on the path to success. He believes that kindness is the single most important factor when it comes to how successful we will be in our lifes" [54] He also says that true kindness is when you want to be good and act accordingly--or at least try. We try to take an action that corresponds with the other person's needs, I would add. If we want to be kind, we must first find out how the other wants to be treated. Otherwise, we can do very wrong, for other person may not experience what we offer as positive. Many times we have a tendency to give gifts that *we* want others to have – again, we mix up ourselves with others. We must remember: You are not I. And then we need to ask questions like, "What do you need from me? What do you appreciate? Did I understand you correctly?"

The road to happiness goes through the corridor of kindness. We need to be a source of joy to each other. It is said that laughter is the shortest distance between two persons, because unstoppable, infectious joy immediately creates a social bond or, if we wish, limbic resonance. This is important to remember, since it's so easy for us to believe that we have to sort out difficulties before we can have fun together. But we can choose to place laughter, play and joy in the space between us. Then it will also be easier to face the challenges that we also have to address.

The Dalai Lama believes that we can choose to be kind for purely egoistic reasons. We don't have to be kind for any other reason than our own, because, what we give always comes back.

There is a lot to this idea. But I believe that we need to go one step further and *choose* to create safe attachment and new neural tracks, *regardless* of what we get in return. When we choose to step out of ourselves and into another person's world, miracles happen. We differentiate, are linked together again and experience that you and I have the same value. When we do that, there is integration between us and also within us, inside our brains.

When we choose to give gifts that feel a bit challenging, we shall of course not abuse ourselves, but we can give and be generous, because

---

54 Stefan Einhorn, *The Art of being Kind*, location 51 (kindle)

at the same time, we get the chance to develop further as partners and human beings.

Strangely enough, our close ones often seem to need what is most difficult for us to give them. Not out of malice, but because their needs automatically force us to take off our Armani suits! Mostly, it feels difficult, nasty and threatening. We feel naked. But when we do it, we also give ourselves a big gift.

Hi, Bag!

In our marriage, Sven and I have given each other many, many chances to develop – gifts in both directions. I'm thinking especially of a gift that wasn't so hard for him to give but meant the world to me. For a period of six weeks, he chose to give me the experience that I could change and make a difference. It was about that damn beer can again.

At this time in my life, the presence of alcohol was a serious negative trigger for me. Whenever Sven went to the fridge to open a beer, my amygdala woke up. The "snap" of the can opening was like a gunshot; to me, it was a battle signal. I lashed out at him as if he had done something terrible!

After Sven had crossed the bridge to me and started to understand my memories of my father's abuse of alcohol and my own horror of it, he chose to help me for a while. We decided that when I got afraid and worried, he would stop drinking. Every time I used our secret code: "Hi, bag!" (rather than "don't drink any more!" or some other command that could easily trigger his anger and defiance), Sven put down his glass. Right then and there. Sven is not an alcoholic and not a particularly big drinker, but this gift was a very loving and generous act. At first we did this for six weeks, bur since this was such a strong trauma for me; he offered it again and again and again.

Even now, as I'm writing this, I get tears in my eyes, so much did Sven's act of kindness mean to me. It wasn't really so much about the alcohol, but rather that I got to experience that I could make a difference;

that I was heard, that I meant so much to my husband that he listened to me and put down his glass. My father was in total denial, and because of it, he didn't listen to me, and that "dog bite" lingered on in the space between Sven and me. He often got the blame for things that I carried around – not because I was mean but because my brain reacted in panic. Now he could instead *heal* me and help me integrate my implicit memories with present reality. And I understood that my reptile-run tantrums were really about a fear that I *projected* onto my husband. Now I could see that I did have the power to change. After a while, I just had to think, "Hi, bag!" to relax, because those words had become a positive trigger in my mind -- a trigger to safety and relaxation.

It has been many years now since I said, "Hi bag!" But I'm sure that if I did, my husband would listen.

For his part, Sven's opportunity to develop wasn't to give up drinking, but to let go of his allergy to being controlled by someone else. In his old crater, he felt powerless, criticized and controlled. But by consciously giving me a loving gift, he became less defensive about these issues. In this way he gave himself a loving gift, too--a chance to heal, integrate and make new neuron tracks.

Before this breakthrough, when we struggled for power at home in our living room dressed in our most elegant suits, Sven became closed, insensitive and impossible to reach. *Just like my father used to do when he was drunk and my mother when she was sad.* In response, I became even more controlling, critical and invasive, the very qualities that had most harmed Sven earlier in his life. Neither of us had parents who wanted to do any harm. But this is how bad things can get, generation after generation, when we don't wake up and become conscious of the connection between past and present.

Good and Generous?

The feeling of having influence is a great experience. As adults, we need to realise that we always can influence ourselves, and that we also sometimes receive a gift that heals. And while we wait for a gift to arrive, we can always give one. What luck!

It's an interesting thought that when we are generous and willing to face another person (though it may feel uncomfortable to us); we do wonders for the world. For many years, I thought that I was generous with gifts, but thanks to the stubbornness of my husband I realized that I sometimes gave just because I wanted something back! Everything was about me then, and I couldn't quite receive Sven – which makes complete sense. To him, my gifts turned into demands.

I think that we do this often. We feel good and generous, but we have a hidden agenda. Maybe it's because we are closest to ourselves, and therefore tend to see everything through the I-lens? But when we can grasp another person's world and realize that we can do well for someone else, we have, in a way, created a foundation for world peace. It is a foundation that makes it easier to continue and to think further about including others--not just those who are close to us, but also those who are not.

It takes skill to give without self-interest, and just like anything else, it may take some practice. But it's worth it. To be kind changes you and your self-perception. If you do good for other people, you begin to look on yourself as a helpful and compassionate person, an identity that makes you feel more optimistic and useful. In short, doing good increases your self-esteem.

Kindness is contagious. When we choose to be kind, respectful, generous, emphatic, and playful with our partner (and everyone else, including ourselves), our actions generate even more kindness and generosity. New research shows that it takes only *witnessing or hearing about* a kind act for us to feel happy and loving inside and feel an urge to do good deeds.

Isolation Lessons

In our part of the world, we often live by mottos like, "It's every man for himself" or "if you want something done well, do it yourself" or "don't interfere." In a hundred ways, we've been told that independence is a must. Some of this, of course, is good--we must put up limits when someone actually hurts us. But some of our responses, unfortunately, are just the dance of the Armani suits – a dance that leads to conflict, war and untold misery. In spite of our individualistic ideals, we still need each other very much.

When we experience that people walk all over us and feel the need to defend ourselves, we should start by listening to our inner signals. This is because we often react to what we *think* is happening, not what is actually happening, and then naturally respond by putting limits on what we *think* is happening. When we do that, we don't listen to our own core, or that of the other person. We are lost in struggle and fighting.

When we defend ourselves against something that we *think* is happening, the other naturally responds with his or her own defence – and where does that lead? We can see it in conflicts between couples and friends, but also between nations and different groups. As I write this, I can't help being curious about what some important people with power (for instance, political, religious and financial leaders) carry along in their implicit memories. Of course, I'm aware of the fact that worldly conflicts are based on more than the childhood trauma or lack of safe attachment in an individual leader, but *the way to solve conflicts* may be affected more by this than we think.

It's an interesting thought, isn't it?

In our own lives, if we don't listen to our own implicit "existential scream," we may be forced to leave many partners and friends – or they will leave us -- due to conflicts. As I've mentioned, I usually say to clients seeking my aid: "If you like the results you get, continue to do what you do. If you don't like the result, do something else." I think that is a key concept. We always have the power to choose something else.

"Let's take a new road.... Yea!!" (Translation from Swedish to English by Eva Berlander)

Choosing Connection

We *can* choose kindness, appreciation and praise. We can choose caresses, hugs and smiles. We can choose to cross the bridge and really listen to our partner, our children, parents, friends, and colleagues. If we choose to make a friendly visit to the other, we not only give him or her a fantastic feeling of being important and valuable, but – interestingly enough – we let go of our own feeling that we are responsible for the other's pain, anger or sorrow. It means that we are valuable, too, no matter how the other feels or behaves. It's quite miraculous.

When the middle part of our prefrontal cortex works well, we can regulate ourselves. We act calmly, soberly and clearly. We feel no need to defend ourselves. We put up clear, friendly and simple limits. Unfortunately, there is the risk of mixing up "putting limits" and think that we're standing up for ourselves when we respond with a strong and even violent defence. In some cases, this may be necessary in order to save our lives, but usually not when we argue about who is supposed to take out the garbage. When we go into defence or attack mode, we have fallen deep down into our crater – and the dance is on. We can see this at home, in psychotherapy, in TV debates (which promotes this kind of battle dramaturgy since it makes for "better" TV) and in war and conflicts in the world.

Peace of Mind

A lot of people know the peace of mind prayer, which is said to have been written by the American theologian Reinhold Niebuhr and often is used in Alcoholics Anonymous' twelve-step program.

> *(God), grant me the serenity to accept the things I cannot change,*
> *Courage to change the things I can,*
> *And wisdom to know the difference.*

This text has been very important to me. Many of us have put incredible energy in trying to change others (which is an Armani suit as well), without success. Not so very strange – since we *can't* actually change others. What a waste, considering all the time and energy we spent and which came to nothing. And how fortunate we are to have realized that! It means that we can let go of trying to control other people's behaviour, feelings and thoughts and use our powers to change the one person we can change – ourselves. As the old saying goes, you can lead a horse to water but you can't make him drink.

We're in Charge of Our Joy

Everyone wants to be happier, but is that really possible for everyone? Sonya Lyobomirsky writes:

> "Any major life-changing endeavour must be accompanied by considerable sustained effort, and I would speculate that the majority of people do not or cannot continue putting in that kind of effort. What's more, all new happiness-enhancing or health-boosting strategies have something in common, and that is that each one bestows on the person a specific *goal*, something to do and to look forward to. And having goals in and of themselves is strongly associated with happiness and life satisfaction. That's why, at least for a time, any new happiness strategy does work! In a nutshell, the fountain of happiness can be found in how you behave, what you think and what goals you set every day of your life. There is no happiness without action." [55]

Happiness primarily comes from limbic resonance, appreciation and loving relationships. We need to help ourselves, so that others dare to come close to us. Knowledge is one thing, but competence comes from practice, practice, and more practice. And we need to wish ourselves good luck on the journey towards this goal. Sometimes it is painful to live. We cannot have an influence on everything that happens, and at times it can be easy to fall down a ravine of hopelessness. Then we have to accept, try to go with the flow and trust in life. A client said something very wise:

[55] Sonja Lyubomirsky, *The How of Happiness; A Practical Guide to Getting the Life You Want,* page 67, 68.

"Everything turns out good in the end... and if it isn't good, it isn't over yet."

My Mother's Wisdom

My beloved mother always looked at things as challenges and possibilities. She was a remarkable woman in many ways and her conviction that there is a positive side to everything has had a profound impact on me and my way of looking at life. I will never forget the painful moment when her heart doctor, who had been treating her for many years, said:

"Now, Carin, you don't have much time left to live. Your body can't take it much longer and you will soon die."

I sat with her and cried, hugging her. I wanted to scream: "Damn doctor, don't take the hope away from her now that she's so frail!" Or did I really want to scream: "Damn doctor; don't take the hope away from me now that *I'm* so frail!"

With her rough, pale, shaking hand, mother caressed me softly on the cheek and whispered: "Imagine, Eva, this is a journey that I have never taken. I have never had to die before. That is what is coming now, and I think it will be exciting."

My mother had a curious soul. I'm convinced that she is still enjoying the trip. Perhaps riding a bike among the clouds? Maybe together with her parents--my beloved grandparents--who are also cycling there. My mother's consistently positive attitude was a choice. It was a loving gift to me, to everyone who knew her, and to life itself. And it was contagious.

I would like to beg you, as well as I can,
to have patience with everything unresolved in your heart
and to try to love the questions themselves
as if they were locked rooms
or books written in a very foreign language.
Don't search for the answers, which could not be given to you now,
because you would not be able to live them.
And the point is, to live everything.
Live the questions now.
Perhaps then, someday far in the future, you will gradually,
without even noticing it,
live your way into the answer.

--RAINER MARIA RILKE, FROM "LETTERS TO A YOUNG POET"
NR FOUR, SIXTEENTH OF JULY   1903

Afterword

The model for "Crossing the Bridge" (also known as contingent dialogue) that I present in this book is not the only way to create loving relationships. Others may present different, equally-valid opinions and models. My goal here has been to offer information, enthusiasm and inspiration by sharing my own fairly extensive experience as an intimate partner, mother, daughter, sister, friend, teacher, therapist, mental trainer, woman and human being. I have shared the approaches that have worked best for me and for hundreds of people with whom I have worked as a therapist. *But remember, everything that I have said and written, may say more about me – then about you!*

I hope that I have inspired you to think "bigger than biggest" when it comes to living *your* questions and making choices that will enhance your life. My best wishes to you.

Acknowledgments

Writing *You Can Make it Happen; How Breakthroughs in Neuroscience Can Transform Relationships* has been a challenge, but an instructive one. It has been both inspiring and a chance for rewiring, as Dan Siegel would say. But without loving support and help, this book would not have been possible. With great affection, I would like to thank:

Lars-Eric Uneståhl, who inspired me to discover my vision and for teaching me mental training and positive psychology;

Harville Hendrix, for the beautiful structure of Imago Relationship Therapy;

Hedy Schleifer, for your friendship, for being you, for your way of playing with words (such as "Armani suit" and the dialogue name "Crossing the Bridge") and for helping me to transform the Imago structure into a form of art;

Pat Love, for all of your laughter, generosity, friendship and invaluable knowledge in research and the sciences (and for helping me with the manuscript);

Daniel Siegel, for developing Mindsight and IPNB (interpersonal neurobiology) in such an inspiring, playful and respectful way, teaching me more about how the brain, mind and relationships work together to form a triangle of well-being. You have taught me discover a greater capacity to nurture the heart with the brain in mind.

Tim and Helen Atkinson, you beautiful couple, for letting me use the happy picture of you on my book cover!

Rose Draper, psychotherapist and Imago therapist in the UK, for reading and checking the manuscript,

Esther Perel, beautiful woman, colleague and newfound friend, for your help and open heart. You inspire me!

My colleague, Jette Simon, together with her husband, Rich Simon, are great visionaries for world peace.

All of the researchers and authors who are dedicated to understanding this subject, and upon whose shoulders I unsteadily placed myself.

All of my brave and beautiful clients, for all I learnt from you.

Lisen Norén, my best friend, for reading the manuscript and giving me honest, valuable and encouraging comments.

Ditte Dunge, for your friendship, your concern, your laughter, and for being the first colleague to read my book in Swedish.

Elsa Gottfridsson, my sounding board, for your warmth, your calmness, and wisdom.

My brother, Robin Brittain-Long, for reading from a doctor's point of view. You ought to write yourself.

My aunt, Eva Ritzén, as well as Monica and Mats Havström, for your valuable thoughts on the material.

Eva Dozzi and Marian Sandmaier, for you honesty, appreciation, writing skills and revision of the text. Without both of you, it would not have become a book in both Swedish and English.

I also want to thank you, Mom, Carin Ritzen-Sick, up in heaven, for your love, and for teaching me that everything is possible. Thank you also for being a role model, with your extraordinary skills as a therapist.

Thank you, too Anders and Nicholas, the most wonderful teenage sons in the world, for enduring a mother who writes, writes, and writes. Thank you for your sense of humour, as you and your friends shout, "You must use your prefrontal cortex!" You both challenge me to be the best mother and person possible.

Thank you, my beloved Sven, for giving me space to write, both financially and time-wise. For reading my manuscript and helping me with it. Thank you for your enveloping love. You inspire me to shine!

Eva (Brittain-Long) Berlander

www.evaberlander.com / www.svenskimago.com

354

Literature

Almqvist-O´Connor, Dagmar, *How to make love to the same person for the rest of your life; and still love it* (1985, 1998)

Amen, Daniel, *Change Your Brain, Change Your Life; The Breakthrough Program for Conquering Anxiety, Depression, Obsessiveness, Anger, and Impulsiveness,* Three Rivers Press (2000)

Amen, Daniel, *Sex on the Brain; 12 lessons to enhance your love life,* Three Rivers Press (2007)

Applegate, Jeffrey S & Janet R. Shapiro & Janet R. Shapiro, *Neurobiology for Clinical Social Work: Theory and Practice*, W. W. Norton & Co (2005)

Badenoch, Bonnie, *Being a Brain-Wise Therapist: A Practical Guide to Interpersonal Neurobiology,* W.W Norton & Co (2008)

Badenoch, Bonnie, *The Brain-Savvy Therapist´s Workbook; A Companion to Being a Brain Wise Therapist,* W.W Norton & Co (2011)

Bauer, Joachim, *Warum ich fuhle, was du fuhlst, Random* (2005)

Beattie, Melody, *Codependent No More*, Hazelden Trade (1989)

Begley, Sharon, *Train Your Mind, Change Your Brain: How a New Science Reveals Our Extraordinary Potential to Transform Ourselves,* Ballantine books (2007)

Beveridge, Martha Baldwin & Harville Hendrix & Helen Hunt, *Loving Your Partner Without Losing Yourself,* Hunter House Publishers (2001)

Blackmore, Susan, *Consciousness; A Very Short Introduction,* Oxford University Press (2005)

Boorstein, Sylvia, *Pay Attention, for Goodness Sake*, Ballantine Books (2002)

Brazier, David, *The feeling Buddha* ,Constable and Company Ltd (1997)

Brown, Rick & Toni Reinhold, *Imago Relationship Therapy" An Introduction to Theory and Practice*, John Wiley & Sons (1999)

Buber, Martin, *Ich und Du*, Martin Buber Estate (1923)

Cassidy, Jude, Philip R Shaver & Mary Main, *Handbook of Attachment; Theory, Research and Clinical Applications*, Guildford Publications (1999)

Chopra, Deepak, *The Spontaneous Furfillment of Desire*, Deepak Chopra (2003)

Chopra, Deepak, *The Path to Love,* Deepak Chopra (1997)

Ciaramicoli, Arthur. P & John Allen Mollenhauer, The *Hidden Challenges to a Balanced, Healthy, High-Achieving Life,* Morgan James Publishing (2009)

Ciaramicoli, Arthur. P & Katherine Ketcham, *Power of empathy; A practical guide to create intimacy, self-understanding and lasting love,* Dutton Adult (2000)

Ciaramicoli Arthur. P, *Treatment of Abuse & Addiction,* Jason Aronson (1997)

Colgrave Melba, Harold Bloomfield & Peter McWilliams, *How To Survive the Loss of a Love.* Prelude press (1993)

Cozolino, Louis & Siegel, Daniel J, *The Neuroscience of Psychotherapy: Healing the Social Brain,* W. W. Norton & Co (2010)

Cozolino, Louis, *The Neuroscience of Human Relationships; Attachment and the Developing Social Brain,* W. W. Norton & Co (2006)

Csíkszentmihályi, Mihály, *Flow, The psychology of optimal experience*, Haper Collins (1990)

Dalai Lama & Howard C Cutler, *The Art of Happiness; A Handbook for Living,* Hodder (1998)

Dalai Lama, *How to Expand Love; Widening the Circle of Loving Relationships,* Atria (2005)

Dalai Lama, Geshe Lobsang Jordhen ,Losang Choehel Ganchenpa & Jeremy Russel, *The Stages of Meditation*, SnowLion Publication (2001)

Damasio, Antonio, *Descartes' Error: Emotion, Reason, and the Human Brain*, Penguin Books (1999)

Damasio, Antonio, *Looking for Spinoza: Joy, Sorrow, and the Feeling Brain*, Mariner Books (2003)

Damasio, Antonio, *The Feeling of What Happens: Body and Emotion in the Making of Consciousness*, Harvest Books (2000)

Decety Jean & William Ickes, *The Social Neuroscience of Empathy*, MIT Press (2009)

Einhorn, Stefan, *Konsten att vara snäll*, Forum (2005) *The Art of Being Kind*, Pegasus Books, LLC (2007)

Ekman, Paul & Daniel Goleman, *Emotional Awareness; Overcoming the Obstacles to Psychological Balance and Compassion, A Conversation Between the Dalai Lama and Paul Ekman*, Times Books (2008)

Epstein, Mark, *Going to Pieces Without Falling Apart; A Buddhist Perspective on Wholeness*, Broadway Books (1999)

Epstein, Mark, *Psychotherapy without the self*, Yale University Press (2008)

Feinberg, Todd E, *From Axons to Identity; Neurological Explorations of the Nature of the Self*, W. W. Norton & Co (2009)

Fontana David, *Learn to Meditate" A Practical Guide to Self-Discovery and Fulfilment,* Chronicle Books (1999)

Fogel, Alan, *The Psychophysiology of Self-Awareness; Rediscovering the Lost Art of Body Sense*, W. W. Norton & Co (2009)

Fisher, Helen, *Why him, Why her; Finding Real Love By Understanding Your personality Type*, Henry Holt & Co (2009)

Fisher,Helen,, *Why We Love: The Nature and Chemistry of Romantic Love*, Henry Holt & Co (2005)

Fisher,Helen, *The First Sex; The Natural Talents of Women and How They Are Changing the World*, Ballantine Books (2000)

Fosha, Diana, Daniel J. Siegel &Marion Solomon, *The Healing Power of Emotion: Affective Neuroscience, Development and Clinical Practice*, W. W. Norton & Co (2009)

Frankl, Viktor E. *Man's Search For Meaning*, Beacon Press (1959) *Ein Psycholo erlebt das konzentrationslager*, Viktor E Frankl, (1946)

Gawin, Shakti, *Creative Visualization*, New World Library (1985)

Germer Christopher, Ronald D. Siegel & Paul R. Fulton, *Mindfulness and psychotherapy*, Guilford Publication (2005)

Germer, Christopher K & Sharon Salzberg, *The Mindful Path to Self-Compassion; Freeing Yourself from Destructive Thoughts and Emotions*, Guilford Publication (2009)

Goleman Daniel, *Ecological Intelligence*, Crown Business (2010)

Goleman Daniel, *Social Intelligens*, Bantam (2006)

Goleman, Daniel & Jon Kabat –Zinn, *Mindfulness @ Work; A Leading with Emotional Intelligence;Conversation with Jon Kabat-Zinn*, (CD-book), MacMillan Audio (2007)

Goleman, Daniel, Richard Boyatzis & Annie McKee, *Primal Leadership; Realizing the power of Emotional Intelligence*, Harvard Business School (2004)

Goleman, Daniel, *Emotional Intelligence*, Bantam Books (2000)

Goleman, Daniel, *Working with Emotional Intelligence*, Bantam Books (1998)

Goleman Daniel, *Healing Emotions*; *Conversations with the Dalai Lama on Mindfulness, Emotions, and Health*, Shambhala Publications (2003)

Gordon, Mary, *Roots of Empathy: Changing the World Child by Child*, Thomas Allen (2005)

Gorski, Terence. T, *Understanding the Twelve steps*, Fireside books (1991)

Gottman, John. M & Nan Silver, *The Seven Principles for Making Marriage Work*, Three Rivers Press (2005)

Gottman, John. M, *What Predicts Divorce?; The Relationship Between Marital Processes and Marital outcomes,* Psychology Press (1993)

Gottman, John M, Julie Schwartz Gottman & Joan Declaire, *Ten Lessons to Transform Your Marriage: America's Love Lab Experts Share Their Strategies for Strengthening Your Relationship,* Three Rivers Press (2007)

Hawkins, Jeff & Sandra Blakeslee, *On Intelligences,* Times Books (2005)

Hendricks, Gay & Kathlyn Hendricks, *Conscious Loving; The Journey to co-commitment (1990)*

Hendrix, Harville, *Doing Imago Relationship Therapy; The Definitive Method,* Jossey-Bass (2010)

Hendrix, Harville, *Getting the Love You Want,* Henry Holt Company (1988)

Hendrix, Harville, *Keeping the love you find: A personal Guide,* Atria (1992)

Hendrix, Harville & Helen LaKelly Hunt, *Receiving Love, Transform your relationship by letting yourself be loved,* Atria (2005)

Hendrix, Harville & Helen LaKelly Hunt, *Giving the Love that Heals; A guide for Parents,* Atria (2003)

Hotchkiss, Sandy & James F. Masterson , *Why Is It Always about You?; The Seven Deadly Sins of Narcissism,* Free Press (2003)

Houston, Jean, *A passion for the possible,* Harper One (1998)

Iacoboni, Marco, *Mirroring People; The Science of Empathy and How We Connect with Others,* Picador (2008)

Johnson, M Susan & Valerie E.Whiffen, *Attachment Progresses in Couple and Family Therapy,* The Guilford Press (2003)

Johnson, M Susan, *Hold Me Tight; Seven Conversations for a lifetime of Love,* Little, Brown and Company (2008)

Johnson, M Susan, *Emotionally Focused Couple Therapy with Trauma Survivors,* The Guilford Press (2002)

Juul, Jesper, *Dit kompetente barn, Denmark* (1995) *Your Competent Child; Toward New Basic Values for the family,* Farrar, Straus and Giroux (2001)

Kabat-Zinn, Jon & Hor Tuck Loon, *Letting Everything Become Your Teacher,* Delta (2009)

Kabat-Zinn,Jon , *Wherever You Go, There You Are,* Hyperion Books (1994)

Kabat-Zinn,Jon & Hor Tuck Loon, *Arriving at your own door;108 lessons in mindfulness,* Hyperion Books (2007)

Kabat-Zinn,Jon, *Coming to our senses; Healing ourselves and the world through mindfulness,* Hyperion Books (2005)

Klein, Stefan, *The Science of Happiness; How Our Brains Make Us Happy – and What We Can Do to Get Happier, Da Capo Press (2006) Die Tagebücher der Schöpfung,* Rowaohlt Verlag GmbH (2002)

Kornfield,Jack & Daniel J,Siegel, *Mindfulness and the Brain: A Professional Training in the Science & Practice of Meditative Awareness, (cd book), Sounds true(2010)*

Kornfield, Jack, *The Wise Heart; A Guide to the Universal Teachings of Buddhist Psychology,* Bantam (2008)

Kornfield, Jack, Amy Schmidt & Sharon Salzberg, *Dipa Ma; The Life and Legacy of a Buddhist Master,* Blue Bridge (2005)

Kornfield, Jack , *After the Ecstasy, the Laundry; How the Heart Grows Wise on the Spiritual Path,* Bantam (2001)

Jack Kornfield, *A Path with Heart; A Guide Through the Perils and Promises of Spiritual Life,* Bantam (1993)

Layard, Richard, Happiness; *lessons from a new science,* Allen Lane (2005)

Legato, Marianne J, *Why Men Never Remember and Women Never Forget,* Rodale Books (2005)

Lillas, Connie & Janiece Turnbull,*Infant/Child Mental Health, Early Intervention, and Relationship-Based Therapies: A Neurorelational Framework for Interdisciplnary Practice*, W. W. Norton & Co *(2009)*

Loehr, Jim & Tony Schwartz, *The Power of Full Engagement,* Free press, (2003)

Love, Patricia & Jon Carlson, Never Be Lonely Again; The way Out of Emptiness, Isolation and a Life Unfulfilled, Health Communications, Inc. (2011)

Love, Patricia & Steven Stosny, *How to Improve Your Marriage Without Talking about It,* Broadway Books (2007)

Love, Patricia, *The Truth About Love; The Hights, the Lows, and How You Can Make it Last Forever,* Fireside Books (2001)

Love, Patricia & Jo Robinson, *Hot Monogamy; Essential Steps to More Passionate, Intimate Lovemaking,* Dutton Adult (1994)

Love, Patricia & Jo Roinson, *The Emotional Incest Syndrome*; *What to do when a parent's love rules your life,* Bantam (1991)

Lyubomirsky, Sonja, *The How of Happiness; A scientific Approach to Getting the Life you Want,* Penguine Press, (2007)

McGilchrist Iain, *The Master and His Emissary*, Yale University Press (2010)

Mendes-Aponte Emely, *When Mom and Dad divorce,* Abbey Press *(1999)*

Marks-Tarlow, Terry, *Psychès Veil; Psychotherapy, Fractals and Complexity,* Routledge (2008)

Monkton, Edward, *A Lovely Love Story,* Harper Collins (2004)

Monkton, Edward, *Happiness,* Harper Collins (2007)

Nelson, Tammy, *Getting the Sex You Want; Shed your inhibitions and Reach New Heights of Passion Together*, Quiver (2008)

O'Connor, Joseph, *Coaching with NLP; How to Be a Master Coach,* Element Books (2004)

O'Connor, Joseph & John Seymour, *Introducing NLP, Aquarian (*1990)

Ogden, Pat, Kekuni Minton & Clare Pain, *Trauma and the Body: A Sensorimotor Approach to Psychotherapy,* W. W. Norton & Co (2006)

Panksepp, Jack, *Self-Agony in Psychotherapy; Attachment, Autonomy, Intimacy,* W. W. Norton & Co (2010)

Pert Candace B & Deepak Chopra, *Molecules of Emotion: Why You Feel the Way You Feel,* Scribner (1997)

Pittman, Frank, *Grow Up! How taking responsibility can make you a happy adult. St. Martin's Press (1998)*

Pollak, Kay, *Growing Through Meetings* (Audible Audio Edition), Earbooks AB (2010) *Att växa genom möten,* Hanson & Pollak (2001)

Robbins, Anthony, *Unlimited Power*, Simon &Schuster (1986)

Schleifer, Hedy, *The Miracle of Connection; Transform Your relationships / Crossing the bridge; transforming Your Relationships* (cd-books) Schleifer & Associates (2007)

Schore, Allan N, *Affect Regulation and the Repair of the Self & Affect Dysregulation and Disorders of the Self, (Two –volume set),* W. W. Norton & Co (2003)

Schore Allan N, *Reader's Guide to Affect Regulation and Neurobiology,* W. W. Norton & Co (2010)

Schwarts, Jeffrey. M & Begley, Sharon, *The Mind and the Brain; Neuroplasticity and the Power of Mental Force,* Harper (2002)

Seidenfaden, Kirsten & Piet Draiby, *The Vibrant Relationship: A Handbook for Couples and Therapist, Karnac (2011) Det levende parforhold" – fra konflikt til naervaer.* TV 2 *Forlag (2007)*

Seidenfaden, Kirsten & Piet Draiby & Susanne Søborg Christensen, *The Vibrant Family: A handbook for Parents and Professionals*, Karnac (2011) *Den levende familie,* Lindhardt & Ringhof (2009)

Senge, Peter, Scharmer, c.Otto, Jaworski, Joseph & Flowers, Betty Sue, *Presence; Human Purpose and the Field of the Future*, Sol (2004)

Siegel, Daniel J, *Mindsight; The New Science of Personal Transformation,* Bantam (2010)

Siegel, Daniel J, *The Mindful Therapist: A Clinician's Guide to Mindsight and Neural Integration.* W. Norton & Co (2010)

Siegel, Daniel J, *The Neurobiology of "We"; How Relationships, The Mind and the Brain Interact to Shape Who We Are,* (cd-book) Sounds true (2008)

Siegel, Daniel J, *The Mindful Brain; Reflection and Attunement in Cultivation of Well-Being,* W. W. Norton & Co (2007)

Siegel, Daniel J & Mary Hartsel, *Parenting from the Inside Out,* Tarcher (2003)

Siegel, Daniel J, *The Developing Mind" Towards a Neurobiology of Interpersonal Experience, How Relationships and the Brain Interact to Shape Who We Are,* Guilford Press (1999)

Sinkjaer, Simon Jette, *Imago; kærlighedens terapi,* Dansk psykologisk Forlag (2005)

Solomon, Marion F & Daniel J. Siegel, *Healing Trauma: Attachment, Mind, Body and Brain,* W. W. Norton & Co (2003)

Stern, Daniel N, *The present moment in psychotherapy and everyday life,* W. W. Norton & Co (2004)

Stern, Daniel N, *The Interpersonal World of the Infant; a View from Psychoanalysis and Developmental Psychology,* Basic Books (1990)

Stern, Daniel N, *Diary of a Baby; What Your Child Sees, Feels, and Experiences,* Basic Books (1990)

Tolle, Eckhart, *The Power of Now; A guide to Spiritual Enlightenment,* New World Library (1999)

Tolle, Eckhart, *Stillness speaks,* New World Library *(2003)*

Tronick, Ed, *The Neurobehavioral and Social-Emotional Development of Infants and Children,* W. W. Norton & Co (2007)

Van Der Hart,Onno, Ellert R. S. Nijenhuis & Kathy Steele, *The Haunted Self; Structural Dissociation and the Treatment of Chronic Traumatization,* W. W. Norton & Co (2006)

Wilkinson, Margaret, *Changing Minds in Therapy: Emotion, Attachment, Trauma, and Neurobiology,* W. W. Norton & Co (2010)

Zukav, Gary, *The Seat of the Soul,* Simon & Schuster (1999)

Made in the USA
Charleston, SC
21 August 2012